D0913115

GUARDING THE BORDER

Number Thirteen:
Canseco-Keck History Series
Jerry Thompson, General Editor

GUARDING THE BORDER

The Military Memoirs of Ward Schrantz, 1912–1917

E D I T E D B Y J E F F P A T R I C K

Texas A&M University Press
College Station

This paper meets the requirements of ANSI/NISO Z39.48-1992
(Permanence of Paper).
Binding materials have been chosen for durability.

Library of Congress Cataloging-in-Publication Data

Schrantz, Ward L.
    Guarding the border : the military memoirs of Ward Schrantz, 1912–1917 / edited
    by Jeff Patrick. — 1st ed.
        p. cm. — (Canseco-Keck history series ; no. 13)
    Includes bibliographical references and index.
    ISBN-13: 978-1-60344-096-7 (cloth : alk. paper)
    ISBN-10: 1-60344-096-8 (cloth : alk. paper)
    1. Schrantz, Ward L. 2. Mexican-American Border Region—History, Military—
20th century. 3. Mexico—Hisotry—Revolution, 1910–1920—Personal narratives,
American. 4. Soldiers—Mexican-American Border Region—Biography. 5. Soldiers—
Rio Grande Valley—Biography. 6. Soldiers—Texas—Biography. 7. United States.
Army—Military life—History—20th century. 8. Missouri. National Guard—Military
life—History—20th century. 9. Soldiers—Missouri—Biography. I. Patrick, Jeffrey L.,
1963–   II. Title. III. Series
    F786.S34 2009
    355.3'7092—dc22
    [B]
                                                            2008034789

Contents

Illustrations and Maps

Illustrations

Maps

Acknowledgments

F IRST AND FOREMOST, I WOULD LIKE to pay tribute to those who initially preserved the archival legacy of Ward Schrantz. His immediate family recognized the historical value of his reminiscences, maps, and photographs and guaranteed that the collection remained intact. Jasper County historian Marvin VanGilder of Carthage, Missouri, who worked with Ward Schrantz, was given the Schrantz scrapbooks by the family, then generously donated these materials to the Jasper County Records Center and made them available to researchers.

Jasper County archivist Steve Weldon, the current custodian of the Schrantz materials, along with records center volunteers Marjorie Bull and Doris Wardlow, are likewise dedicated to the preservation of this and many other primary source documents relating to the rich history of Jasper County. During this project, all three cheerfully answered my questions, located and copied important materials, and provided much-needed support.

I owe a great debt to Drs. William Garrett Piston and Herbert W. Jackson of Missouri State University, who read the manuscript and offered valuable suggestions and words of encouragement, and to Kip Lindberg, who scanned all of the photographs used in this work.

Special thanks are due to Sharol Higgins Neely, local history librarian at the Springfield–Greene County (Missouri) Public Library, who was particularly helpful in locating a microfilm copy of the *El Paso Herald*.

I would also like to acknowledge the assistance of staff members at the State Historical Society of Missouri in Columbia, the National Archives and Records Administration (National Personnel Records Center, Military Personnel Records) in St. Louis, and the El Paso Public Library.

And finally, I would be remiss if I did not thank my wife Tammy and children Joseph and Rebecca for their tireless patience and understanding. Although they have not come to know Ward Schrantz as well as I have, they have cheerfully tolerated my desire to see the old soldier live again in print.

Notes on Editorial Method

W ARD SCHRANTZ WROTE THREE DIFFERENT VERSIONS of his memoir of regular army service on the Mexican border. These accounts, in addition to the narrative of his time in the National Guard, are preserved in the Marvin VanGilder Collection at the Jasper County Records Center in Carthage, Missouri. It is difficult, if not impossible, to determine precisely when he penned these recollections, as all three are undated. The most lengthy account, detailing Schrantz's entire regular army service, is typed on stationery from the U.S. Army transport *John Ericsson,* his World War II command, and was likely written either at the end of World War II or just after Schrantz's return from the war. The other two versions, although similar, are much shorter (they end with his regiment's move to Texas City in early 1913) and likewise contain no dates or clues as to when he composed them. All three versions have been combined into one continuous narrative in this work. Schrantz's accounts appear here largely as written. Minor changes in spelling have been made for clarity's sake and are indicated by brackets "[ ]." Redundant words have been omitted. Ship and newspaper names have been italicized. Capitalization and punctuation have been retained from the original documents, along with nonstandard capitalization. Brackets and a question mark [?] indicate unclear or unreadable words. Schrantz's letters from Texas in 1913–14 to the *Carthage (Missouri) Evening Press* and an essay on the U.S. Army, the National Guard, and Mexico have been included as appendices to this work.

GUARDING THE BORDER

Introduction

WARD LOREN SCHRANTZ OF CARTHAGE, MISSOURI, was a newspaper journalist, author, and historian, but he also faithfully served his country as a soldier for nearly half a century. He began his unusual military career in the Missouri National Guard in 1909, then joined the regular army three years later. Discharged in 1914 after serving on the Mexican border, he returned to the Missouri National Guard. He went back to guard the border once more from 1916 to 1917. During World War I, Schrantz led troops in combat as a captain in command of Company A, 128th Machine Gun Battalion, in the Thirty-fifth Division. As a reserve infantry officer, he endured the military doldrums of the 1920s and the stagnation of the depression in the 1930s. He watched as Americans ignored a growing fascist menace, but after Pearl Harbor, despite being in his fifties, he made a minor but significant contribution toward the liberation of Europe by commanding a troop transport on numerous trips overseas during World War II. He finally retired from the army reserve in 1950 with the rank of colonel.

Schrantz began his soldiering during the twilight years of the old frontier army, a time when few disputed a continued role for horse cavalry. He ended it in the atomic age, when the possibility of nuclear war raised questions about the viability of any conventional forces in future conflicts. Schrantz's service took him from the fields of Missouri to Texas in the turbulent days of the Mexican Revolution to the trenches of France with their machine guns, barbed wire, and mud. Throughout it all, the highly literate Schrantz recognized the unique nature of his army service, and at various times he recorded his experiences while in uniform. He assembled the typed reminiscences of his travels in the United States and throughout the world in several large notebooks, forming a record that provides an important witness to the American armed services in transition.

One of the most valuable portions of Schrantz's memoirs documents his service in the United States' regular army (1912–1914) and the National Guard (1915–1917). Although both organizations were relatively large at the time (approximately 100,000 and 120,000 men, respectively), few enlisted men who served during that period had the opportunity or inclination to document their military careers in significant detail. Those who fought Native Americans in the 1870s and 1880s and the Spanish in 1898 left behind a number of narratives, while American soldier "doughboys" who served in World War I wrote and published many memoirs. There is a noticeable lack of soldier reminiscences during this "middle" period of 1898–1917, however. Ward Schrantz, on the other hand, filled dozens of pages with a record of what it was like to be a private in the regular army and a noncommissioned officer in the National Guard during the crucial years leading up to America's entry into the "Great War."

In addition, Schrantz had the good fortune, as he saw it, to be assigned to the Texas-Mexico border—not a quiet, remote army post or mundane recruiting station but a volatile region where he experienced potential danger on a daily basis. He enjoyed a wide range of experiences on the border. He helped guard El Paso, watched battles between Mexican revolutionaries, served with the provisional "Second Division" in Texas City while his comrades were fighting in the port city of Veracruz, and, as a member of the Missouri National Guard, guarded the border while General John J. "Black Jack" Pershing chased the Mexican revolutionary Francisco "Pancho" Villa. Schrantz extensively documented all of these activities in his reminiscences.

Ward Schrantz's writings are significant for a number of other reasons, however. Although he was not a professional writer, Schrantz's education and small-town newspaper experience allowed him to craft a well-written and entertaining narrative. Because there is no evidence that he prepared his memoir for publication, the Missourian wrote in an honest, unpretentious, and unassuming style, with extensive detail, vivid descriptions, and occasional humor. Although he did not hesitate to criticize his fellow enlisted men, his superiors, and even civilians, Schrantz also included self-deprecating remarks and anecdotes. For example, Schrantz freely admitted an occasional twinge of fear, or at least anxiety, as he performed lonely nighttime sentry duty or faced down a group of armed Mexican revolutionaries along the Rio Grande.

For historians of military material culture and society in general, Schrantz recorded important aspects of the enlisted soldier's life during this neglected period. He described in detail the daily life of a soldier, including living conditions, rations, training, and weapons. He painted literary portraits of the varied collection of officers and enlisted men who populated the "Old Army," from career soldiers to new recruits, from rogues and slackers to determined, reliable, professional warriors. Schrantz also recalled the civilians he encountered, including characters such as a Civil War veteran in El Paso determined to defend his property against revolutionaries across the border and the Hispanic inhabitants of a small West Texas village who one day found Missouri soldiers not only living among them but also building elaborate defenses to protect them from bandit attacks.

Any reader of Ward Schrantz's account will quickly realize that there was clearly a difference between how soldiers were required to behave, according to army regulations, and how troops actually behaved on and off duty. Although the majority of the regulars and National Guard members took their business seriously, some were also not above sleeping on guard duty or sneaking across the border to enjoy the temptations of a Mexican border town. Such colorful details of army life in Texas simply did not find their way into official histories.

Finally, because he served in both organizations, Schrantz provided a fascinating study of the contrast between life in the regular army and the National Guard during a period when both organizations were undergoing tortuous changes to increase the professionalism of both career and citizen-soldiers.

Through his writings, the candid Ward Schrantz not only recalled his service but also kept alive the memory of countless other regular army and National Guard soldiers, men now gone and all but forgotten. These nameless, faceless individuals protected U.S. interests and helped manage an overseas empire amid the struggle between the great powers in Europe and the revolutionary turmoil in Mexico.[1]

The young soldier who found himself caught up in these dramatic international events began with a modest upbringing in a small midwestern town. Born in Stark County, Ohio, on November 13, 1890, Ward Loren Schrantz moved with his parents to Carthage, Missouri, a short time later. Located about 150 miles south of Kansas City, in southwestern Missouri, Carthage had been founded in the 1840s and had experienced great unrest and devastation during the Civil War, but following the war impressive commercial growth and the arrival of railroads had made it one of the most important towns in that part of the state. By the 1890s, Carthage was known for rich deposits of zinc, lead, and building stone. In 1900, the town's population stood at more than nine thousand.[2]

Tragedy struck the Schrantz family not long after their arrival in Carthage. Thirty-four-year-old Henry Schrantz died in late January 1893, leaving behind a thirty-two-year-old pregnant wife and five children. Although it must have been quite difficult for her to keep the family together, by 1910 Catherine (Kate) Schrantz had remarried and all but one of her children were employed, including her son Ward, who had joined the business department of the *Carthage Evening Press* (one of the town's two newspapers) the year before.[3] Schrantz actually began his career as a carrier boy with the *Carthage Democrat,* then went to work for the *Press,* becoming a printer's devil in 1908, then a reporter, and finally circulation manager.[4] Rather than continue working for the newspaper, or in one of the other prosperous commercial enterprises in Carthage, young Schrantz was soon convinced that he needed to make soldiering his profession.

Such a desire must have been relatively common in the town of Carthage. During the Civil War, Carthage and Jasper County were bitterly divided between Unionists and secessionists, and units from both sides found recruits in the area. In addition to being the scene of a major battle on July 5, 1861, Carthage was devastated twice by Confederate forces before peace returned in 1865. After the conflict, the fertile soil and numerous business opportunities in southwestern Missouri made the region an attractive one for settlement by Union veterans. A local Grand Army of the Republic post flourished, and young Schrantz had frequent contact with veterans from both sides of the conflict. "Veterans of the great civil war [sic] were all about in my home town at that time," he recalled, "and many of them willing enough to tell their experiences to an interested small boy." Despite the often unromantic and vicious nature of the guerrilla war in southwestern Missouri from 1861 to 1865, veterans who had served in various campaigns could still recount tales of glory, honor, and heroism for impressionable youths. As one historian explained it, veterans "remained powerful arbiters of popular values" who urged the young to treat "war as an adventurous and romantic undertaking, a liberating release from the stultifying conventions of civilized society."[5]

Even if the Civil War had not affected Carthage, young men could look to the events of 1898 for inspiration. Company A of the Second Missouri Infantry, known locally as the "Carthage Light Guard," had enthusiastically marched off when the United States went to war with Spain. Schrantz himself was part of the crowd that gathered to see the volunteers off at the local train station. "In memory, looking back at them," he noted many years later, "they still seem huge," with their blue uniforms, knapsacks, and breech-loading rifles.

Although the company remained stateside and saw no combat, that very fact probably reinforced the belief in the glorious nature of war. The city's citizens did not have to hear of the horrific combat deaths of local sons or the other hideous aspects of battle, and it is quite likely that few members of Company A returned to Carthage deeply scarred or disillusioned by their military experience. Instead, the one notable casualty from the town was Charles P. Wood, the unofficial "soldier-correspondent" for one of the local newspapers, who kept readers abreast of the company's activities. Wood did not suffer terribly from a battlefield wound but died of disease at a training camp in Georgia. He was returned to lie in state in the rotunda of the local courthouse, a shining example of heroic sacrifice by a promising young resident of the city. Later in 1898, another volunteer infantry company left Carthage for the war, and a third served in the Philippine insurrection. All these units returned from the "glorious adventure" to the cheers and praise of the local citizenry, having maintained the proud tradition of volunteer service.

Schrantz's decision to pursue a military career was apparently not a sudden one—he had always been enamored with the military. "Nature, kindly or otherwise, endowed me with an innate interest in military subjects and in military history and my boyhood in Carthage, Mo. was filled with thoughts along that line," he wrote years later. Schrantz played "war" with his schoolmates (one friend recalled he was always a leader). The *Carthage Evening Press* explained that "in younger years, it is said that he actually cried because he had not lived in the time of the civil war and had missed an opportunity to obtain actual war experience."[6] The same newspaper praised Schrantz when he enlisted in the regular army, noting that he was "an enthusiastic militiaman and anxious to enter the service of Uncle Sam," well informed regarding army duties, and one whose friends predicted he would advance rapidly in the military. "Young Schrantz is well deserving of success," the *Press* article continued. "He is an industrious worker, is thoroughly dependable, has no bad habits and does everything thoroughly which he undertakes. The PRESS and his many friends wish him success in his new undertaking."[7] With the encouragement of family and friends, at the age of twenty-one Ward Schrantz resigned his newspaper job and set off on a military odyssey that was to last, with some interruptions, for nearly fifty years and through two world wars.

Ward Schrantz's first destination in his martial career was Jefferson Barracks, a permanent military post and recruit depot a few miles south of St. Louis and about 275 miles from his hometown of Carthage, where he received his initial training. Recruit Schrantz recalled his time there as "something of an amusing nightmare," where new men were the "lowest of the low," for "the one unforgiveable [*sic*] sin at that time in the army was being a recruit."

After a few weeks of instruction, Schrantz joined Company F, Twenty-second U.S. Infantry, in the Texas border town of El Paso. It was, according to Schrantz, "a unit which believed in itself," composed of "field soldiers," mostly career men, veterans of the Spanish-American War and the Philippine insurrection, and even some who had participated in campaigns of the Indian Wars. "Everyone was quite human here," Schrantz remembered, "and we soon felt that we were members of the family."

Company F was charged with patrolling the border to prevent armed parties from entering or leaving Mexico, to keep arms or ammunition from being taken into that country, and to protect American property along the border. Over the next few weeks, Schrantz and his fellow regulars did exactly that, without incident. That is not to imply, however, that the young Missouri soldier found his task entirely unexciting or without danger. On one occasion, he confronted a group of armed Mexican bandits, but fortunately for Schrantz, their leader either "decided that I was harmless or it was not his day to shoot at Americans" and allowed the soldier to retire unmolested.

In early 1913, with the murder of Mexico's president and a revolt against the government in that nation's capital, Schrantz and his comrades found themselves on a train to Texas City, Texas, to prepare for possible offensive operations south of the border. The young soldier was elated by the prospect of combat: "Off to the wars! Altogether I was in a most happy frame of mind—possibly because I had never yet seen war."

After the Twenty-second Infantry arrived in Texas City, "a vigorous training period" followed, according to Schrantz, with "constant maneuvers too, battalion, regimental, brigade and eventually division," so that the men were "toughened and in as good physical condition as it is possible for men to be." Although other troops sailed south to seize the Mexican port city of Veracruz, Schrantz's regiment remained behind in Texas City. Finally, after nearly two years in Texas City, Schrantz became disillusioned with the regular army. It did not appear likely that more American troops would have an opportunity to see action against the Mexicans. Unable to obtain an officer's commission and with a lucrative job offer at home, Schrantz decided to leave the service. Taking advantage of a decades-old option available to enlisted men, Schrantz purchased his discharge and left the regulars in November 1914, his career as a professional soldier over.

Back in Missouri, Schrantz rejoined Company A, Second Missouri Infantry, part of the Missouri National Guard. The guard labored under "many handicaps," Schrantz explained, but the new noncommissioned officer participated in regimental maneuvers and tried his best to make sure that Company A would be prepared to form a framework of professional soldiers around which a larger wartime force could be built when needed. "I added my efforts to those of the others to build the unit up," he proudly recalled, knowing that "it was certain that it would be called if America needed more troops."

Major sites associated with the travels of Ward Schrantz, 1912–17

In March 1916, Schrantz got his wish. That month, Mexican revolutionary Pancho Villa and his followers slipped across the border and launched a surprise attack on the town of Columbus, New Mexico. Two months later, President Woodrow Wilson ordered the National Guard units in Texas, New Mexico, and Arizona to the border to protect against bandit incursions while the regular army pursued Villa. In June, he ordered the rest of the National Guard into service. Schrantz returned to the Texas-Mexico border the following month, as Company A and the entire Missouri National Guard went into camp at Laredo. Weeks of inactivity sapped the morale of most of the guardsmen. Schrantz's unit, however, remained optimistic: "In my own company, morale was good enough. . . . We made a point of pride in being punctiliously military with our officers, however well we had known them at home. We had, in fact, a very good opinion of ourselves."

By early 1917, the Missourians had participated in numerous drills, patrols, maneuvers, and other worthwhile training but had not actually traded shots with Mexican regulars or bandits. With the border relatively safe, and relations deteriorating with Imperial Germany, the National Guard troops came home. That January, Schrantz and the other members of the Second Missouri were mustered out of service. Although Schrantz, ever the eager soldier, "would have been pleased to stay on the border," most of his comrades had had enough of border service. The Missouri troops had gained valuable experience that would soon be put to good use, however, for, as Schrantz wrote, "within less than three months after the return of my own company to civil life, the United States was at war with Germany." The citizen-soldiers from Carthage were no doubt grateful that dedicated, determined former regulars like Ward Schrantz were available to lead them into combat in France in 1918.

1

The Missouri National Guard

NATURE, KINDLY OR otherwise, endowed me with an innate interest in military subjects and in military history and my boyhood in Carthage, Mo. was filled with thoughts along that line.

Veterans of the great Civil War were all about in my home town at that time and many of them willing enough to tell their experiences to an interested small boy.[1] This, together with the outbreak of the Spanish-American War in the spring of 1898, with the epidemic of wars [in] various places in the world the next six years, all liberally treated in newspapers and magazines, fostered and encouraged the natural inclination. Campaigns in Cuba and in the Philippines; the Boxer rebellion, the Boer War, and the Russian-Japanese war, all were subjects of boyhood conversation and games. These things naturally influenced mental trends and most of the small boys with whom I "played war," eventually served in the national guard, army or marines in the next 15 years even before our entry into the First World War put so many men in uniform.

As a boy between seven and eight years old I saw the local national guard company—the Carthage Light Guard—march away as Company A, Second Missouri Volunteer Infantry, to the railway station to entrain for Jefferson Barracks.[2] They appeared huge men to me, a small boy, as I stood in the muddy street watching them—blue uniformed, their long 1872-model caliber 45 Springfield rifles, sloped off their shoulders at what seemed neat angles to me but probably were not; their knapsacks on their backs with the blankets in a small roll transversely across the top.[3] In memory, looking back at them, they still seem huge—viewing them as I still do mentally from the altitude of a seven-year-old boy.

I did not know then—or I would have been happier at being too small for the war—that years later I would march away myself in the same company and from the same armory as a sergeant to the Mexican border troubles, or that I would again march away with it as its captain at the beginning of the First World War and would command it when it first went into battle. In later years I became well acquainted with Col. W. K. Caffee, then the commander of that volunteer regiment, and of Capt. John A. McMillan, then company commander, and heard from their own lips the story of the regiment's activities and trials in the months that followed.[4]

It was an old unit, as Missouri national guard organizations went, having been formed in 1876 under the influence of Col. Caffee, then one of the gilded youth of the town and fresh from Shattuck, military school, but with its first officers and a nucleus of its rank and file veterans of the great Civil War, some of the Confederate army, some of the Federal. And as commander of the company in later years I took pride in the fact that within 11 years after the Civil War closed, in this town of southwest Missouri which the hostilities had reduced to ashes and around which the border war was most bitter, veterans of opposing armies could get together in the same military organization.

And still as a seven-year-old boy I watched a second volunteer unit— Co. G, 5th Missouri Volunteer Infantry—march away, unarmed and in civilian clothes, for the train to Jefferson Barracks. I was to hear much of Capt. George P. Whitsett, its commander, later. After his company was mustered out he gained publicity in connection with some proposed fil[i]bustering expedition to Nicaragua, nipped in the bud by our own government but for which he had signed up a number of his volunteer soldiers. Then he became an officer in the 34th (?) U.S. Volunteer Infantry in the Philippines and wrote letters to the home newspapers about fighting in northern Luzon.[5] Still later he was connected with the constabulary there and was some kind of a judge in the administration of the island. Newspaper readers in tho[s]e days heard much of the "water-cure," a form of torture said to have been inflicted on suspected native guerrillas in the Philippines to make them confess their offenses, and in my imagination

I connected him—and probably quite unjustly—with those. In World War I, I knew him as judge advocate of the 35th Infantry Division and later of a corps staff and cited for gallantry in action. At the time of his death some years after that war he was a major in the regular army.[6]

My early military interests had a rather adverse and now amusing influence on my high school career. Naturally interested in history I narrowly avoided flunking out in that subject due to my inclinations to dig into reference books containing more details of military movements than the textbooks possessed. Hence of the allotted pages I knew relatively little and was in consequent disgrace, quite humiliating at the time. But despite it I have since always congratulated myself on my tangent-directed energy and poor scholarship in this regard. A less laudable high school fault my senior year was an interest in the writings of Karl Marx which did not influence me very long but which ran somewhat counter to my natural trend. But even that probably has its value since in my vigorous spasm of reading I acquired a good deal of knowledge of communist doctrines which have in later years given me a certain foundation on which to argue against them, and at the same time helped toward an understanding of the stuff out of which the formidable Red Army of the Second World War was built.[7]

However my military inclinations soon won over my early Socialist leanings and three months after I was 18 I enlisted in the national guard, an organization which was anathema to my erstwhile Socialist associates who had picked me as a promising young radical—I becoming instead one of those young men approbviously [sic] referred to as "scab-herders" by my late associates.

I always have remembered with a smile a comment one of my elderly Socialist friends made to me a short time later.

"Ward," he said sadly, "I always thought you were a pretty good boy—until," concluding with energy, "you went and joined the damn milishy."

And another one said to me not long afterwards when he dropped into the newspaper office where I was employed:

"Ward, if you were on duty with the militia and you were ordered to fire on a crowd and your brother was right in front of you, would you shoot your brother?"

"Of course," I replied brazenly to shock him, "that is exactly what he would do to me if the situation were reversed."

He had no answer to that, but it was a reply I could make easily since both of my two older brothers were and are violently loyalist and strong law-and-order men and if they ever have had any inclinations to shoot me it probably was during that brief period when I was reading Karl Marx and Frederick Engels.[8]

On the evening of Feb. 5, 1909, I went to the local national guard armory, asked rather timidly how one went about enlisting, and was ushered promptly to the company office where I was put through a form of physical examination by Capt. W. E. Hiatt, the company commander, and sworn in forthwith, my physical examination by a civilian physician following a few days later. Capt. Hiatt was a national guardsmen [sic] of some 15 years or so service and had been a second lieutenant in the volunteer unit during the Spanish War. He was a courteous gentlemen [sic] and able soldier and I liked him as well as any officer, regular or national guard, under whom I later served.[9]

I was issued immediately a tight-fitting blue uniform with bright buttons, a bell-topped cap with cross-rifles on the front and a 1903 Springfield rifle with bayonet, the clothing to be taken home and the rifle and bayonet kept in the arms rack. I did not do so well a short time later when I drew khaki. There was a blouse with bright buttons, a pair of straight trousers, and leggins large enough for a man with twice my caliber of legs so that the first practice march I took they were bagging down around my ankles. Shirts were not then an article of issue in the Missouri National Guard and each man bought his own of blue chambray. The straight trousers, I learned, were already obsolete—the regular army wearing khaki breeches. About 30 years later, after a great deal of wandering around with other types, the army came back to trousers and leggins not unlike those then out of style. The hat issued was the high crowned campaign hat, creased in the center, and with blue hat cord.

This organization—Company A, Second Missouri Infantry, officially, and still the Carthage Light Guard locally—was in the doldrums though I learned later it was still one of the best units in the regiment. The high social status it had once enjoyed had been lost back in the late 'nineties though something of the old reputation of a crack militia outfit still lingered. There was no pay attached and attendance at drill was more or less voluntary. A small nucleus of enthusiasts inspired more or less by the example of the captain worked hard and drilled faithfully every Friday night while the rest dropped in when convenient or a date with the girl friend did not interfere. According to my count there were usually 20 or 25 there at that time. However some time later seeing some drill reports I noted that according to them we always had between 35 and 40. There were 58 on the muster rolls but of those a number had been away from town for a year or two, I learned.

I have said the captain was an excellent officer and he was, but then as now there was sometimes a difference between being an excellent officer and being a successful national guard company commander in dull periods. The professionally skilled captain did not always have the best turn-outs. But Capt. Hiatt kept the unit going and trained his faithfuls for noncommissioned officers, and so even in this low period a volunteer unit could have been formed quickly if war came.

After I had belonged to the unit for about a month there was the annual federal inspection. To pass this it was necessary [to] actually have 35 or 40 men on the floor. This was done by getting "substitutes" from ex-members who came down for the occasion, donned a vacant uniform and answered to an absentee's name. Men stood at right shoulder arms until their names were called, then came down to the order. There was some embarrassment on this occasion when some of the substitutes forgot the names which had been assigned to them and had to be nudged by the next man in ranks before coming down to the order.

My first camp was at Nevada, Mo., 60 miles north of my home town in the summer of 1909—an eight-day camp with army pay. It was devoted to simple drills, maneuvers and parades, and all of the Missouri National Guard was present. Brief and rudimentary as it was, it was helpful training in camp life and organizational functioning in the field.[10]

I found the period very interesting though my zealousness and my newness might easily have made it a tragic one for me—though possibly less tragic for me than for another.

I took my military duties very seriously, and guard duty, quite properly, most serious of all. As a sentry on post along one side of the camp

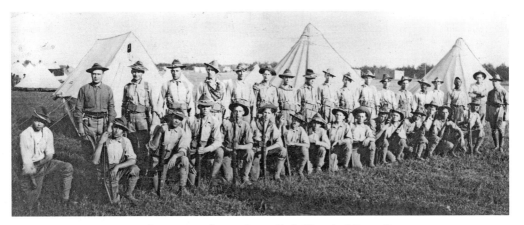

Company A, Second Missouri Infantry, Camp Clark (Nevada, Missouri), summer 1909

one night I was under orders to stop all men trying to enter the camp after taps and to hold them for the corporal of the guard. The previous night, I learned in guard tent gossip, some out-late rowdies had avoided the embarrassment of going to the guard house by engaging sentries in conversation, then brushing the bayoneted rifle aside suddenly, smiting the guard violently on the point of the jaw, then strolling in while the sentry recovered.

That night a man tried to cross my post long after taps. I held him for the corporal of the guard. He chatted pleasantly while waiting for the corporal, then attempted to push my rifle aside and step toward me. Unfamiliar with the use of the gun butt I knew only one answer. I jerked my rifle back, then advanced the point of the bayonet near his belt buckle and commented, rather inanely and probably in a quavering voice: "Wait a minute." Quavering or not, I was poised and steeled to drive the bayonet into his body at the first aggressive movement on his part. He obviously sensed that, for he waited very quietly and both of us silently, the bayonet point at the pit of his stomach, until the corporal of the guard arrived. The next day I heard the man telling someone else confined in the guard tent that a sentry came near killing him the previous night. He was quite correct and maybe the word spread, or perhaps he was the only one who attempted to slug sentries, for I heard of no more cases of the sort.

As for me I learned a lesson I remembered in reference to others— there is no one in the army more dangerous than a scared recruit.

A battalion of the 13th Infantry was at the camp from Fort Leavenworth, Kans., where that regiment was then stationed to serve as a model for the state troops. Mostly it was a good example—a well drilled organization, its men swarthy with the sun and apparently tough as nails. But I remember their crap games, with a great many $20, $10 and $5 gold pieces on the blanket, for the regular army at that time and for years afterwards [was] paid in gold.

And I discarded my ill-fitting uniforms and replaced them with modern breeches, leggins and khaki blouse purchased from miscreant members of the 13th trying to raise funds by sale of their uniforms.

Back home again, and not quite such a recruit as national guardsmen of the day went, I became one of the nucleus of enthusiastic young soldiers which kept the guard alive. Since for economic reasons I still could not go to college, where the military training of Missouri University interested me more than anything else anyhow, and lacking the political influence necessary to secure an appointment to West Point, I put all my spare time, thought and energy into military work and study. In the spring I became a corporal and at the annual inspection apparently did very well in a little quiz that the inspecting officer conducted for noncommissioned officers afterwards. Col. W. K. Caffee, who as previously mentioned had commanded the regiment during Spanish-American days, was present and at the conclusion of the examination gave me some kind words of praise. It was most encouraging to me, and its effect lasted for a long time. It has always been a lesson as to how much a few encouraging words can do for one who is trying.

There was a noncommissioned officers camp in 1910, with all the noncommissioned officers of the regiment gathered together into two provisional companies for training at Nevada under the tutelage of the 13th U.S. Infantry. The affect was most healthful. There was also a maneuver that year at Fort Riley [Kansas] which I, for reasons connected with my civilian employment, was unable to attend. This fact I always regretted since it is my observation that every bit of military experience, however tiny, is of ultimate military value.[11] In the spring of 1911 I became a sergeant and was immediately made quartermaster sergeant—the equivalent of supply sergeant of later years—and served as such at the 1911 encampment at Nevada.[12] This was uncongenial work but doubtless

Company A, Second Missouri Infantry, Carthage, Missouri, July 3, 1910

educational and was the more difficult for me in the field since I acted as duty sergeant besides.

The year 1911 was important to my military training in another way. I began interviewing old soldiers and studying the official records of the Union and Confederate Armies to write a series of newspaper articles about Civil War engagements and skirmishes in my home county. This interest continued for years, resulted in publishing a modest volume on this field in 1923.[13] Since war changes only as weapons and circumstances change, I feel that many important lessons in irregular and guerrilla warfare lie hidden and neglected in the dusty tomes dealing with such phases of our own Civil War.

When the 1911 drill regulations came out I and a group of fellow enthusiasts purchased some of the first copies issued by the *Army and Navy Journal* and studied them most carefully, trying them out in our own little nucleus on Sundays and any night in addition to drill night we could get possession of the armory. Our efforts were soon helped by the War Department which sent drill sergeants from line regiments to be stationed for a time with National Guard units for instructional purposes. We first had one named Johnson from Company A, 15th Infantry, and later one named Foster from the Fourth Infantry.[14] These men had committed the regulations to memory and we did the pertinent portions likewise. This was of assistance to me until after the First World War. I can still quote paragraphs from memory.

In the summer of 1912 our Second Missouri Infantry was sent to Kansas to participate in maneuvers—the Seventh U.S. Infantry, stationed at Fort Leavenworth, our regiment, and a squadron of the 15th U.S. Cavalry, all commanded by Col. Daniel Cornman, maneuvering against the Kansas and Oklahoma National guard regiments, the 13th Cavalry, then at Fort Riley, and some other regular artillery units.[15] It was both an interesting and worthwhile maneuver, invo[l]ving actual marching, bivouac and simulated combat over some 60 miles of Kansas terrain, terminating at Lansing, south of Leavenworth, Kans. Still a combination, supply, mess and duty sergeant, I had a busy time.[16]

One unpleasant feature of the maneuver for me was connected with hard tack which with raw bacon was the nearest equivalent of the day to the C and K rations of the Second World War. We breakfasted one morning at 4 A.M. and did not have a cooked meal again until the days maneuver was over about 5 P.M. In our haversacks we had hardtack and raw bacon. I ate maybe a box of hard tack. It swelled after I ate it. The result was uncomfortable in a big way, as I recall, and as we bivouacked that night east of the Kansas State Penitentiary I groaned in agony.

The maneuvers were reasonably realistic and made the more interesting because of an abundance of blank cartridges issued the men. In my opinion they were excellent training. The Mexican troubles were already absorbing the attention of most regular troops and as I recall no more combined army and national guard maneuvers were held. Even after the First World War they were not resumed on any large scale until—if my memory is right—about 1937. Our army was sadly in the doldrums to permit any such long intermission of a training feature so important.

By the summer of 1912 I had reached a place where national guard activities—however much increased interest the federal government was manifesting and however much additional clothing and equipment was arriving—ceased to satisfy me. I decided either to enlist in the regular army in the hopes of gaining a commission in the Philippine Scouts or to join one of the factions in the Mexican revolutionary troubles in order to get war experience preparatory to service in the American army.[17]

My mother—my father had died when I was two years of age—agreed I should join the regular army. Wisely she felt that a young man with a trend like mine had better get into the army and stay there. She had no enthusiasm about Mexico yet offered no objection. She could see the value of war experience for a soldier. I am proud of my fine Spartan mother—an ideal mother for a soldier. I am only sorry that a more or less erratic military career failed to live up to her probable hopes and expectations.

My application for a discharge from the national guard to join the regular army being slow to go through, I resigned from the newspaper where I was employed, visited for a time with a brother in southwest Oklahoma, and then went to El Paso to look into the matter of joining in the wars in Mexico.[18]

A Civilian Visits Mexico

MY ORIGINAL INTEREST in the Mexican wars had hinged in part on my sympathy for Francisco Madero in his successful revolt of 1910 and 1911 against President Porfirio Díaz. It seemed to me—quite ignorant of details as I was—that he had not dealt fairly with the leaders who had helped him to make that revolt successful. When Pascual Orozco raised the standard of revolt against him in 1912, Tracy Richardson who lived at Lamar, Mo., who once had been a member of the Second Missouri Infantry in which I had had my national guard experience, and who later had served under Lee Christmas in Nicaragua, gained a good deal of publicity as a machine gunner in Orozco's army. This gave me a rather favorable impression of the Orozco effort.[1]

By the time I reached El Paso the Orozco revolt was broken and such of his former forces as remained were in the field only as bandits under the name of "Colorados" or, as Americans called them, "Red Flaggers." It did not take much enquiry around El Paso to decide me that they were not the right side to be on anyhow. But I decided to go over to Juárez to take a look, although El Pasoans to whom I talked advised me that just then was a good time for all good Americans to stay on the American side of the line. In point of fact the only Americans I saw in El Paso that day was [sic] an old Iowa couple looking at the bullet-chipped statue of Benito Juárez, and an American post card salesman who told me that it was unwise to wander about Juárez alone.[2]

One of the first things I did in Juárez after looking at the monument

Benito Juárez Monument, Juárez, Mexico

and church was to wander down by the jail, garrisoned and loop-holed for rifle fire. This was interesting and I stopped to stare. In the Mexican army [in] those days the women constituted the commissary department, each man being paid daily and his wife, or the woman camp follower who served as such, getting and preparing food for him. It was lunch time and these women, some far gone in pregnancy and others with children accompanying them, were bringing food to the soldiers. A stack of Mauser rifles inside the main entrance interested me also. My acquaintance with military rifles was limited to the 1903 Springfield and the obsolete 1872 [sic] single-shot Springfield. All this display of interest was no doubt indiscreet and the sentry studied me suspiciously. I decided it might be as well to walk on.

Walking on past the jail about a block I found nothing but adobe houses and turned back. As I neared the jail on my return the sentry called out an officer. The two studied me closely as I passed. Despite an uneasy conscience caused by the fact I had come down there in expectation of bearing arms against their side, I ambled past, trying to look as innocent and unconcerned as possible. The officer apparently decided I appeared harmless and so I was not stopped. Otherwise it is possible my future might have been an unhappy [one], the Mexican custom of the time, according to reports, being either to shoot suspects or to put them in jail and forget about them.

This little experience caused me to remember the old post card man and seek his counsel. He told me that the regular soldiers, clad in blue grey such as those at the jail[,] were a part of the army that President Madero had taken over from the Díaz regime. Many of them, he surmised, ought to feel at home garrisoning that jail since they had been recruited from jails in the first place. The rest of the soldiers in town, those wearing khaki, were Maderista volunteers—mounted troops who were largely ranch hands who had volunteered to help Madero, a good many of them English-speaking and from the Mexican population on the American side of the border. He suggested that if I was determined to look around the town that he get one of those—a good many of whom he knew—to show me about. To this I was agreeable.

A pleasant young Mexican who in consequence I soon had as a guide told me that his name was Umberto Tabares and that he had worked on a ranch near Marathon, Texas, until he joined the Maderista volunteers. He thought he was to fight for Mexico, he said, but that the way it was there was no fighting at all. The Mexican regular army commanders would not let them fight the Red Flaggers about the town. They would be sent out from time to time but once outside the town some distance, would be required to halt and do nothing. In his opinion these regular army troops were not at all loyal to Madero. As for him, in view of that situation, he was considering slipping back across the border and returning to Marathon.

His estimate of the situation, I noted later, was about correct. When Victoriano Huerta revolted against Madero early the next year, the federal troops in Juárez turned rebel, united with the Red Flaggers bands outside the city, and surrounded and captured the Maderista volunteers in the town.

Accompanied by young Tabores [sic] I strolled through the local market and at my suggestion we walked up by the main barracks of which I had read in newspaper accounts concerning some of the fighting in Juárez. These were held by regular troops.

Some kind of ceremony was in progress, possibly guard mount. Gaily-garbed buglers and some troops were maneuvering in the street, then marched back inside where a considerable body of troops were in formation. We stood across the street opposite the entrance looking in.

A portly officer of upper middle age came across to us and engaged my Maderista guide in a wordy exchange, the Marathon cowboy holding up his end of it quite as boldly as if he had been a dignitary of the old army himself.[3] Finally the officer turned away and Tabores turned to me.

"He says we can't stand here," he commented.

We walked down to the corner, stayed there until the music stopped [and] he accepted my offer to buy a dinner if he would show me a place and handle the conversation.

He led me to a hotel, argued for awhile with a fat woman in a hotel courtyard who regarded us with obvious suspicion but who eventually agreed to serve us. A waiter stood behind our chairs thrusting lined-up dishes, hot with pepper, in front of us as we cleared the contents from the preceding one. An additional dish of pepper sat in front of us, and since I did not care for mine in view of my feeling there was already a super-abundance in the food, my companion added my spare seasoning to his in flavoring his own food. The waiter impressed me as being there partly to listen to our conversation, and it was with some relief a short time later, after I had told my guide good-bye, that I returned to the American side of the line again, being searched for firearms by the bridge guards as I had been on the way over.

That night I was on an east bound Texas Pacific train, pumping a discharged member of the Second Cavalry about the fight at Bud Dajo, in Jolo, in which he had engaged shortly before returning to the United States.[4] And I was impressed when somewhere near Fort Hancock, a couple of armed cavalry guards passed through the car, carefully scrutinizing each passenger. I supposed they were looking for Mexican bandits or suspicious characters. My companion grunted. "Showing off," he surmised.

Joining the Regulars

BACK HOME I found my discharge from the national guard waiting for me, went to nearby Joplin, applied for enlistment and that night with one other recruit went to Jefferson Barracks where after final physical examination we were sworn in with a group of men from various other recruiting stations.

It apparently frequently happened that men applied for enlistment but their nerve failed them and at the recruit depot they did not want to join. The club the army held over their heads was that if they did not go ahead and take the oath they were guilty of getting railway transportation to the depot under false pretences [sic]. The reluctant ones thereupon tried to fail the medical examination.

One man in my group professed to be unable to read any letter of any size on the eye chart. And he could not hearing [sic] the ticking of a watch behind his ear or even loud whispers.

"You can't see very well, can you?" said the medical officer.

"No sir," answered the man, "I can't see skeercely at all."

"And you can't hear very well?" continued the medico.

"No sir. I can't hear skeercely at all."

"Well," said the officer, "I guess you can see and hear well enough to soldier. Get over with that group of men who have passed."

This was on October 23, 1912, and we enlisted for three years.[1] On November 1 a new law went into effect by which men enlisted for seven years—either three or four with the colors and the rest in reserve. We congratulated ourselves on getting in just under the wire.

Generally speaking, the recruit depot was something of an amusing nightmare. Recruit companies consisted of a training cadre of permanent party men—"general service infantry," I think they were called—and the recruits. The permanent party men lorded it over the recruits in a big way, impressing on the newcomers that they were the lowest of the low. A corporal ranked about as high as a colonel in the line and even a private was an important personage. As for us we officially and unofficially were "'Cruits," so listed on the roster. One gathered that the one unforgiveable sin at that time in the army was being a recruit. I was rather surprised the first time I did a guard and became acquainted with some of the noncommissioned officers to find that they were quite human and rather pleasant fellows when away from routine in barracks.

Since I suspected that telling I had been a national guardsman would not add to happiness of life in the army, I carefully remained silent about any military background. Since obviously I already knew the recruit drill I was subjected to some appraising stares but no one questioned me. Presumably a man's past was his own business until he was exposed. But the noncommissioned officers evidently came to certain conclusions.

One evening the corporal in charge of my squad room in the 27th Company, a man who never honored a recruit with anything but a scowl, came into the room and direct to my bunk, affable and smiling.[2]

"Your name is Jones, isn't it?" he asked.

"No," I said. "That is Jones yonder."

He scowled at me as of old and smiled on Jones.

"Get your blankets," he said pleasantly as to an equal, not to a contemptible recruit, "we are going to the guard house."

And so "Jones" who, we soon learned, had served in the army before, deserted and reenlisted under a false name, passed out to prison and punishment.

If there were any chaplains about Jefferson Barracks I never saw them but I went once to a religious service conducted by some ministers from St. Louis. They addressed us as if, it seemed to me, we had been convicts in a penitentiary. A soldier in the ranks was not rated very high by ordinary civilians in those days and I have no doubt these good ministers regarded us as about convict social level.

We did not see much of our officers but occasionally they gave lectures of one sort or another and since they talked to us as if we were soldiers and not mere recruits we were pleasantly impressed. Only one of these officers remains in my memory and of his talk only one section. He was a jovial old cavalry major named Quinlan. Dennis P. Quinlan I think.[3]

"Don't get the idea that you are heroes because you are in the army," he told us. "No man is a hero just because he joins the army and no man is a hero in his first war. But if he ever volunteers to go back to a second war—ah then he is a hero."

The recruits in the 27th Company as I remember them was not a bad lot. My principal friends were a man named Percy Lang from Chicago who had been a cook on lake steamers, a quiet ex-laundryman named Dennis from somewhere, some six or seven years my senior, and a young farmer named Apple—"'Crut Apple"—was always the first name called on our roll call. Lang like I had enlisted for the infantry, Dennis was in for the coast artillery, and Apple for the cavalry.[4] My own preferences were for the cavalry but I had a somewhat exaggerated idea of the value of my previous infantry training and thought I would have a better chance there. I wanted first to be in the infantry therefore, and second I wanted to get out to the Philippines.

All the men at the recruit depot had enlisted for some particular arm or service and changing to any other was optional. Requisitions came to the depot from time to time for so many men of such-and-such an arm or service for such-and-such a point. If there were not enough enlisted for such arm to fill the requisitions, others were invited to volunteer and many did. Everyone was anxious to get away, and services such as the medical corps for which few had signed up thus obtained their quotas. I was tempted once to transfer to the field artillery for there was a group going to the Philippines. Had it been a cavalry group I would have done so probably. But I held off, waiting in hope. My main fear was that I would be sent to the 7th Infantry at Fort Leavenworth, and my fear was based not on any objection to that famous regiment but to the fact that Fort Leavenworth was a bit too close to my own home. Could I have seen what

Pvt. Percy Lang (*right*), Company C, Twenty-second U.S. Infantry

the future held for the Seventh, I would not have minded. Less than a year and a half later that regiment boarded transports at Galveston for Vera Cruz while my own waited on the beach for orders that never came.

In early December there came a bunch of requisitions for replacements and most of us "old timers" in the 27th Company moved out—the infantry to Fort Bliss, the coast artillery to Fort Morgan, Ala., and the cavalry to the Third Cavalry on the Rio Grande somewhere.[5] Bidding goodbye to Dennis and Apple, Lang and I with a couple of carloads of others were soon speeding across Missouri, Kansas, the Texas Panhandle and New Mexico down to El Paso where a few short months before I had been pondering the idea of joining some army in Mexico.

Noncommissioned officers of the Jefferson Barracks permanent party conducted us on our jaunt so the atmosphere on the train was much the same as at the barracks except that we were happy and elated at being on the move.

Our food was a bit scanty but I had been in the national guard too long where it was still scantier at camps to grouse about that. I ate slowly, masticated the food thoroughly, and hence—believing something I had read somewhere—was better satisfied than if I bolted it. Carefully, from policies sake, I refrained from complaint. One evening as we crossed the Panhandle there was, for a wonder, plenty of hash. Just as we were finishing eating, the sergeant in charge came up the aisle and spoke to me.

"Did I hear you say you were not getting enough to eat?" he queried.

"You never heard me make any complaint," I answered truthfully.

"I don't know whether I complained or not," spoke up Lang, "but anyhow I haven't been getting enough to eat."

Someone carrying the receptacle with the hash was with the sergeant and the noncommissioned officer filled Lang's meat pan heaping full.

"Now I want to see you eat that," he said. "Eat every bit of it."

Lang ate the food leisurely—all of the huge pile. Next he took a piece of bread, swiped up his mess kit with it and ate the bread. Then he spoke.

"Sergeant," he asked, "may I have some more hash?"

El Paso

ARRIVING AT FORT Bliss on the north edge of El Paso on Dec. 7, 1912, the detachment of recruits from Jefferson Barracks were lined up near the railway and counted off to go to various infantry units.

Fort Bliss, Texas, lies on a high sandy plateau three miles northeast of El Paso and just around the shoulder of Mount Franklin. To the north and east is a rolling, sandy waste, covered with sagebrush, mesquite, Spanish bayonet and low growing cactus. To the west are grey, rugged mountains, a few houses climbing part way up the bare foot hills. South of the post the ground drops to the fertile valley of the Rio Grande, criss-crossed with irrigation ditches and dotted with low, adobe houses half concealed by tall cottonwood trees. Through the center of this valley flows the Rio Grande, marking the boundary between the United States and the turbulent republic to the south. Beyond the valley and on Mexican soil, the ground again rises, forming grey foothills, and merging finally into the barren mountains whose jagged, irregular peaks are silhouetted against the sky.

Fort Bliss[,] at the time of which I am speaking, was more of a camp than a fort or barracks.[1] The only barracks there consisted of quarters for four troops of cavalry while the garrison of the post consisted of a regiment of infantry, a regiment and one squadron of cavalry and several batteries of artillery. All of these were housed under canvas except several troops of cavalry, which, more fortunate than their comrades, occupied long sheds which offered more protection from the cold winds that sweep around the mountain than did the worn tents of the remainder of the soldiers.

A number of soldiers lolling around some huge wood piles near the railway looked us over approvingly as we were divided off into two parties, one of which went to the first battalion of the 18th Infantry and the other to the 22d.[2] We were marched up the sandy road between the tents until we reached the tent which served as headquarters and here we were assigned to our companies. To my delight I and two others were assigned to Company "F," 22nd Infantry, which we were informed was not at Fort Bliss but was one of the organizations which were stationed along the border, enforcing the neutrality proclamation forbidden [sic] the taking of arms and ammunition across the line.

The troops at Fort Bliss and in the El Paso vicinity at that time consisted of the 22d Infantry, commanded by Col. D. A. Frederick, the first battalion of the 18th Infantry, and the Second Cavalry. Col. (or Brig. Gen.) E. Z. Steever was in command of the whole.[3] "Easy" Steever some of the soldiers good-naturedly called him, I learned later, because they thought he was too willing to accede to the request of El Paso for troops for parades. That Col. Steever might have had a sound military reason for making a display of his strength in El Paso whenever occasion offered in view of the disturbed conditions along the border did not seem to have occurred to anyone.[4] But there were no parades while I was there, so far as I recall. Certainly my company participated in none.

The infantry units had been sent to El Paso from their home posts at the time the Orozco revolt started. The 22d was guarding the international bridges and had outposts at other key points along the border, with headquarters at Fort Bliss.[5] The battalion of the 18th, as I recall, was all at Fort Bliss, as was all of the Second Cavalry at that time. The reason for the cavalry being at the post instead of on patrol, I was told, was that it had recently returned from the Philippines and had been filled up with recruits, whom it was necessary to train before going on anything even approximating active duty.

In the assignment of recruits I was in the group allotted to the 22d Infantry and the genial sergeant major of that regiment, an old soldier named Jans, detailed several men including myself to Company F.[6] My friend Lang went to Company C of the 22d where he soon became a cook

Brig. Gen. Edgar Z. Steever, from *Fifty-first Annual Report of the Association of Graduates of the United States Military Academy* (Saginaw, Mich.: Seemann & Peters, 1920)

and so far as I have knowledge of his life lived happily thereafter in that capacity. "You fellows are lucky to be assigned to F Company," he told us. "You'll have a good captain, a good first sergeant and be in an outfit that feeds well. I don't know what more a soldier can want." Neither did we. It all sounded good—especially about the food—and with the driver[']s favorable comment in our ears we were at Washington Park a few minutes later getting checked in.

Company F was stationed at Washington Park in East El Paso near the Rio Grande and we were taken there in a mule-drawn escort wagon jolting over dusty roads. From the high ground before we started downward I remember staring over the valley at the distant and often captured Juárez, dominated by hills to the south so that it looked from there like it might have been founded with the specific purpose of making its capture easy. A noncommissioned officer in the wagon explained that we were joining the best regiment in the army and being assigned to the best company of that regiment. Capt. L. A. Curtis, the company commander, he further asserted, was a fatherly individual, deeply interested in his men, and an ideal officer under whom to serve.[7] We were favorably impressed, particularly after we were told the same thing by other men of the company. It was a unit which believed in itself.

Capt. Curtis, a slow-spoken Spanish-American War veteran 40 years of age, welcomed us himself, and we were then taken in charge by a heavily-bearded, middle-aged first sergeant. Beards had gone out of military fashion before this but when the regiment left its quarters at Fort Sam Houston the preceding February he had stated that [he] wasn't going to shave again until it returned—and he hadn't. His whiskers gave a Civil War aspect to the scenery.

Company F was billetted, along with Company E, in a long adobe building at the front of the park in a long room evidently used in normal days for fair exhibits of some kinds. At the head of the bunk allotted to me was a huge crude mural of an ailing chicken with the words "Conkey will cure you." Each morning when I awakened this work of art was the first thing to greet my vision and at night it was the final object I contemplated before lights were switched off. Even yet it is photographed indelibly on my memory and I never think of El Paso but I think of this afflicted specimen of poultry, waiting for that magic remedy to make it whole.

We were issued field equipment and rifles, with 30 rounds of live ammunition to carry in our belts and we settled down feeling quite field-soldierish and warlike. Along each wall was placed a row of cots, at the head of each, a rifle and a cartridge belt, worn and white with many washings and crammed full of steel jacketed cartridges. About forty men were in the room and their gaunt, unshaven appearance told of hard service. These were no spick and span barracks soldiers but men who had been on the arduous duty of border patrol for almost a year and they were not so punctilious about appearances as they would have been under more peaceable circumstances. These were field soldiers. Everyone was quite human here, we soon ascertained, even the non-commissioned officers, and we soon felt that we were members of the family. A bearded first sergeant gave us a few words of advice, a grizzled quartermaster sergeant issued us equipment and cots and we made ourselves at home, feeling as if we had fallen into a bunch of old Indian fighters or something of the sort.

The 22d Infantry had been stationed in barracks at Fort Sam Houston at San Antonio the February preceding but a threatened clash at Juárez across the river from El Paso had sent it hurrying from its comfortable and cozy quarters to the scene and since then it had been in the field on border guard. The first sergeant's carefully tended beard, I afterwards ascertained, had started on leaving Fort Sam Houston, he having remarked that he was not going to shave until the regiment had returned to barracks or had been in the field a year—and he did not.

There were two companies of the 22d Infantry stationed at Washington Park at this time, Company "F" and Company "E." Company "E" maintained an outpost I was told, at San Lorenzo ford, a crossing of the Rio Grande about two miles to the southeast.

Company F, we found, maintained an outpost about a mile to the west on the international line which here was a former channel of the Rio Grande, the river having cut a new channel inside Mexican territory. This was the region later called "the hole in the wall" and I have heard its ownership was disputed but at that time all south of the old stream bed was considered Mexico.[8] From the outpost tent single sentries by

Billets, Company F, Twenty-second U.S. Infantry, Washington Park, El Paso, Texas, December 1912

day and double sentries by night patrolled a beat which on the west ran to the foundry and on the east along the old streambed to where it ran into the river. The company was low in strength and about a third of it was on duty nightly. Consequently there was not much doing in the way of company drill, about an hour a day being all that was devoted to this work. This little drill did not apply to recruits, however. It was with some disappointment that I learned that recruits were to be given special training a week or so before being turned to duty. We were assigned an old time drill sergeant, whose long drooping mustache made him appear more like an old time pirate than like a soldier, and he drilled us from morning until night. It was Sunday before we had an opportunity to look around and see much of the country in which we were stationed.

Less than a quarter of a mile south of the park ran the muddy Rio Grande, winding its way through yellow, sandy flats overgrown with willows and grease wood and with its channel full of shifting quicksands and ugly, treacherous mudbanks. The American side of the river at this point was low and was quite evidently subject to overflow in high water. The Mexican side was higher, was bordered with an occasional clump of willows of a fair growth and to the south stretched away grassy fields for some miles until they met the grey mesquite growth of the uplands. Several whitewashed houses surrounded by cottonwood trees were visible in this valley land and there was one long building which might have been a barracks of some sort as occasionally a Mexican flag could be seen flying above it.

Some distance to the southeast of the park the river turned to the south for a half mile or so, then to the east again making a broad loop, at the southern end of which was San Lorenzo ford where "E" Company kept watch on one side and an old Spanish mission[,] in a clump of cottonwood trees and surrounded by a huddle of adobe huts, seemed to stand sentinel on the other.

El Paso with its atmosphere of Mexican intrigue was an interesting city at this time as was Juárez across the river, a town barred of course to American soldiers but which I had visited a few months prior to enlisting in the army when I had been down in this country as a civilian. Among the things of especial interest in El Paso was an old muzzle loading cannon in the center of the city on San Jacinto plaza which had been stolen by insurrectos during the Madero revolution and had been used against Juárez in the attack which captured that place for Madero and resulted in making him president of Mexico. Down near the city hall was another gun which had been used by the Maderistas in this campaign and later presented to the city of El Paso after the triumph of the revolutionaries. It was a small caliber piece which had been bored out of an old axle of a railway coach by American soldiers of fortune serving with Madero and which was said to have done good service in the attack on Juárez. I myself had seen the small holes in the buildings in the Mexican town which were said to have been made by this gun and I therefore viewed it with much interest as I had not seen the gun itself on my first visit.

My first glimpse at a regular army organization from the inside naturally interested me. The noncommissioned officers, unlike those at the recruit depot, were friendly and human. Most of them were old soldiers—the junior of them being on his third three-year enlistment, and a number of them being veterans of the Spanish-American War 14 years before as well as the later Philippine campaigns. While the general educational level was low, by modern standards, there were exceptions in some obviously well-educated men whose presence in the ranks I presumed to be the result of love of soldering or love of liquor, or both. It was only at pay-day they showed the liquor trait. When a private drew $15 a month, a corporal $21 and a sergeant only $30, normal sobriety was a necessity as well as a virtue.

My own position in the company was pleasant from the start due to a reticence about the past which fitted in with military ideas of the day. The reticence was entirely due to my feeling that it would be tactful to conceal a national guard background so long as I was new in the regular army[,] but whatever interpretation was put on it by my new comrades the result was favorable. A man's past was his own business. What he had been or done in civil life did not matter[,] only what he was and did in the army.

The first evening I had unpacked my gear from the Jefferson Barracks recruit bag to stow it away in a box underneath my bunk[;] my well-worn infantry drill regulations of national guard days was lying on my bunk. A sergeant picked it up curiously, and noted that I had torn out the flyleaf where a man usually wrote his name and organization.

"Where did you get this?" he asked.

"It is one I had left over," I replied.

He grinned and asked no further questions, for this reason or others but I found myself accepted henceforth as a soldier instead of a recruit.

The days were comparatively warm in this region but the nights were cold and out in Washington park the men off duty shivered around the two tiny stoves in the huge barnlike room in a vain endeavor to keep warm. Incidentally this was the time at which the old soldiers spun endless yarns of Cuba, the Philippines and of China and engaged in long arguments about things that had happened in those far away places many years before. There was a large number of old soldiers in the outfit— one bugler had been continuously in this one company since the days of the Philippine insurrection and there were a number of men, eight or ten I should say from memory, who had entered the army prior to the Spanish-American War. Two, I learned, were entitled to Indian campaign badges and one, a corporal, had been doing border guard in 1890, the year I was born. Then there were a bunch of second and third enlistment men and a goodly number of first who had joined the unit at the beginning of the first border mobilization in 1911. The younger men on their first enlistment did not engage much in these conversations but told reminiscences of their own of happenings on border guard the summer before at the various points along the international line where they had done duty. In such company the talk ranged widely and we recruits took it in with open mouths, much to the gratification of the old soldiers who I expect were rather appreciative of a new and eager audience. And after taps everyone went to bed and covered themselves with their overcoats and various articles of civilian bed clothing purchased down town and did their best to keep warm until morning, a very difficult task.

And the company had its gay Lotharios also, I soon noted, who were conspicuous by their absence from these impromptu evening sessions. There was "Silk Hat Harry" Elam who hummed popular songs constantly and walked with a swagger. He came from North Carolina, as indeed did so many others that it seemed to me that that state must have furnished half of the enlisted men of the old army. And then there was "Cholly" Perry, a gentleman with carefully oiled silky hair and with an amorous propensity that was always getting him into trouble.[9] He had already faced a summary court for his custom of applying terms of endearment to strange Mexican girls, and about the time I joined the outfit he had gotten into trouble again.

One sunny day "Cholly" had been strolling in the park back of the billets and he chanced to meet a nice looking and well dressed young American woman alone—the park was a pretty place with a little zoo at one end and El Paso people citizens [sic] visited it frequently even at this season of the year. It was more than the dashing Cholly could stand to see this charming damsel without an escort so as he met her he removed his hat.

"How do you do," he said.

"Why, how do you do," the lady replied, smiling sweetly, "What is your name?"

"Cholly Jones," beamed the gay masher, jubilant at the brilliant start he had made.

"Well, Cholly Jones," replied the fair one, "I am Mrs.——.[10] I will take pleasure in reporting you to the lieutenant."

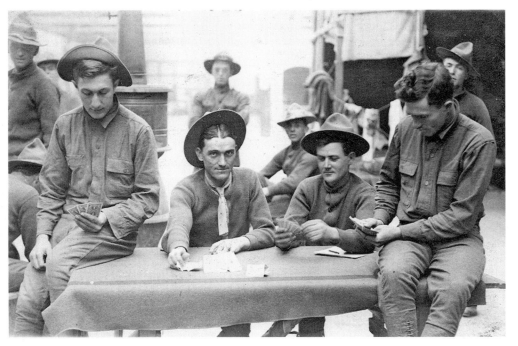

Men of Company F, Twenty-second U.S. Infantry, Washington Park, El Paso, Texas, 1912

And so Cholly Jones [Perry] was in bad again. Lieut.——being commander of Company E. Result another summary court and another "blind."[11] But the victim was never cured. Up till the time he deserted a month or so later after being caught trying to sell a comrade[']s overcoat so as to keep up his gay life he played up in his fancied role as a smasher of hearts.

At the recruit depot the dread of my young life had been kitchen police. Peeling potatoes and scrubbing greasy pots and pans had never appealed to me somehow and it was with no particular pleasure that I realized that before long I was certain to be detailed upon this duty. So it was with some pleasure that I received the news one day that I had been made assistant to the company clerk and in return for the little work that I did in the office from time to time would be excused from the kitchen detail. I am afraid that this to me pleasant news did not go to make me popular with some of the privates who were less lucky and I heard one old timer grumblingly remark that I was "getting my hand out early," meaning that I had been "hand-shaking" or currying favor with the first sergeant, but I was not guilty and if there was any feeling that I was it soon wore off because I never afterwards heard anyone allude to it directly or indirectly.

Probably a word as to the international situation in the El Paso vicinity might not be amiss at this point. Juárez, like all of the cities in northern Mexico, was held by federal troops, consisting in part of the old regular army of the Díaz regime and in part of volunteer troops, mainly mounted, who were known as Madero volunteers and many of whom had come from the Mexican population on the American side of the border. There was not much love lost between the volunteers and the regular army but the volunteers appeared to be better type of men and better fighters even if obviously less disciplined than the men of the old army.

Outside of the towns, roving around through the mountains and across the wastes, were small groups of "Coloradas" [sic] or Red Flaggers, most of whom had served with Orozco in his rebellion against Madero during the summer of 1912 and now that the Orozco movement had been broken up still kept the field as guerrillas. At times these small bands operated close to the garrisoned cities and occasionally united into a force large enough to menace some of them with capture. When I had been in Juárez some months before as a civilian, I had been told by a member of the Madero volunteers that the commanders of the old regular army were in sympathy with the Red Flaggers and made no actual attempts to clear them out of the country. He stated that secretly these officers were still opposed to Madero, against whom they had fought as parts of the old Díaz army, and though now supposedly serving him were in fact not much enclined to fight anyone opposed to him. Later events indicate that this man's estimate of the situation was not far wrong. So far as the duty of the American border guard was concerned it was merely to prevent armed parties entering or leaving Mexico, to prevent arms or ammunition being taken into that country and to protect American property along the border.

When we new men had been with the company a week or so we were deemed fit for guard duty and so one morning rolled up our blankets and comforts and wandered seven or eight blocks down a big irrigation ditch through an unkempt Mexican section of the town to the company guard tent on the border, all set to take our part in border guard, a la 1912.

As I have stated, Company "F" maintained an outpost on that part of the border formed by the former river bed of the Rio Grande and from the outpost patrolled the line along a stretch of about a mile and a half, the outpost tent being centrally located as regards the portion being patrolled. The sector was split in two long posts along which single sentries walked in the daytime and double sentries at night. One post, known as No. 1, was to the west of the guard tent through the streets and allies [alleys] of the Mexican section of town and the other was along a less settled stretch ending near the place that the old ditch joined the river. Both of them were lonely enough at night, particularly the last named. It was on this last named post that I served my first tour.

Being a recruit I took life and my duty very seriously. I was detailed to the outpost about nine o'clock in the morning and as I walked my post I diligently studied everything that moved and many things that did not on both sides of the line and was much surprised that a stirring adventure of some sort did not at once occur. However nothing happened and, aside from the Mexican dogs that snarled at my heels as I passed the adobe huts of their owners, the only thing that caused me any concern was when an old Mexican woman some distance in front of me started to carry a large basket of clothing across the line. I halted her and required her to remove the clothes from the basket but much to my disappointment there was no ammunition concealed in the bottom, nothing but clothes, and I reluctantly let her proceed on her way unhindered. The only trepidation that I could see I caused among the natives was with the children. They frequently crossed back and forth across the line but invariably waited until I had passed a hundred yards or so and then dashed over at top speed.

Tours of duty were four hours on and eight off. By day I strolled along under cottonwood trees in which mistletoe was profusely growing, studied the Mexican side alertly for signs of activity and the American side curiously to observe the habits of the local Mexicans. And in the long tours at night there were long conversations with my companion about his military experiences or about his home regions. Under orders we carried our rifles with empty chambers but with a full clip in the magazine so that there was a minimum danger of accident but only a movement of the bolt necessary to prepare for action. I fell in the habit of a mountaineer friend and habitually carried my rifle in the hollow of my left arm. Orders were not to fire, even if fired upon, except in self-defense. The restraining order was not taken too seriously. The "except-in-self defense" clause seemed broad enough to cover all eventualities.

To me it seemed that the duty itself was not taken as seriously as it might be. The first night I was on post from 10 to 2 A.M. and was amazed to see the 2 to 6 o'clock relief turn out with blankets. The nights were chilly and the custom was for the men on number 1 post to the west to sleep in the foundry at the west end of the post and those of No. 2 relief to sleep in the plant at which El Paso garbage was burned which was within the territory of that patrol post. The only man of the whole out-post awake during those hours was the non-commissioned officer of the guard dozing over a magazine at a lantern much of the time at the guard tent within 50 feet of the border. As I have already said, the nights were cold and soon after a companion and I went on post at 10 o'clock, I found that walking post at night was the exception rather than the rule. At the point where the two posts joined some blocks distant from the guard tent, there was a little reentrant angle in the northern bank of the old river bed where a fire was perfectly concealed from the American side although it must have been visible for a considerable distance in Mexico. Here the two patrols were wont to meet and warm their shins between patrols and in fact warmed considerably longer than they patrolled. I warmed my feet at the fire with the others but I never became so bad as to go to sleep when I was supposed to be on duty and many a time after this first guard when I found myself on third relief I traded reliefs with some one who was scheduled for the second so I would not be on the one where it was customary to slumber instead of walk post. This was long before the days of the Columbus, N.M. raid and the average soldier was convinced that patrolling the border was not only as safe as going to church but that it was a silly sort of a thing that might as well be omitted anyhow.[12]

My expressions of surprise drew amused rejoinder that there was no danger—that the officers never came around after 2 o'clock. As for the Mexicans "those fellows know better than to attack Americans. Now if they were Filipinos, it would be different." I wondered, perhaps unjustly, a few years later if a similar attitude was responsible for the surprise of the garrison at Columbus, N.M. by Pancho Villa.[13]

Now Company F was not the sort of an outfit that would ordinarily do this sort of thing. It was a smooth functioning and really efficient sort of organization as a rule. It contained an abnormally large number of old soldiers and for some reason was almost entirely free from that atmosphere of petty jealousy and intrigue that is often found in a military unit. I was told then and still believe that it was one of the best outfits in the army. But the border guard was distinctly fed up with its task and from what I heard I received the impression that this sort of thing was not particularly uncommon at this time.

This carelessness in patrol due to the bored attitude of the rank and file was only a passing phase and ended with renewed activity across the line which caused renewed activity of our own officers in checking up. But while it lasted I was never on the 2 to 6 o'clock relief, always trading it off, when I drew it, to someone who had drawn the 10 to 2 watch and preferred the later one where they could sleep.

After this first guard, others followed so rapidly that it seemed to me like I was on guard most of the time but I rather liked it except for the loss of sleep. In the daytime I would think that the service was a good place to be but when an unsympathetic non commissioned officer stirred me out of my sleep in the middle of the night to go out into the cold and walk post I always wondered why anyone was such a fool as to join the army when he might as well stay in civilian life where he could get some sleep.

Occasionally on guard there was a little false alarm or something else that caused some excitement and varied the usual monotony. On one occasion I and a tall Tennessean who was my companion on No. 2 post, rounded up a Mexican who we found sneaking through the mesquite in our vicinity and our suspicions as to his character were not allayed any when he produced a bottle of whiskey and tried to make friends by offering us a drink. A search of his person revealed nothing more dangerous than the whiskey bottle however and after he had proved to our satisfaction that his only object in lurking in that neighborhood was to keep a rendezvous with a senorita who lived in a nearby hut we let him go. He was rather badly scared and if the senorita later appeared at the agreed upon place of meeting I am afraid that she found her lover absent.

On another occasion when I was walking post in the daytime along the portion of No. 2 where there were no houses, I observed a Mexican squatting behind a bush on the Mexican side of the dry river bed and regarding me intently. Now I had heard many times how a Mexican would kill a man for his arms if he had a chance and somehow I did not like the idea of the stranger regarding me so closely. It did not seem right and proper to me that I should give him a chance to shoot me in the back by continuing to walk on down my post so I slipped the safety catch of my rifle to the "ready" and, carrying it in the hollow of my arm ready for instant use, I strolled over into Mexico to look him over.

The Mexican did not know quite what to make of this invasion of his native land and remained in his squatting position while I came over and looked down at him. He appeared to be unarmed and seemed more scared than dangerous so after eyeing him in turn for a few minutes I returned to the American side of the line where I belonged and continued walking my post. I suppose he was simply watching me out of curiosity.

As for me I tried to be alert, being young and comparatively ambitious, and once for a few moments I thought my vigilance was about to be rewarded by action.

Going on patrol as a single sentry at 6 o'clock in the morning I was strolling along No. 2 post when I saw to the east two horsemen[,] in civilian clothes, ride toward a Mexican farmhouse on the American side just to the east. In the early morning light I caught the glint of the butts of rifles in boots attached to their saddles.

My instructions covered a situation such as this appeared to be. Working my rifle bolt and slipping a cartridge into the chamber, I ran across the field to intercept them, the safety catch up and with my thumb against it to knock it down to "ready." The horsemen drew up to wait for me without making any motion toward their weapons. As I neared them I saw they were Americans, and smiling. In fact I had already met both of them. One, I knew, was a retired first sergeant of cavalry and the other a Texan of gun-antecedents. They were men of the customs border patrol which at that time were ununiformed save as their heavy revolvers in western holsters and their Winchesters indicated their calling. My recognition of the two was attended with a combination of relief and disappointment but happily not of chagrin since, without mentioning it, they obviously considered my zeal in intercepting a couple of gunmen as most commendable.

These were indeed gunmen, though on the right side. In all the history of border patrol of that and subsequent periods I suppose there was no duty as dangerous as theirs. As activity increased we saw more and more of them. Though few in numbers they undoubtedly were a very effective guard against the kind of banditti then along the border. I felt at the time that the army patrol as I saw it needed some such supplementation.

As the weeks went on, alarms of one sort or another became not unusual, usually reaching us in the form of an alert for which we knew no reason, requiring that all men off duty remain in camp available for call.

One day when I was on outpost duty we noticed a number of horsemen riding rapidly back and forth near a clump of trees a mile or so south of the border. A few moments later a cannon opened fire toward to [sic] the south and for about four hours shots were fired at intervals but we h[e]ard no other firing, and all we could see was the flash and smoke of the discharge and an occasional horseman riding off rapidly to one flank or the other. A few American civilians drifted down to the border to watch what was going on but that apparently was all the interest the affair created. Curiously enough nothing further developed from this and we never learned the least thing about the affair. It may have been target practice or it may have been Mexican artillery shelling some distant point where it was thought there were rebels but where no one wished to go to investigate. It was not even mentioned in the usually voluble El Paso papers—much to my regret since I had spent most of the time perched in a tree observing proceedings.

One night we had a brief false alarm which taught me a lesson. I had been on first relief, had come off post and had turned into my bunk at a little after 11 o'clock, fully dressed of course in accordance with regulations on the subject but unbuckling my cartridge belt for greater ease. About 11:30 a rattle of shots on the Mexican side close at hand brought us out of our sleep, off our bunks and out in the open in an instant, rifle in hand and ready for whatever might happen. But there really was no cause for excitement. A wedding celebration was in progress at a Mexican house just across the dry river bed and, Mexican fashion, some of the guests were expressing their hilarity by firing into the air. And it was just as well for me that this was the case for about the time the shooting was explained to us I discovered that I had left my belt of cartridges on my cot and had answered the alarm without ammunition other than the five rounds in the magazine of my gun. I slunk back in and put on my belt while the others were staring at the house and so no one noticed—and I saw no occasion for mentioning it.

One morning a little after daylight when I was shivering up my beat on the Number 1 post about three blocks west of the guard tent, two mounted Mexicans wearing long serapes muffled about their faces rode across the border from the direction of an adobe hut where I had been told two cowpunchers lived who worked on the American side. I let them pass unquestioned with a "good morning" exchanged in English with the leading one. After they passed it occurred to me that I should have made them throw back their cloaks so that I could see that they were unarmed. It was not too bad a slip since our orders principally concerned the smuggling of arms into Mexico but obviously armed men should not be permitted to cross either direction and the men might have been wearing revolvers under their cloaks. I reflected that I too was getting careless. That night in the *El Paso Herald* was an item saying that Pancho Villa, formerly a bandit but later an officer in the army of Madero and still later a prisoner in the penitentiary at Chihuahua City where he had been confined by Gen. Victoriano Huerta, had with the assistance of some friends made his escape from the prison and that morning with a single companion, both fully armed, had crossed the border and was then at such-and-such a hotel in El Paso.[14] According to the newspaper report he was at that time in an El Paso hotel where a number of his friends had gathered around him to protect him from any attempt on his life by his enemies in the American city. Villa was not as prominent at that time as he later became, but I have always wondered if I let an opportunity to bandy words with that redoubtable character [?] escape me. It might not have been Villa who had crossed my post but it can be imagined what conclusions I naturally drew. Even if it had been he, I could have done nothing unless he had been armed and then nothing except disarm and turn him over to the sergeant of the guard who in turn could have done nothing but find out who he was and release him, but it would have been some comfort to have even disarmed this noted outlaw and I regretted that I had let the chance slip so easily by. Think what a yarn it would [have] made—

"Throw back your coat," I said to old Pancho, and there he was a-wearing a revolver strapped to him. "Now get off those horses, I told 'em—"

And unlike most reminiscences the story would have gained in interest with age for Villa was just at the threshold of his career so far as his acquaintance with the American army was concerned. But, justly punished for being asleep on the job and neglectful of duty, I sat silent by the guard tent fire or around the stoves in the billet at Washington park and listened to the old timers spin yarns of the attack on El Caney, the march to Malolos, skirmishes with wild Moros and other kindred tales.[15] I had nothing to say but I resolved to be ever alert in the future. I had learned my lesson—"too late, alas, too late."

I later regretted it still more when he became such a noted chief in Carranza's campaign against Huerta and more yet when he raided an American town and caused an expedition to be sent into Mexico in pursuit of him.

A considerable portion of the time that I was not on guard I devoted to taking long walks, sometimes over to the stock yards where there were usually large herds of long horned Chihuahua cattle which had just been brought into this country, sometimes down the river past San Lorenzo ford and often to the east along the concrete highway leading out past Alfalfa.[16]

On this latter road I frequently stopped at a little fruit stand run by a weazened old Mexican man to buy apples, as I rather enjoyed munching them as I walked. Incidentally I was painfully trying to acquire some knowledge of the Mexican tongue and I would frequently test out some of my vocabulary on the old man. I generally managed to make myself understood but it was probably due more to the sign language than to my knowledge of Spanish.

One day he was joking me about going up the Alfalfa road so often, intimating that I probably had a Mexican girl up there somewhere. During the course of this discussion he used the word "pelon," apparently applying it to me, chuckling as he did so. When he found out that I did not know the meaning of the word he laughingly repeated it and apparently tried to explain what it meant but his explanation was too deep for me. I tried later, from men who talked a little Spanish, to get the meaning of it but all I could find out was that it meant "bald-headed." Now I had a full crop of hair and I could not imagine why the old man should have applied the word to me. Some years later I found out that the word "pelon," which also means "cropped head," was applied to the soldiers of the Mexican regular army in reference to the fact that they were to a large extent recruited from jails. The old scoundrel of an apple seller was probably insulting me all the time and I did not know it.

Soon after this a considerable band of Red Flaggers chased the federal garrison out of Guadalupe, some distance down the river, began to talk about an attack on Juárez, and sent patrols up toward it. A detachment of federal cavalrymen—five or six men as I recall it—took post at the Mexican end of the unguarded ford just south of Washington Park, and there was considerable riding of patrols back and forth. The federals who as usual were not anxious for a fight seem to have withdrawn toward Juárez and contented themselves with sending cavalry patrols in the direction of Guadalupe, the rebels meanwhile sending mounted patrols in the direction of Juárez. The region across the border from us thus became a sort of no mans land traversed by patrols of both factions. A flag was flying on some white buildings some distance south of the river and I suppose troops were stationed there, probably the force from which the ford outpost came. Partly for exercise and partly out of curiosity I was accustomed to stroll along the American side down there when off duty and I recall that the Mexicans at the ford were rather careless with firearms, firing at objects in the river occasionally and in such direction that now and then a richocheting [sic] bullet which had probably struck a sandbar went singing off on the American side to the eastward somewhere.

Around a third to a half of our company of about 60 men were on guard duty daily and the remainder not on detail of some sort drilled, maneuvered or took short practice marches in the forenoon. One of these jaunts, one morning, was eastward along the border road leading toward Alfalfa a few miles further on. As we rested just west of the village there came from the brushland in the valley across the Rio Grande the sound of a rifle shot, followed by four or five more, increasing to the patter of a lively little irregular fusillade which soon dwindled away into a few scattering shots then ceased. Mexicans in vehicles of one sort or another going by us toward El Paso were thrown into consternation. Quite possibly they thought our presence had some connection with the firing and that bullets might soon be coming in our direction. Some of them flailed their burros into sharp trots, others impelled their animals into accelerated speed by gouging them with sharp sticks where it would do the most good—the whole group clattering down the road toward the city trying to get away from our vicinity as rapidly as possible. Soon we were hiking back to our position at Washington Park but we enlisted men at least never knew what started the fireworks. Probably a Red Flagger patrol had clashed with some of the federals.

That afternoon I strolled down by the river as usual. The federal outpost, I noted, was no longer in the bunch of willows on the other side of the ford. As I stood there, whittling on a cane I had cut from the brush a few moments before, I noted seven mounted men trotting around the bend of the river on the Mexican side of the stream to the southeast. They were in single file with intervals of about 20 paces between horses and I could not see what uniform, if any, that they wore. For some distance around where I was standing the ground was perfectly flat and bare, as this was the low bank and the river flowed over it in time of flood. I was therefore quite visible to the approaching patrol and when it had drawn a little nearer, the leader, followed by the others in file, veered away from the course of the river and directly toward the clump of willows in such manner as to keep it between them and me.

I did not like this maneuver very much, and liked it still less when I saw through the willows as they approached that they were clothed in nondescript garb, no part of which suggested either the khaki of the Maderista volunteers or the bluish grey of the Mexican regulars. Obviously they were Red Flaggers. I remembered with some disquiet that a day or two before some of Salazar's band had fired at some members of the 13th Cavalry in the Guadalupe vicinity for preventing recruits from crossing to join them, and I would have been glad if I at least had had my rifle with me.[17] However since retreat would have been undignified and perhaps not entirely to the credit of the American army I remained where I was, whittling on my stick and endeavoring to appear indifferent.

The patrol rode up to the clump of willows and the leader drew rein behind it, staring at me over the top of the bushes. Then, drawing a rifle from a boot on the right side of the saddle he dismounted, threw his reins to a companion, and, with his rifle and free hand pushing away the willows, came through the clump and stood staring at me across what seemed at the moment a lamentably narrow stream. I continued to whittle, but with one eye fixed on a nearby depression in the sand which I figured I could reach quite promptly if he raised the gun to his shoulder. But either he decided that I was harmless or it was not his day to shoot at Americans, for after a short scrutiny he returned to his companions; all dismounted, and began to prepare a meal. I then felt free to continue my stroll. About an hour later the men departed, trotting toward Juárez.

The only guard maintained at Washington Park itself during this time, completely unprotected though it was in the direction of the ford directly to the south, was a single sentry post. Three privates and a non-commissioned officer were detailed alternately from E and F companies for this duty, the N.C.O. going to bed at night, though fully clothed, and the sentries waking each other up when time came for the reliefs. During daylight hours the sentry walked back and forth inside the building to prevent any soldier inclined to do so from taking out any bundle of clothing to sell to augment $15.00 a month pay. But at night post was outside the southern portion of the long adobe building—the section of it occupied by troops—encircling the southern end and cutting through the lighted sally-port in the center. At each round he also was required by his orders to walk south of the buildings a short distance along the front of some adobe stables where a few race horses were kept.[18]

For some reason the custom was for this quarters-guard to be armed with a revolver instead of a rifle—the 38-caliber service weapon of the time being passed from one sentry to another at the end of the period of each on post. The first time I walked this post there had been five cartridges transmitted. The night after I saw the Red-Flagger patrol at the ford and I went on this duty there was only two. This seemed to me a rather meager armament in troublous times for a sentry who was the only man awake out of a hundred or so soldiers sleeping in a rather ex-posed situation, but having no inclination to invite ridicule or accusation of timidity by protesting I accepted the situation as I found it, though I would have been much more comfortable if I had carried my rifle and worn the cartridge belt that hung by the head of my cot inside.

There was more or less movement, all the early part of my tour of duty, along the Alfalfa road, north of the park and this was somewhat disquieting since usually at that hour [there was] little. Also my youthful imagination pictured lurking Red-Flaggers in the blackness by the stables and I walked that part of my post with revolver in hand.

Now the Alfalfa road north of the park was paved at that time with about a nine-foot strip in the center and along about two A.M. while in front of the stables I heard a tremendous clatter of galloping horses coming down this highway from the east. It sounded to me as if half the Red Flaggers in Chihuahua had crossed the border and were galloping in. I raced for the sally-port, believing that if I ran fast enough I could reach it by the time the horsemen did and make a two-cartridge stand in this entrance, deriving gloomy satisfaction from the thought that after I had done so my exit from the world would be directly in front of my captain's door, his quarters opening up on this entrance. My [immediate] and more practical purpose however was to reach the sally port in time to throw off the light switch so my brief resistance would at least have the protection of darkness.

As I reached the sally-port and ran through with revolver in hand the horsemen swept by to the north, continuing toward town. They were American cavalrymen, and only five or six of them at that. And rankest recruits too, I reflected sourly—who else would gallop horses on concrete when there was gravel road alongside. Anyway there went my excitement, clattering on towards town while I resumed my leisurely patrol, glad that all was peaceful and serene, yet disgusted at the anti-climax. It was time for my relief. I went in, woke up the sentry whose turn was next, gave him the revolver and two cartridges, felt for my rifle and ammunition belt to see that they were convenient, and went to sleep.

The next morning I was told that soon after I had gone off duty all the border posts had been alerted with word that the Red Flagger forces south of the Rio Grande had started movement westward toward Juárez. The patrol which had given me a few pseudo-heroic moments quite possibly had been carrying information of some sort.

The band at Guadalupe had continued all through their stay there to make verbal threats against Juárez and a night or two later when they left the Mexican village and rode up the river toward the town every American outpost along the border was on the alert. They kept to the river until after they had passed San Lorenzo ford and then seemed to have turned to the south and made no attempt at all to attack Juárez.

The Red Flagger bands, I further learned, had not come west along the river as far as Washington Park, turning south instead when about opposite the Company E outpost at San Lorenzo ford. As soon as I was relieved from guard I borrowed the first sergeant's field glasses and climbed to the top of a shoot-the-chutes structure at the south end of the park to see what I could see across the river. It was not much. There was a distant scurrying about of mounted patrols, apparently federal, but no signs of conflict. A little later I saw the smoke of four trains moving south from Juárez on the Mexican Central Railway and in about an hour the occasional sound of a distant cannon could be heard, probably "El Niño," a light piece mounted on a flat car and frequently mentioned in the newspapers as used for patrol on the railway. So far as I ever heard there was no real fighting—and the El Paso newspapers would probably have had the story if there had been. My recollection is that the reporters said that seven troop trains had been sent out but that the Red Flaggers continued moving to the south and the federals returned to Juárez.[19]

A period of quiet followed this brief flare of excitement. The first battalion of the 18th Infantry had left El Paso for Fort D. A. Russell (later Fort Francis E. Warren) at Cheyenne, Wyo. The 22d Infantry, it seemed, was also scheduled for station at that post instead of its previous post at Fort Sam Houston and much of the company gossip had to do with the possibility of such a move.

Then came new developments in Mexico—this in the early part of February, 1913. A portion of the garrison of the city of Mexico under leadership of General Bernardo Reyes revolted and attempted to capture the palace. General Reyes was killed but his followers, now commanded by Felix Díaz, a nephew of Porfirio Díaz, the president whom Madero had ousted, stood siege in the arsenal 10 days. Then on Feb. 18 General Victoriano Huerta, reaching an accord with the rebels, arrested President Madero and the vice president, forced their resignation, and took over the government, the episode being climaxed by the murder of the former president and vice president the night of February 22.

These things had caused intense excitement in El Paso and Juárez, and in the Mexican town the old-army federals declared for Huerta, made prisoners of the Maderista volunteers who formed part of the garrison and were joined by the Red Flaggers, their late enemies.

The uproar and excitement increased as the days went on. The El Paso papers, particularly the *Herald,* worked the situation to the limit, issuing extras in rapid succession, though some, as I remember it, had but little different from the preceding one save one or two inconsequential paragraphs. But they went like hotcakes. Whenever I went down town I invested all my spare change this way—every renewed burst of shouting of "Heerol, Heerol," the newsboy equivalent for *Herald,* sent me automatically reaching into my right hand breeches pocket to see if I had any nickels left.[20]

The counter-revolution and the murder of Madero made a very unpleasant impression on American public opinion and there was widespread talk of intervention and war.[21] Possibly there was some natural concern as well as excitement in El Paso, since the papers assured their readers that the 22d Infantry would remain in El Paso to protect that town, regardless of what happened. Our Philippine and Cuba veterans laughed at this. El Paso would be much more comfortable in case of war, they said, than Chihuahua, but we younger and less experienced men raged. We would be "the El Paso Home Guards" we grumbled.

Down on our Company F No. 1 patrol post east of the foundry there lived an old Civil War veteran who was a friend of mine and with whom I discussed the local situation. It amused and pleased me when the old man confided that he was re[a]dy to take the war path. The more turbulent part of the Mexican population of El Paso was preparing for hostilities against the American population in case of war, he said, and he had made plans all of his own.

"I have a mighty good gun and know how to use it," he confided. "There are five Mexicans in this part of town I am going to get just as soon as a war starts. They have made their brags but they are going to have to shoot fast if they shoot first when I go after them." I have often wondered if in the various times of tumult that El Paso has had since then if the old veteran started on the trail of his chosen victims. How dangerous he was I cannot say but at least he certainly was anxious.

President William H. Taft had only a couple weeks of his term of office remaining—since President-elect Woodrow Wilson would be inaugurated March 4—but it was reported that he would order the concentration of an American division in Texas ready for his successor in case he decided on intervention.

This interested us. A paper divisional organization announced some time previously had listed the 22d Infantry in the 2d Division. Maybe—just maybe.

A morning or two later after calling the roll as usual at reveille, First Sergeant Elbert C. Russell stared at us belligerently with bristling beard, a sure sign that something of import would be forthcoming.[22]

"Hurry over and get your breakfast, then roll your packs and fold your cots," he said. "We are going to move."

A short time later as we completed our preparations, a troop of the Second Cavalry rode up at Washington Park. A detachment moved down to relieve our outpost. The remainder dismounted and unsaddled and carried in armloads of saddles, rifles, sabers and other paraphernalia, while the escort wagons which had accompanied it began unloading supplies at our kitchens. Our old soldiers looked at these troopers appraisingly and patronizingly. They were principally recruits it seemed and had been training up at Fort Bliss for some months while the infantry and other cavalry units had been doing the border guard. Now they were going on active duty for the first time since their return from the Philippine Islands some time before. Anyhow they looked picturesque and ambitious and I have no doubt performed their duty well.

The move of our unit from Washington Park to Fort Bliss where the regiment was assembling was chiefly memonetous [momentous] to me because I was a half innocent, half guilty party [to] the stealing of a sack of beans from the cavalry, an incident which impressed me somewhat because of the fact that I was somewhat tender of conscience in those days.

The cavalry troop was to use the same kitchen that had been ours and as our property was loaded on escort wagons assigned for the purpose, theirs was being unloaded from other wagons. I was on loading detail and after the greater part of the kitchen equipment and rations had been stowed away noticed a sack of beans that I had not seen before. I picked

First Sgt. E. C. Russell, Company F, Twenty-second U.S. Infantry, 1912

it up and started to swing it on the wagon when I noticed it bore a tag stencilled "Troop L, 2d Cavalry."

"Not ours," I commented as I lowered it. "Troop L, Second Cavalry." "Throw it in! Throw it in!" forcefully whispered our mess sergeant. I did, and so we were ahead a sack of beans and the horse-soldiers short.

That night at Fort Bliss where the regiment was being concentrated was a most miserable one. The other was between five and six years later in Montrebeau woods near Baulny—but that is another story.[23] A merciless wind whipped around the shoulder of Mount Franklin, driving before it a cold steady rain. Shelter tents would not stay up in such a gale with only loose sandy soil to hold tent pegs and we sought what shelter we could. I huddled in the lee of a canvas sidewall of an old kitchen but, thoroughly drenched, gave up the fight in due time and joined hundreds of other men gathered around huge fire[s] down by the railroad track. Sleep was out of the question and until daylight roasted on one side and froze on the other and tried to dry our sodden bedding whenever the rain slackened. I slept toward morning and was awakened by some women searching for acquaintances, or husbands maybe. Just then first call sounded. The mounted detachment of the regiment loaded its horses on cars nearby but for the men no transportation had yet arrived.

"First call for a move," commented a grizzled corporal grinning grimly. "There's an old saying. 'It pays all debts and divorces all women!'"

There was a day of shifting about and waiting, and night found us down in east El Paso somewhere shivering with cold and still waiting for cars. Eventually as evening approached we were loaded onto street cars and taken down to a railway station in the eastern central part of the city. Some of the older non commissioned officers pointed out to me as we went, the homes where they were leaving their wives and childrens [sic]. Our artificer—mechanic—had just purchased one but he had only a year to do toward retirement and could confidently look forward to returning to spend the rest of his life.

Darkness found us waiting at the station, huddled around fires trying to keep warm for the cold wind still continued. Some baggage cars were there and the word was passed around that the cooks had the range installed on one of them getting us some supper. That sounded good and soon we lined up with our mess kits, looking forward [to] hot coffee and a warm meal. But, alas, it was not to be.

Our cooks, in an attempt perhaps to forget the handicaps under which they had to work, had gotten hopelessly drunk and that meal we looked forward to consisted of a single cold beef sandwich per man—stale crumbly bread and tough meat. And the delivery of these was accompanied by jangling and quarreling. Everyone's nerves were on edge and the drunken cooks were mumblingly defending the slender rations. One of them kept muttering over and over inanely in answer to complaints: "Well, we're all American soldiers, aren't we?" He was an old soldier who had served with Funston in the 20th Kansas in the Philippines and a good friend of mine—but I did not feel friendly to him that evening.[24] It was perfectly true but as I gnawed at the "bulls neck" and bemoaned the hot coffee I had longed for I could not see but what an American soldier was as much entitled to a reasonable meal as anyone else in the wise world. In my heart I could not blame the cooks for getting drunk. Possibly we all felt like it. Confusion everywhere, discontent, oaths.

"The army on the move," sneered someone caustically, "The army on the move."

But everything must come to an end—even disagreeable episodes like this—and in due time our cars arrived, officers penetrated the mob giving instructions. Discipline reasserted itself and a few moments later we filed aboard and were on our way. Snugly ensconced in these tourist cars which seemed to us almost palatial after the rude billets of the border guard we felt as we curled up in our bunks and roared away into the night as if we had been transferred from some bleak, freezing, lower region into paradise. I chuckled in self congratulation forgetting my recent misery and discontent, felt that the army was a very fine and comfortable place indeed. Off to the wars! Altogether I was in a most happy frame of mind—possibly because I had never yet seen war.[25]

Morning found us near Alpine, at the top of the Big Bend country, traversing a rugged region greener than that around El Paso and to me new and delightful. Steep, boulder strewn hills lay all about for though in the night we had passed the rougher portion of Texas, this portion which lies between Alpine and Sanderson has a wild and rugged grandeur of its own that can hardly be excelled. Now and then on the very summit of these hills could be seen crosses, silhouetted against the sky. Mexican graves, a companion told me. A beautiful custom this, it seemed to me, burying the dead on a summit where they could overlook the beautiful land where they had lived, but how it originated or why it was continued, none could tell me. Farther to the eastward the country became lower and greener, covered with a luxurious growth of mesquite, cactus, Spanish bayonet, a plant I took to be Yucca, and various other forms of vegetation common to the southwest. Great canyons wandered across the rolling plains and meandered leisurely southward toward the Rio Grande, and at spots we could see the blue mountains of Coahuila standing out in relief against the southern horizon. This was the "big bend country" of border fame. I stared at it through a haze of romance.

At the stations where we paused we found the cowboys and other loungers who greeted us as expectant of war as were we, and obviously, as men of the exposed frontier, expecting to be concerned in it, and in the case of the young men at least apparently looking forward to it with some relish.

Marathon, [where] the young Mexican Maderista volunteer who had once guided me about Juárez had told me was his home; Sanderson— Langtry. Much publicized as Judge Roy Bean has been in the intervening years, I had never up to that time heard of him. A large sign on a building plainly visible from the train window announced "Justice of the Peace. Law West of the Pecos" and such of our men as were familiar with this country told many tales of the quaint old character who had placed it there; of how he had fined a man found dead all the money he had on his person on the ground that a revolver had been found on the body, and of how he had once [r]endered a decision to the effect that there was no law in the state of Texas forbidding the killing of a Chinaman.[26]

A number of miles east of Langtry the railway crosses the Pecos River on the highest bridge in the United States and peering out as the train crept across the structure at snail[']s pace we stared down at the green water at the bottom of the canyon 300 odd feet below. A detachment of cavalry was stationed here as well as at a number of other points along the railway to prevent destruction by any band of hostile Mexicans who might cross the river, elude the border guard and come north to the railway.

Soon the track turned to the south and after running awhile along the cultivated valley of Devil[s] River came out on the bank of the Rio Grande. It was a different Rio Grande however from the sluggish, yellow stream with the mud banks and quick sands that we had come to know so well at El Paso. Here it was broader and swifter and moved along in a stately manner more in keeping with its importance as an international boundary. Soon we passed through Del Rio and by nightfall were east of Spofford in a flat brushy country full of jack rabbits and with an occasional farm appearing here and there.

Morning found us south of Houston in a region which appeared as southern as El Paso was western. The hut of the Mexican laborer had been replaced by the ramshackle shanties of the southern Negro. Forests of pine trees with long streamers of Spanish moss appeared here and there; once in awhile there were large hayfields, and now and then pretty country houses, with climbing roses, all in bloom, clambering over the front veranda, seemed like pages out of some delightful southern novel. In the air, mingled with the odor of the pines, was the salt smell of the sea. Soon we ran out on a huge, green, floorlike plain and presently reached Texas City which, as it turned out, was to be our homes for many a month.[27]

Texas City

AT TEXAS CITY, Texas, on this February 28, 1913, everything was activity. The sidings were crowded with the trains of eight regiments, some just arriving. Some almost unloaded.

Scores of escort wagons slushed through the mud, their splattered mule teams straining every muscle. Everywhere was seeming confusion, and displeasure at the weather which had turned rainy and the camping ground which under the circumstances seemed little better than a swamp. North of town on this flat, treeless, grassy plain, pyramidal tents were already beginning to rise. Soon ours joined them, our officers frowning at the ground, permitting gaps in the line so as to avoid as many low spots as possible and take full advantage of occasional mounds.

The 2nd Division, the only division assembled at that time, was of the old triangular type which preceded the "square" type of World War I days. There were three infantry brigades which by the paper organization of the day were supposed to have three regiments each.[1] In fact one brigade—the Fifth, which was concentrating at Galveston across the bay, had four regiments, the 4th, 7th, 19th, and 28th. This brigade was soon to be commanded by Brig. Gen. Frederick Funston though I have the impression that at first Col. Daniel Cornman of the 7th Infantry was in command. On the Texas City side was the Fourth brigade, commanded by Brig. Gen. Hunter Ligget consisting of the 23d, 26th, and 27th Infantry regiments, and our own brigade, the Sixth, commanded by Brig. Gen. Clarence R. Edwards, which included the 11th, 18th, and 22d.[2] There was also the 6th Cavalry, the 4th Field Artillery—a regiment of mountain guns—and some odds and ends—a battalion of engineers, a field hospital, an ambulance company, a signal corps company, a bakery unit and an airplane squadron.

Regiments probably ran about 800 men each and the total strength of the division on June 30 after a considerable number of recruits were received is listed as being 517 officers and 10,770 men.

Major General William H. Carter, a medal-of-honor man from Indian-fighting days, was in command.[3] He was quoted in the Texas *State Topics* as saying: "This is the largest concentration of a single command of regulars in the history of the army." It is possible, however, that he was misquoted. The so-called "maneuver division" at San Antonio in 1911 had an aggregate strength of 12,598 at one time, and the command that Major General William R. Shafter took to Cuba for the Santiago campaign of 1898 aggregated 16,887 of whom fewer than 3,000 were volunteers. However it certainly was one of the three largest concentrations of regular army troops in American history up to that time and those of us who were included therein, took considerable pride in being members of such a force, supposing that very soon we would be on our way to Mexico.

As for the armament of the day, the infantryman's weapons [were] the 1903 Springfield rifle and bayonet, except that each regiment had a regimental detachment of two Benet Mercier machine guns carried on pack mules. The cavalry, of course, had rifle, pistols, and sabers—the slightly-curved 1906 model—and I think two Benet-Merciers on pack horses. The artillery was armed with 2.95 [inch] pack howitzers.[4]

The expectation of immediate war did not last long. When President Woodrow Wilson was inaugurated on March 4 it became quite clear that he had no ideas of intervention, and the soldiery at Texas City settled down dejectedly in the mud while the high command pondered a better-drained camp site.

The camp site matter was a somewhat serious one in the Sixth brigade at least. Probably someone had made some sort of preliminary reconnaissance before we were assigned to the ground on which we had pitched our tents, but rather obviously that reconnaissance had been made at some time in dry weather. Now it was raining more or less continuously and there was no drainage. Ditching the tents did no good.

Gen. William H. Carter and staff reviewing the army, Texas City, Texas, 1913

Diking was more appropriate but rain at night usually overflowed the dikes. In my tent we fastened our weapons and equipment onto the central tent pole and kept all else on our cots. At night we tied our shoes up onto the cots to keep them out of the couple of inches of water we could count on covering the dirt floor by morning. All tents were not this bad, of course, but on the other hand some were worse, and getting to the mess hall at the head of the company street meant wading two or three lakes.

Meanwhile the engineers were busy working out the official solution to the problem on the beach a mile and a half to the east, staking out lines of proposed ditches—about 17,000 feet to a regiment, someone said. Soon we were going out on working parties to this trench net-work and a little later the entire brigade floundered through the mud to the new site and re-pitched the camp. The engineers had figured well. Thanks to the ditches which drained onto the beach itself—perhaps a fall of four or five feet at high tide—the camp was livable and while at first the roads were quagmires they were soon graveled and the place became excellent for its purpose.

It was while on one of the working parties digging ditches that I first saw General Edwards who became well known a few years later as the

World War I commander of the 26th Division. He and his staff were out riding horseback watching the work on his brigade area. As the general rode up we saw our Corporal Chapman—a lean, ramrod like soldier of Indian mien and perhaps 45 years of age—come stiffly to attention and salute then to our surprise we saw the general lean over, shake hands cordially with him, and dismount and chat for awhile.

"He used to be my company commander," was the corporal's complete explanation in response to a query as we trudged back to camp.

The episode gave me a good opinion of generals in general which I have never had any occasion to lose. It was maybe 8 or ten months later that I had my own first and only conversation with General Edwards. A corporal by that time I was corporal of the guard, and the only non-commissioned officer at the guard tent, on an occasion when the general was making one of his frequent rides around the camp. He stopped and chatted for a time, remarking mildly, among other things, as he surveyed the scene that the camp of the 22nd Infantry looked like "a camp of Pennsylvania militia." I laughed, as he probably meant for me to do, for in truth the camp was somewhat irregular in shape but it was a most sensible one shaped to fit the terrain. Perhaps the Pennsylvania state troops used sensible camps too.

The lessening of the rains brought on a vigorous training period. Our earlier drills included battalion formations on the plain west of our first camp. My remembrances are chiefly of the huge mosquitoes which annoyed us and of the terrified rabbits which frightened from their hiding places by the march of one column dashed off at top speed only to run into another column and then veered off only to run into still another, for the ground was covered with troops. This continued until the animal finally found its way out or was pulled down by the crowd of canines who as company mascots were with the troops and who gave chase with as much vigor as was possible in view of their habitually overfed condition. I also have a vivid remembrance of one occasion when "F" Company, doing close order drill, was marching along in company front when the center of the line stirred up a nest of snakes. This much disturbed the drill and I suspect rather tried the patience for which our fatherly company commander was noted.

There were constant maneuvers too, battalion, regimental, brigade

Aerial view of the camp of the Twenty-second U.S. Infantry, Texas City, Texas

and eventually division.[5] The early ones were accompanied by a certain awkwardness and a tendency of one unit to get in the way of others indicated that regular army units of the day had been accustomed to operate singly instead of in conjunction with others, but it was not long until all habitually flowed smoothly; and the men were toughened and in as good physical condition as it is possible for men to be.

This constant activity made life at Texas City interesting and livable enough. I remember no particular boredom, and that was a time when no one outside of the army tried to furnish entertainment to soldiers on other than a commercial basis. One could always go into Texas City in off-duty periods, a town pleasant enough but small and where I entertained myself usually by strolling along the docks and looking at the ships, the Wolvin line vessels which ran into Tampico and Vera Cruz putting in there, a good many British steamers carrying cotton and also some coasting line to New York.[6] Ferry boats ran at convenient intervals to Galveston, and those who felt ambitious enough could go to Houston by street car.

Entertainment in the camp seemed to depend upon the chaplains principally and in the 22nd there was for a long time no regimental effort along that line. There was a pleasant Y.M.C.A. tent back of the 18th Infantry camp, however where I went frequently to read or write, and there was an 11th Infantry enlisted men's club in another tent, run by the chaplain, which I liked most as a loi[t]ering place, perhaps due to the variety of reading matter there including military magazines.[7] Probably most of the soldiers at Texas City came to know or know about Chaplain John T. Axton of the 11th Infantry. I was much pleased when, some years later, he was made chief of chaplains for the entire army.[8]

At the time, Major General Wm. H[arding] Carter[,] commanding the division, seemed to me a rather colorless figure but in point of fact he must have been an excellent officer however much he failed as an

Mess hall, Company F, Twenty-second U.S. Infantry camp, Texas City, Texas, 1913

individual to impress his personality on the troops—or at least on me. Looking back, I know that discipline in the division was excellent, morale high and that training progressed rapidly. What with constant drills, maneuvers, practice marches and target practice, the division must early have been considered in full readiness to perform any mission it might have been given in connection with the Mexican situation.

That there were still possibilities in this respect was shown by the fact that all through the months there laid in readiness at Galveston wharves four small army transports of the day—the *Sumner*, the *Meade*, the *McClellan* and the *Kilpatrick*.[9] Though most countries had recognized the Huerta government in Mexico, our own country had refused to do so with the result that there was diplomatic bickering throughout the year while in Mexico civil war continued without getting much of anywhere except into the newspaper headlines—Carranza, Villa, and Zapata against the government.

The airplanes—something of a novelty at that time—had added interest to the early part of the maneuvers. The army, I have read, owned 15 planes at that time and I think most or all of them were at Texas. Two non-stop flights of 240 miles were made, which was quite an achievement at the day and a great deal was said about their success in war if used as scouts or messengers. In my scattered notes about this-and-that, made at the time, I find this one:

"One reads much in magazines about various styles of artillery made for the purpose of bringing down these aerial craft and to me it is unknown whether there are any such weapons in the United States army. It is certain however that there is none in this division. As one watches one of the 'enemy's' aeroplanes on maneuvers, circling about out of rifle range, observing every move of the column, it is easy to understand what a disconcerting effect such actions would, or will, have when war is real instead of mimic."

On the morning of July 8, 1913, when the men of my company gathered at the head of the company street for the daily police of camp we watched one of the planes which circled over and flew west, chatting about how pleasant it would be to be in the air on a hot day like that was already starting to be. Then something went wrong with the machine. It

Plane crash, Texas City, Texas, July 8, 1913

nosed upward, then forward and straight down, both wings collapsing before it crashed near the 4th Artillery camp. A Lieut. Call was killed in this crash.[10] So far as I recall there was never another airplane flight from the Texas City camp.

A curious accident happened in E Company of my regiment about this time—a man's life saved by his moustache. Hunting had been encouraged and there were a number of shotguns in camp. One soldier in that company had a little moustache of which he was quite proud and which he [was] constantly twisting into a curl with his hands. One morning as men were returning from the mess hall, there was a shotgun blast in the Company E area just back of my tent. I ran out, with others, to find this man whirling about with a ghastly wound in his right forearm and a shot-torn spot in his shirt in the right chest. Another soldier, seated on a cot, working with a shotgun, had accidentally discharged it, the charge striking the man with the moustache. Happening to be curling his moustache at the moment, his chest was partly shielded by his forearm which caught the full effect of the charge. It was said at the time—when reports

Kitchen row, Twenty-second U.S. Infantry camp, Texas City, Texas, October 1913

came back from the hospital—that he would lose his arm but that the wound in his chest was not serious due to the position of his arm when the shot was fired.

Mustaches were of course quite common and there was even an exceptional case where there were beards. I recall how a soldier of my company came to grow one of the latter. Shaving in the field was not particularly stressed except that it was necessary to be neatly shaved for Saturday morning inspection. A certain Private Reynolds had neglected this for some reason, and must have been casting about desperately for an excuse as Captain Curtis came down the line inspecting arms.[11]

"Reynolds, why-didn't-you-shave?" the captain demanded in slow inexorable voice when he reached him.

"Sir," answered Reynolds, "I 'lowed to grow a beard."

"Then-see-that-you-do," replied the company commander as he passed on.

So Reynolds grew a beard—a thin, Van-Dyke-appearing affair that gave him a rather distinguished look.

Along in October, 1913, opportunity came my way. Capt. Curtis had been sent to the Army School of the Line at Fort Leavenworth and was succeeded by First Lieut. James E. Ware, another 40-year-old Spanish War veteran.[12] Lieut. Ware made several changes in the company and tried a series of men out for corporal, by making them lance corporals, observing their work, then relieving them of duty as lance corporals and trying someone else. In time I was selected for such trial.[13]

At the time of my initial assignment in charge of a squad, squad drill was being stressed, each corporal drilling his own. My lot on this day was to drill my squad—this I assume by chance—directly in front of the company commander's tent and under his eye. Normally this would have been my ruin since it was the first time I had drilled anyone in the regular army. But in my national guard days, under tutelage of regular army sergeants visiting my unit in Missouri, I had practiced myself in this. I not only knew how to drill a squad but I knew every movement by rote as laid down in the drill regulations. It was my morning to grandstand. We had had but little close order squad drill in the 22d—which was a field soldier organization—and the first sergeant, keeping an eye on me because it was my first effort, thought I had explained one movement wrong. "No, sir," I was able to say positively, "that is correct. I am quoting the exact words of the regulation" and so left him thumbing through his book, and went merrily on my way.

My warrant as corporal came [in] 1913 but not until Lieut. Ware had interviewed me to find how it happened that a first enlistment man[,] with only a year's service, could drill a squad like one who had often done it before. So it behooved me to confess my national guard service, explaining why I had been silent on the point. The lieutenant understood. "I was in the national guard once too," he said.

I was immensely, though I hope secretly, pleased at this promotion. To be a corporal in the regular army seemed to me a very important position—as it doubtless was, and is. It was a big aid to my morale which had sagged somewhat as intervention in Mexico appeared to grow less probable.

The winter of 1913–14 was one with many field firing problems—a thing relatively new in the army at that time—in which little tactical exercises were worked out with targets and ball ammunition, and my note books of the time contain details of many such, I having attended voluntarily as a wandering observer those held by many units besides my

Cpl. Ward L. Schrantz, 1st Sgt. B. D. Coleman, and 1st Lt. James E. Ware, Texas City, Texas

own. The Second Division was being as well trained as the knowledge and means available at the time permitted. It was also kept oriented by means of occasional lectures and motion pictures concerning events in Mexico—those of my knowledge being for the rank and file and there must have been many more available only to officers. Lectures were by returned missionaries or refugees. Pictures I recall include a detailed one showing the federal (Huertista) army. At this picture, shown in the open air near the 11th Infantry or 18th Infantry recreation tents, I was seated with a mass of other enlisted men in front of some chairs later occupied by General Edwards and other officers, and I remember hearing the general comment on "the latest French artillery" in the possession of the Mexicans. Another picture shown at the newly-erected 22nd Infantry club was taken in the Big Bend country of Texas, showing Mexican Red Flaggers forced across the Rio Grande at Ojinago. The close-ups of wounds, I recall, were big and vivid enough that they should have constituted some seasoning for what battle wounds were.

American and other allied war vessels were at this time lying in Mexican harbors and on February 28, 1914, the British cruiser *Essex* came into port in Galveston, bringing Sir Lionel Carden, the British ambassador to Mexico, on his way to Washington for a conference with somebody.[14] Aboard was the commander of the British fleet in Mexican waters, Vice Admiral Sir Christopher Craddock.[15]

On March 7 there was a review at Texas City in which the division passed in review before Brig. Gen. Frederick Funston, then in command of the division, and Admiral Craddock. "The Admiral is about the same size as General Funston and wears a short beard," I noted in my diary. Eight months later Admiral Craddock went down fighting with his fleet 40 miles off Cape Coronel, Chile, against the German squadron of Admiral Von Spee in one of the initial naval actions of World War I.

The next day the *Essex* was open to visits by the public and I was among the Texas City soldiers who went to Galveston to go aboard her. I was quite impressed with the nattiness of the British Marines, the glittering brass water-jacket of a machine gun mounted on a tripod, with the racks of rifles and cutlasses, and with the British short rifle used by the Marines—then new but later to become familiar to millions of Americans as the British regulation rifle of World Wars I and II.[16] I was less favorably impressed—being an American without previous contact with the British armed forces—with mottoes appearing here and there—"Fear God and Honor the King," "The King, God Bless Him," and others of similar import.

On April 9 the Mexican situation again flashed to the foreground. The Mexicans seized and held as prisoners an American paymaster and some sailors who had landed in a launch at Tampico. Rear Admiral Mayo, commanding our fleet off their port, immediately demanded their release and the firing of a salute of 21 guns as an apology to the American flag. The prisoners were released but General Huerta refused to fire the salute.

In the midst of the hub-bub incidental to this situation, the Second Division departed on a march to Houston to participate in the San Jacinto day parade, the Fifth brigade leaving Galveston the 15th and the Texas City troops moving out to join them on the morning of the 16th.

It was a march of much interest to me, the entire division moving by one route in a long column, an exercise no doubt affording valuable and probably much needed practice in logistics for the division staff. My own regiment camped the first night at Hulen Park, 11 miles from Texas City; the second night at Webster after another march of 11 miles and the third night at Dumont, also called South Houston, 12 miles farther on. At this latter camp we heard that President Wilson had issued an ultimatum to President Huerta demanding that he salute the flag in apology for the Tampico incident and we younger soldiers were quite elated at the prospects the situation seemed to offer for active service.[17]

On the morning of the fourth day my own unit remained encamped for about two hours as the forward parts of the column moved by, and I remember distinctly the impressiveness of the scene as the 6th Cavalry, in column of twos, with its band mounted on white horses in the lead, passed up the road, the white horses standing out against the background of pine woods. For us that day's march was only seven miles, we going into camp about noon in Magnolia Park south of Houston.

Crowds from town thronged our camp during the afternoon, most of us much flattered at this most unusual interest in the army on the part of the civilian populace. This was April 19th and we were scheduled to rest on the 20th, then participate in the Houston San Jacinto day parade on the 21st. A good many of our men departed for town, with proper leave until taps, as soon as the evening meal was over but I was among those who remained in camp, planning to visit Houston on the next day's holiday. Speculation of course was on what Huerta would do, as President Wilson's ultimatum expired at 6 o'clock, P.M.

Soon after 8 o'clock the regiments nearest the street car line suddenly began cheering, and soon shouting news boys invaded our own camp. "Huerta Refuses to Salute!" Our own regiment took up the cheers and others followed until the whole camp of the division seemed cheering in unison.

At 3:30 A.M. the next morning an orderly stumbled over the rope of my shelter tent looking for headquarters. In a few moments officers call was sounded, and as the camp stirred in excitement, first call and reveille followed.

"Hurry up, hurry up," the word was passed along. "Breakfast at once. We march at 4:30."

It was a beautiful still morning in the black pine woods and soon thousands of candles were burning in the open as men hastily tore down their shelter tents and rolled their packs. Somehow the cooks had risen to the situation and a hasty breakfast was ready by the time the packs were rolled. The company escort wagons came rolling up, the teamsters cutting fences in their haste—the government probably paid for that. By 4:30 my own company and all others so far as I could see, was ready, and wagons were completing loading, the field ranges being jammed in still hot.

Then we waited for orders, and kept waiting. "We are going back by train," was the report. At daybreak the Fifth brigade swung by on the way to the railway. We kept on waiting, grumbling, soldierlike, at what we deemed someone's inefficiency. As to the time necessary to put a division in motion on unexpected orders, we of course had no idea. We were ready. What was the matter with headquarters? Where were the railway cars on which we were to load?

About 8:00 the 6th brigade received orders—to march. The railway report was a dream so far as we were concerned. In point of fact only the Fifth brigade moved by rail, the remainder of the division returning by marching.

The citizenry had already gathered to watch and an incident at the first halt amused me. We halted by bugle, and in accordance with custom all men immediately turned to the right and trooped off the road to rest. We were in a pine woods and off to the right were a number of women with baby carriages watching. As the column halted, and all men with one accord left the road en masse toward them, the mothers snatched their infants from the carriages and fled. I have often wondered what thought was in their mind. When, glancing apprehensively back in flight, they saw everyone sit or lay down on the ground, they returned in obvious relief to the baby vehicles they had abandoned.

Later in the day, about 10 miles south, as we perspired along an asphalt road by the railway track under a blazing sun, the Fifth Brigade passed us in special troop trains—passenger cars, box cars and flat cars on which escort wagons were blocked. There was a shouted chorus of banter and genial mutual vilification, drowned in the roar of the cars, but the Fifth Brigade men were the victors in the tilt as they rolled by, raising and lowering their clenched right fist rapidly and mockingly in the army signal for "double time," and also throwing off to us copies of Houston newspaper extras saying that the Fifth brigade would board transports for Vera Cruz immediately on arrival at Galveston.

We camped at Genoa after a march of 14 miles. The mail came and with it my copy of the *Army and Navy Journal* dated the preceding Saturday. War was inevitable, said that authoritative publication.[18] I believed it and was jubilant. What the *Army and Navy Journal* said was gospel to me. I still read that dignified publication, and have ever since, but also ever since I appraise its editorials before believing them.

Being in an exuberant mood that evening I broke into an old silly song as I went down the line of shelter tents after mess—"I'm going to get married, ma-ma, ma-ma; I'm going to get married—."

"If you were married, Schrantz," commented First Sergeant Basil D. Coleman not unkindly, "[y]ou probably would not be singing that way."[19]

In truth a sudden move to Mexico or elsewhere would cause some worry and embarrassment to our married noncommissioned officers who had their wives at Texas City. And that evening, to further impress me with the idea that war was serious, an old corporal narrated his experiences after the Philippine Insurrection of helping dig up bodies of dead soldiers for shipment to the states. But I crawled into my blankets still happy.

The night of the 21st we camped near Dickinson after another march of 14 miles. No officers or men were permitted to leave camp. The wares of the newspaper vendors who visited the camps informed us that the Marines and bluejackets of the fleet had seized the customs house at Vera Cruz with a loss of four men killed. War! Knowing nothing of shipping problems I wondered if we would return to our Texas City camp before going to Galveston to board transports. I had four five-dollar gold pieces secreted in a corner of a wooden box in which I kept my belongings and was worried about them.

The next day we marched the remaining 14 miles to our permanent camp. The Fifth brigade, to my surprise, was reported still at Galveston but the Marines and blue jackets had completed the capture of Vera Cruz with the loss of a good many more killed and wounded. A few days later the Fifth brigade sailed on the four army transports and by that time we too were packed, with our company property marked for shipment or for storage, as the case might be.

We kept on waiting. General Funston who had commanded the Fifth brigade in the movement, had taken command in Vera Cruz, we read, extending his lines to take in El Tejar and the water works. Two troops of the 6th Cavalry and some miscellaneous troops had gone from Texas City. On April 25th I saw a battalion of the 4th Field Artillery sail on the SS *Saltillo* from Texas City, leaving a horde of canine mascots barking on the piers, no dog being allowed on ships. The newspapers now talked of an international conference and peace instead of war. My balloon of hopes subsided. No war, no campaign ribbon, no nothing. I was disgusted.

Preparations for a possible move of the remainder of the Second Division to Vera Cruz continued, however, a number of small merchant vessels being chartered and moored at convenient piers in readiness. At the end of May the ships available, together with their tonnage, was [sic] as follows: At Galveston: U.S.A.T. *Kilpatrick,* 2380; U.S.A.T. *Meade,* 2376; U.S.A.T. *Sumner,* 2182; SS *City of Macon* 3999; SS *City of Memphis* 3081; SS *Colorado* 2025; SS *Denver* 2819; SS *Kansan* 5131; SS *Minnesotan* 4067; SS *Panaman* 4064; and the SS *San Marcos* 2168, all at Galveston, and the SS *Ossabow* 2043 and the SS *Saltillo* 2044 at Texas City.[20]

The 22nd Infantry, we were told, was scheduled to go on the *City of Memphis,* in case of movement, my own company, I recall to be assigned to standees being put up in the tween deck section. Conversion work was pushed on these and I watched with interest in my spare time the conversion of the *Ossabow,* a vessel with engines aft, to carry horses or mules, some to be in stables below deck and the others to be carried in stalls built on the open deck.

The *City of Memphis,* in which we were so interested at the moment, did not carry troops to Vera Cruz but was later to have an unhappy part in a real war, being one of the American vessels sunk by German submarines prior to our entry into World War I.[21]

While the Vera Cruz excitement was still fresh, Maj. Gen. J. Franklin Bell, another famous soldier of the Philippine campaigns, appeared at Texas City and took command of the division.[22] He addressed each regiment of the division in turn, talking to the 22d Infantry on June 1. He explained President Wilson's policy which intended to avert a war but added that he thought war was probable and that therefore he wanted to talk to all of the men in the division telling them how he wanted [them] to conduct themselves in campaign. The inhabitants of Mexico were to be treated kindly. So long as members of the armed forces had arms in hand they were to be killed but enemy soldiers too were to be treated kindly, once they had surrendered. He gave counsel on military precautions and on conduct in battle and in campaign. He warned against making a march with a canteen of whiskey—doubtless good advice which struck me as curious since I had never personally known nor have I since known, of anyone trying to make a march on whisky instead of water. General Bell urged coffee in the canteen as a thirst-quencher. I tried it on the next march but the results were most unhappy. At each drink I became thirstier. Someone told me that was because I had sweetened coffee whereas it should be unsweetened, but after that I stayed with water. A more pertinent bit of advice was on endurance. "When you are exhausted and feel you cannot go a step farther, keep marching anyway," the general said. "Pretty soon you will get your second wind. And when you are again exhausted still keep on going. You will get your third wind and be all right."

General Bell took a vigorous personal interest in the preparation of the division in training and otherwise for the possible campaign—talks by visitors to Mexico and officers returned from Vera Cruz; familiarization of infantry with the fire of the mountain guns (from the sidelines where the shriek of the shell could be heard without one being near the point of burst) and with more maneuvers.

On July 14, President Huerta, yielding to battlefield reverses at the hands of opposing factions from within and to American pressure from without, gave up power and fled the country. The following month Gen. Venustiano Carranza took over the government and while he was not particularly friendly to the United States, our country had been backing him and it was assumed that peace would come to Mexico.

As July merged into August ultimatums and war declarations crackled in Europe.

The *Galveston News* and the *Houston Chronicle* which were our principal sources of information in the camp broke out in great headlines. There was talk "about-it-and-about" in each of the multitudinous khaki tents at Texas City and perhaps in the higher levels there was excitement as well, akin to that which I have heard existed in the civilian world at that time.

But I recall no particular excitement about the matter among the enlisted personnel of my own unit. We followed events with interest but in a detached sort of way, as I recall, perhaps because our own little balloon of war anticipations regarding Mexico had so recently burst in our faces leaving us more matter-of-fact than before. Those men, of whom we had a good many who had come from homes abroad[,] were naturally concerned about their kith and kin who would be in the armed forces of the various belligerents, but for the rest of us it all seemed rather remote, of interest only from a professional standpoint.

Besides there were other things on our minds, particularly a scheduled march to Galveston.

We made the 17-mile march the evening of August 3, starting shortly before dusk. The road at first was flanked by ponds in which were growing masses of tall cat-tails, and the flat grass lands were a dark yellowish green in the fading light. It was dark by the time the causeway was reached and the moon had risen. The broad expanse of the waters of Galveston Bay, luminant in the moonlight, and the long white causeway with the endless dark column of infantry pouring over it toward the lights of the distant city, made an impressive picture. And here and there companies broke into song, inspired by the scene—"We were sailing along, on Moonlight Bay—." That great day in history was just a peaceful soldier evening for us and with little thought given to the storm breaking over Europe.

It was during the five or six days that we were encamped at Fort Crockett that I first really felt the thrill of the European war.[23] Off duty I went down town to join the crowds at the newspaper bulletin boards. The crowds were of almost as much interest as the bulletins. Reservists of many nations had already poured into Galveston in response to mobilization notices published by the foreign counsels in the newspapers in hopes of getting transportation home. These included Austrian, German, French, Swiss, English, Dutch, and others—for all overseas nations were mobilizing. There was a babel of tongues, discussions, arguments. Back in Texas City on August 11[,] I watched the SS *City of Tampico* from Vera Cruz and Tampico moor, loaded with German reservists who had been in Mexico. I talked to one of them who spoke English. He said that they were mainly engineers and men of similar professions who were working in Mexico and were sent to the United States by the German counsels

Cook shacks, Twenty-second U.S. Infantry camp, Galveston, Texas

when they answered the call to reservists. They had been told that in Galveston they could get a ship for Germany. They were a happy, cheering and apparently high type group. A tender came alongside and took them to Galveston. Later I read in the newspapers that they had been told by the German counsel in Galveston that there were no ships available and he advised them to return to Mexico, offering them transportation. But most of them, not thus easily thwarted, took trains for New York instead, paying their own fare, hoping to get a ship there.

There apparently was no thought by anyone that the United States might eventually be drawn in. The popular idea, based on tables of strengths of armies published in newspapers and magazines, was that the war would be over in three months. I disputed this in our camp arguments. "The German army cannot be defeated within three months," I held, "and it is only on a belief that it will be that this three-months idea is based."

Men of the company who had been in European armies before they came over as immigrants told of their organization and armament, [and] we listened eagerly. A Private Stelmach, recently arrived and recently joined, showed me a picture of his brother in the "Feefty-five regiment" of Austria. The newspapers said the Germans had occupied a certain town in Russian Poland near the border. Private Aaron Nikolonetski showed me the printed item and protested violently: "It[']s a lie. I know that town. The Germans couldn't possibly take it. There is a whole squadron of Cossacks stationed there."[24]

I followed the course of the war with pencil marks on maps. For a while after August 22 the maps told what the headlines didn't. These told each day of British victories—the British being better publicized than the larger French army—but each day the current "victory" was many miles in rear of the victory of the day before. It was the retreat from Mons.[25] News accounts told only of isolated successful rearguard actions, and on them the headlines were based. That there was a retreat was shown only by the map. I believed nothing unless I could check it by town names— which is still the best way of which I know for following a war from newspaper accounts.

In view of what was going on elsewhere, life at Texas City, while pleasant enough, seemed dull. Yet the docks were always of interest to me.

A longshoremen's strike and Negro strike-breakers from Galveston unloading ships under supervision of colored bosses. It was a dangerous job for them. Nets full of cargo were swung over the side by the ship's cargo derricks, lowered to within five or six feet of the pier, then let go— the freight flying in all directions and spools of barbed-wire occasionally bouncing and rolling into the water between ship and pier. I then thought it indifference and it was not until many years later when I had something to do with ships that I realized that it came only from unskilled winchmen. Apparently there were not cargo nets enough. When one had been landed, the hook was switched to as near the bottom of it as could be reached conveniently, and it was hoisted away, dumping the freight in a bouncing clatter onto the decks. The Negroes dodged and jibed and sang at their work. As the cargo nets hung suspended, preparatory to the inevitable crash when the winchman let go, the boss man would shout "Watch out," then "Watch out or the devil will git you." The men, hopping nimbly aside to avoid bouncing spools of wire, were impressed with the phraseology of the latter warning. They began to chant it themselves. Soon they had made up a little song which they sang as they worked.

The strike over, and a deck load of long-horned cattle being unloaded from the SS *Haakon,* in from Tampico. Wooden, cleated gangways had been placed from the deck to the bulwarks and from the bulwarks to the pier, and up and down this runway the long-horns were forced to go by cattle-hands, swearing in southern drawl. The men worked down among the cattle, their shirts wet with sweat and fouled by manure. Now and then an animal would break back down the deck and one of the men would turn it back, by shouting, striking it across the nose with a short stick, punching his fingers in its eyes, or grasping its long horns and forcing it back by sheer strength. Reluctant ones were heaved up the narrow runway by strength of shoulders of several men, or by someone twisting its tail until it started from the pain. And when all other means failed, a rope was looped around the creature's horns and it was swung off by a cargo derrick, collapsing in a heap in bewildered fashion when it reached the dock.

An overnight pass in Houston and a 3 A.M. fire which called me from my bed in a nearby hotel to see the excitement. It was a cleaning establishment in the upper story of a two-story structure adjacent to a one-story structure. Two fire engines puffed in the streets. Firemen on ladders from the roof of the one story building to the roof of the two-story one, stood on their ladders directing a hose at such flames as were emerging above while [the] other hose played from the front through broken windows. It wasn't much of a fire, I thought, standing chatting across the street with a policeman. Waiters in an all-night restaurant beneath the cleaning establishment returned to their counters and starting serving customers. Then a violent explosion showered the street with bricks. Firemen on the leaning ladders leaped straight backward off them. I raced the policeman up the street out of brick range. But almost as I started there was another explosion. The wall on which the firemen[']s ladders had stood collapsed, and tons of brick and debris crashed through the ceiling of the restaurant. The bricks and wreckage had hardly settled until the firemen were scrambling up the ruins, playing their hoses on the fire, seeking to dig out those entrapped by the collapse. It was a fine example of courage. The newspapers said next day that two were killed and 12 injured. The city council passed some kind of ordinance against keeping gasoline in cleaning establishments.

Battleship USS *New York*

The new battleship *New York* up from Vera Cruz and open to public inspection in Galveston. A new ship—the pride of the navy—spotlessly clean and with the crew in white undress lounging about or playing acey-deucey.[26] The battleship [had] some 20 parrots acquired in Mexican waters. I stared at the vessel's great 14-inch guns and peered into gun turrets from which the only exit was steel doors of no great size—like manholes, I thought. A beautiful ship, but I would rather fight on shore than sink penned up in a gun turret. The "new *New York*" then was the "old *New York*" when I next saw her again 29 years later accompanying a troop convoy to Casablanca.

By October the American military future looked drab. It was announced that Vera Cruz would be evacuated and there were rumors that the Second Division would be demobilized. A wave of pacifism borne of reports of tremendous casualties in the European war appeared sweeping over the nation. A new song "I Didn't Raise My Boy to be a Soldier" was popular, in civilian quarters. Morale in the Second Division probably seemed sagging, for General Bell issued an order encouraging men to take furloughs or go on fishing passes.[27]

Back home letters from friends in the national guard told me of changes in my old company. A former national guard corporal, once junior to me, told me that he was now first lieutenant and that I would have been myself if I had stayed in the guard instead of enlisting in the army. A new man to the company had been named second lieutenant because he had been in the regular army and all the old-timers of the company were gone.

I writhed a little at this. Naturally I wanted to be an officer. No officers were being commissioned from the ranks in the regular army at that time or did such appear likely in view of the apparent overwhelming pacifist sentiment in the nation. And no more soldiers were being given commissions in the Philippine Scouts.[28]

At this stage I received a letter from the home town newspaper offering what appeared at the time a promising position if I could and would leave the army. It was not hard, I knew, to get out if I made a request. A man with two years['] service could purchase a discharge for $100 if he had a job waiting.[29]

"You will be making a mistake, Schrantz," my first sergeant told me. "You like the army and you should be a soldier and nothing else. If you leave the army now you are leaving your military career behind."

And he was right as regarded a professional career.

I was discharged on November 4, 1914.[30] Captain Sylvester Bonnaffon III, then my company commander, was kind enough to write in on my discharge "Qualified for a commission as second lieutenant in the volunteer army."[31] This was a high and coveted honor in those days for men being discharged and I realized also that it probably did not go to many men discharged by Purchase. Moreover it was not entirely an empty honor. In April congress had passed a law authorizing the president, in time of war or when war was imminent, to form a national volunteer army with officers commissioned by him.

Captain Bonnaffon's note on my discharge might well serve to get me a volunteer commission in the event of war, I reflected, and in the meanwhile I would go back into the national guard.

Return to Missouri

 ON NOVEMBER 13, 1914, the first national guard drill night after my return to Carthage, Mo., a week earlier from service in the regular army, I reenlisted in my former guard organization, Company A, Second Missouri Infantry.

"Keep on your corporal's chevrons," said the company commander, "I will send in a request for your appointment." However when my warrant came I found I had been appointed sergeant, my former rank in the unit.

The small attendance at drill rather shocked me, as did the apparent state of training—all of which indicated principally, probably, that my memory was poor. The national guard, in the days before there was any drill pay, worked under many handicaps. Yet the group, which was a cadre rather than a company, obviously was a nucleus which could be expanded in case of emergency into a wartime unit, and, however unprepared the national guard was for campaign, it was certain that it would be called if America needed more troops. The regular army was so small it would not even be a start. A part of the older men who had left or dropped out of the company during my absence were now back in uniform again, and the former second lieutenant was now first sergeant— having lost his commission by a temporary change of residence. I added my efforts to those of the others to build the unit up.[1]

Now for the first time I experienced the restlessness and difficulty of adjustment to civil life which all who have ever left the armed forces know. Nor was this eased any by the fact that in late December the 22nd Infantry, with the rest of the Sixth brigade, had left Texas City and was now on border duty at Naco, Ariz., called there by the attack on the Carranzista garrison of Naco, Sonora, by Villista forces under General Maytorena.[2]

And in February, 1915, the war in Europe took a turn which was ultimately to result in American intervention—the inauguration of the German submarine campaign.

At the outbreak of the European war I was a mild German sympathizer for no other reason that I know except my Teutonic name—though my forebears were not German nationals but had come to Lancaster county, Pa., from Switzerland in the early 1700s—both my father's family and my mother's. Stories of German excesses and mistreatment of the populations of France and Belgium during the invasion of 1914 which turned most Americans against that country, I had not believed. Such things happen only in undisciplined armies, I held, and the German army was one of the best disciplined in the world. As is well known now, the German troops, outrunning their food supply system, were in places practically turned loose to forage for their own food, the civil population being left unprotected and at their mercy—the mercy of drunken men who looted wine and liquor as well as food. And that atrocities did occur I later found out for myself by conversations with French inhabitants of villages, overrun in 1914, in which I was stationed in 1918.

But from being a German sympathizer I switched to a questioning neutrality when the submarine campaign started, and became an ardent advocate of war against Germany after the *Lusitania* was sunk in May. Since it appeared from ensuing exchange of notes that our national policy was to be marked by the same strength of words and weakness of action that had characterized it with Mexico, I toyed somewhat idly with the idea of going to Canada, as many Americans were doing, to join the Canadian forces for overseas service. I was deterred principally by a feeling that my German name would be a disadvantage and that I might even be suspect—as I probably would have been had my late sympathies for the enemy been known, mild though they were. As for the name itself, the fear was probably vain, since I have been since told by Canadians that there were many Teutonic names in the Canadian forces.

The 1915 training of the national guard regiment to which I belonged was an eight-day maneuver in July, between Bowers Mill and Aurora,

Mo., a distance of about 40 miles, the first battalion retreating up the valley of Spring River and engaging in a rear guard action against the other two battalions, the regimental commander and Major Charles Miller, U.S. army, acting as umpires. There were about 150 or 200 men in our battalion, so I suppose the whole force participating amounted to between 500 and 600. The conditions gave ample opportunity for training in life in the field, in varied weather, patrolling, outposts and minor combat action and I believe was about as good a preparation as was possible for such a regiment in such a period of time for service such as might have been encountered in Mexico.

So far as I noted, the maneuver was taken seriously and no opportunity for training neglected. One incident which created general amusement was when the battalion adjutant came galloping up from the rear of a part of the battalion marching in [a] column of fours on the road, his mission probably being to take a message to someone at the head of the column. But when he came to the tail of the column, he[,] not being accustomed to horses and this particular tough-mouthed beast hired for the occasion having ideas of his own, could neither check his mount or swerve it around the column. Tugging vainly at the reins he galloped right through on the crown of the road, the men, diving to the ditches to right and left, grinning and shouting wise-cracks at his distressed receding form.[3]

International affairs during 1915 were such as to keep my thoughts focused on military affairs instead of to the civilian matters to which I perhaps might have more sensibly and more profitably directed them. Conditions along the border were turbulent at times. In south Texas, in the lower Rio Grande valley, there was a period of disorder which caused part of the troops remaining at Texas City and Galveston after the hurricane of that year, to be sent down into the area to afford protection and to dispose of any Mexican marauding bands that the Texas rangers had not already eliminated. The 22nd Infantry—my old organization— was now at Douglas, Ariz., and on November 1 I was flattered to receive from my friend, First Sergeant Basil D. Coleman of Company F[,] the following telegram: "Can see Villa's army forming on hills east of Douglas for attack on Agua Prieta. We're entrenched along border. Better join us."

I was tempted as I read of the battle at Agua Prieta which my old associates were witnessing from their border trenches, but I still had hopes both for service and for a commission in the national guard—though the latter was unlikely enough. With war talk in the air there was but a small turn-over of officers and certainly no resignations impending in my own company.[4]

The "continental army plan" broached about this time by the Secretary of War gave me some hope. The pacifists and preparedness people were still engaged in wordy argument but it was generally conceded that some sort of preparation should be made. The Secretary of War proposed the formation of a national reserve organization of citizen soldiers to be known as "the continental army," this force to train in the field 30 days each year. I hoped I might obtain a commission in this but the idea of this kind of army was soon discarded and congressional thoughts began to take the turn which resulted in the passage of the first national defense act the following year.[5]

On March 9, 1916, the Mexican disturbances neared the war stage when Francisco Villa, or some of his bands, raided Columbus, N.M.[,] surprising the 13th U.S. Cavalry stationed there, killing any number of soldiers and citizens and burning part of the town before being defeated by the cavalrymen and chased back across and south of the border. Service even with the national guard now seemed likely but the punitive expedition to pursue the Villistas was organized and invaded Chihuahua without provoking hostilities with the Carranza government.

7

Back to the Border—As a Civilian

BY APRIL I was restive enough that I determined to take a month off from work and wander about.

I had always wanted to travel on a Mississippi River steamer and learning that there were some commercial lines still running, I went to Memphis, intending to go by water to New Orleans. However there were no through boats farther than Vicksburg, so I engaged passage on the *"John Lee"* of the Lee lines for that city and went aboard. The river water-front was all new and strange to me. As I wandered about there was a pistol shot from a group of Negroes nearby. The blacks scattered in all directions, and one Negro with raised revolver backed up the railway embankment, menacing the dissipating crowd, then at the top of the bank lowered his weapon and ran. I walked over to the scene of the disturbance. Two Negroes were supporting a burly third, shot through the chest. He seemed able to walk, and the two half led and half carried him away. No white man other than myself had evinced any visible interest in the affair. I mentioned this later to the first mate of the *John Lee.* "Oh these niggers are always killing one another," he said. "No one pays any attention."

As the *John Lee* wound leisurely around the tortuous channel of the Mississippi two or three days on its way to Vicksburg, stopping to unload passengers and freight at any obscure landings not reached by railway, I found many things to interest me, and among them were the colored roustabouts who handled the freight. Nothing disturbed their good humor long and they mixed their work with non-interfering horseplay, such as cramming their old felt hats upside down on their heads as they trotted back and forth unloading cargo. The mate, whom they called "Mistah Mike" and who they apparently regarded with a mixture of fear, respect and liking, drove them to their best effort with forceful threat and direct expletive, yet without sign of rancor and I suspect with underlying affection despite the violence of word and tone. And the Negroes sprang with quick obedience at his word but without sign of resentment and with grins undisturbed.

"'Bird's-Nest,' you black S.O.B.," he would shout, as a sample, "If I come down and bend this bar over your head you will move," where at "Bird's-Nest" moved with alacrity but with a smile.

The Negro called "Birds-Nest" was completely bald—not a hair on this head. The custom of the roustabouts when they wanted a drink was to lean overside and scoop up a greasy hatful of muddy river water to quench their thirst. But if Birds-Nest was about they always borrowed his hat, perhaps considering it a sanitary drinking cup because of his hairless cranium. Other nicknames I recall were "Burley," "General," and "Monkey-Head," and there was one man who even the mate cursed as "Mister Brown." The roustabouts apparently were heroes to the colored girls along the river as at every small landing a dusky feminine group was on hand to ex[c]hange badinage with them.

There were a good many colored passengers going from one landing to another, they being carried up on the hurricane deck. There was an occasional white man, billeted like myself in a state room, but most of the state rooms remained empty. With these white passengers and with the ships officers I talked concerning the river, the interest of which to me lay in the Civil War atmosphere in which my reading had placed it, and I learned something of river life. They showed me the steamer *City of St. Joseph* hard aground near Luna Landing, Ark., waiting for higher water to float her off. And one passenger had been aboard the steamer *Ben Hur* when she struck a stump a short distance above Vicksburg a week or two earlier, listing and going down immediately in shallow water but deep enough that one woman was drowned in her stateroom and most of the cabin passengers, including my informant, had had experiences with water.

A courtly elderly gentleman, familiar with Vicksburg and knowing many of the people there, talked to me at length, as elderly people will to a sympathetic listener, about the town and its history. Having told him that I intended to go over the old battlefield thoroughly, he narrated an anecdote, which he passed on as hearsay, concerning the placing of the numerous monuments on it showing the points of interest and commemorating the "high water marks" reached by various Union organizations during the assaults in the early part of the siege.

An Iowa infantry regiment, noted for its prowess in marching, had been called "the greyhounds" and on the battle marker its veterans had placed on the field was carved the figure of a greyhound in full motion, according to the story. But through some mistake the marker was placed on the wrong side of the driveway and so, as set, showed the greyhound exerting its speed away from the Confederate line instead of toward it. In two days plodding on foot over the field I saw no such marker—but anyhow it was a story worth remembering.

One other remark this gentleman made amused me. We had landed at Vicksburg and were walking up to the Carroll Hotel together. It was early Saturday and there were many colored women going toward the business district. Some of the mulattoes modishly dressed and trim in appearance were different from any colored women I had seen and I remarked with surprise: "Why some of these women are actually pretty."

"They should be," he answered, "they have in them some of the best blood of the South."

From Vicksburg I went by train to New Orleans, thence to Galveston and Texas City, whence I wandered somewhat disconsolately and very homesick for the army over the deserted flats which had been the camp ground on which as a member of the Second Division I had spent so many months.

The hurricane of 1915 had driven the sea over the camp and far inland. Happily the Sixth Brigade, which had been the most exposed in 1913 and 1914, was out in Arizona in 1915, so the loss of military life, while considerable, was not as heavy as it might have been, the camps being vacated in time.[1] The causeway connecting Galveston Island to the mainland was gone, and instead there was a trestle supporting the railway. Near the lower docks the railways were still twisted like ribbons and along a considerable part of the sea side of Galveston the seawall stood alone, with the boulevard washed out behind it and adjacent houses gone. The troops were all gone now except the garrison at Fort Crockett.

At San Antonio, I wandered around Fort Sam Houston where the 19th Infantry, or a part of it, was now stationed, then took train down to Laredo through a country which at the time was quiet and peaceful enough in appearance. Laredo too was serene and I enjoyed wandering around its quaint Mexican streets and strolling with interest through war-scarred Nuevo Laredo. Many of the building[s] of the Mexican town leading down toward the river were in ruins but so far as I noted were not pock-marked with rifle bullets like walls I had seen in Juárez a few years earlier. I was told by Americans that when our forces took Vera Cruz that the Mexican garrison of Nuevo Laredo, believing that war with the United States had come, had set fire to the city and retreated to the south, attempts to blow up the bridges being frustrated by American army sharpshooters who shot down Mexican soldiers who sought to fire the charges which had been placed under the Mexican end of the structure.[2]

I turned my face homeward—never suspecting that I soon would be back in Laredo as a soldier. It is a curious coincidence that I should have visited El Paso as a civilian in 1912, then soon found myself back there on border guard, and that the same thing should happen as regards Laredo following the civilian visit of April, 1916.

However peaceful the section of the border I had visited appeared, and however little informed the public was on the facts, to those in authority, war with Mexico must have appeared imminent by the end of April.

The Mexican government was ceasing any form of cooperation with the punitive expedition in Chihuahua in pursuit of bandits, was on the contrary shifting to an attitude of open opposition soon to result in armed clashes between detachments of the U.S. forces and federal forces of Mexico, and was soon to demand complete withdrawal of the Americans. Maj. Gen. Hugh L. Scott, army chief of staff, and Maj. Gen. Frederick Funston, commanding the border forces, were in conference with Gen. Alvaro Obregón of Mexico at El Paso.[3] Information of the American generals was that some 17[,]000 Mexicans had concentrated at Pulpito Pass to threaten communications of the expeditionary forces, that

Mexican irregular groups were forming near Victoria in Tamaulipas with the implied consent of local federal commanders to raid the Brownsville section of Texas, and that Luis de la Rosa was openly recruiting men in Monterey for some similar effort along the border.[4]

Practically the entire small regular army in the United States was now on the Mexican border or with the punitive expedition, except one regiment of cavalry, but due to the enormous length of the Mexican border, it was so thinly distributed that the border country was open to raids anywhere. The conference with Obregón proving futile since the tentative agreement reached there was not approved by Carranza, the "organized militia," as the national guard was then officially termed, of Arizona, New Mexico and Texas was called into federal service on May 9. But raids along the border became more frequent.

On June 3 congress finally passed the 1916 national defense act which gave the national guard a federal status above anything which it had previously enjoyed and authorized the president, in event of a national emergency, expressly declared such by congress, the power to draft it as units into the army of the United States. The new law also set the term of national guard enlistment at three years active and three years in the reserve, and for this or other legal reasons, it was required that every member of the national guard sign a new enlistment oath.

In my own company, and elsewhere so far as I know, with a few exceptions, this was done promptly and gladly, and 65 of the 70 odd men on our rolls had taken the new oath before June 17 when urgent directions came from the Missouri adjutant general that the work be completed at once.

The newspapers were now telling of numerous raids on unprotected sections of the border, including some in the Laredo region, and on the basis of these alone it was felt in our own unit that the entire national guard was about to be called into service. What was not known to the public was that General Funston had informed the War Department that information in his possession indicated that the Mexican army was contemplating an invasion of Texas with San Antonio as the objective.

On June 18—which was Sunday—President Wilson called the entire national guard of the United States into service. Congress had not declared an emergency and the call was under the constitutional right of the president to call the militia into service to suppress insurrection, re-pel invasion or execute the laws of the union. It was not until July 1 that an emergency was formally declared. Thereafter, the president was em-powered to draft the national guard and use it in an invasion of Mexico should such be decided upon.

Laredo

IT WAS ON the morning of June 19 that orders to mobilize reached Company A, Second Missouri Infantry, by which time some two-thirds of the company had already assembled in uniform on the basis of newspaper reports. By nightfall the unit was ready to move, but for some reason, probably inability to get railway cars, the companies of the regiment each in a separate town, did not move to the state concentration camp at Camp Clark, Nevada, Mo., until the morning of the 21st.

In the meanwhile we endeavored to recruit. It had always been my belief that while Americans were averse to military service of any sort in time of peace that they would volunteer in great numbers whenever an emergency arose which offered chance of active service. This little recruiting effort banished illusions. We sought 108 men, the authorized war strength of the day. We left with 84, of whom seven were rejected later on a physical examination.[1]

Ours was not a bad company for a national guard organization of 1916 when general efficiency standards were much lower than they were later when the national defense act, federal pay and the prestige of World War I made the national guard a reasonably effective force. Our captain and first lieutenant were guardsmen of considerable experience. Our second lieutenant was a former regular soldier who was commissioned a year later in the regular army; our first sergeant was a former officer; the combined mess and supply sergeant, four of the six duty sergeants and two of the six corporals had been enlisted men in the regular service, as had several of the privates. This was a rather unusual percentage of ex-regulars for that time, when the regular army was quite small, and taken with the small group of experienced national guardsmen who had taken their previous training seriously, constituted a framework out of which an efficient company was quickly built.

We were reminded by association with other units at Camp Clark that the national guard of the time was rather spotty as regarded military attitude, training and bearing. Some companies were very good, some were very bad, more were mediocre. But under tutelage of a fiery and energetic commanding officer, Col. W. A. Raupp who had been a captain in the volunteer army in the Spanish-American War and was of long national guard experience besides, the regiment was soon whipped into serviceable shape. Col. Raupp, highly regarded in his organization and in my opinion a most capable officer, somehow became embroiled in a feud with senior officers of the regular army while on the Mexican border, a circumstance which deprived him of combat service during the First World War and placed him instead in command of a pioneer regiment which did not leave the states. For many years after the war he was a brigadier general commanding the Missouri National Guard and served for a time as adjutant general of Missouri.[2]

The first day we were at Camp Clark, Col. Raupp sent for me and kindly offered me the position of regimental sergeant major, the highest noncommissioned post in the regiment. However I wanted to fight the war, if any, with a rifle instead of a typewriter, so thanked him but told him that if it was a matter of choice I preferred to remain a duty sergeant. He named instead a friend of mine, Battalion Sergeant Major Clyde A. Narramore who had originally been from my own company and who doubtless made a much better regimental sergeant major than I could have done. He was commissioned a few months later while on the border, served as lieutenant of the 110th Trench Mortar Battery during World War I and was a national guard captain for some time thereafter.[3]

The colonel, I felt, rather sympathized with my desire to keep clear of paper work, and I believe that if a vacancy had occurred in the officer personnel of my own company during the border service he would have recommended me for a second lieutenancy—but there was no such vacancy. In the early months of the First World War I served under his command as a captain.

Although the Missouri troops were ready, so far as I could see, to move immediately, after the concentration at Camp Clark, and the issue of additional equipment and clothing, there was a delay that seemed then to be considerable in view of a reputedly critical situation along the border. The adjutant general of Missouri later reported that this was due to the fact that the government furnished only one mustering officer.[4] The first regiment to leave departed July 1 and my own not until July 5.

The mustering in process was accompanied by some amusing incidents. In a newly formed company of my own regiment there were a number of young business men without knowledge of military matters and apparently skeptical of what their officers told them. They had all taken the new federal oath and could not understand an additional mustering-in oath. They acquired the idea that they were to be mustered into the regular army instead of for the emergency and 28 refused to take the oath until a field officer in whom they had confidence was sent for and explained to them that this was just an extra frill that the government required and made no difference in their term of service. In another company some men had refused to sign the new federal oath but had been brought to camp anyhow, as was proper since the call was for "organized militia and national guard." The mustering officer's instructions, however, [were] not to muster anyone unless they had signed the new oath and these seven men were able to evade service. Their uniforms were taken from them, they were given fatigue clothes and told to leave camp. Their departure was something of an event since their late comrades formed behind them with tin wash basins and "drummed them out of camp" by marching along, thumping on the tin pans and chanting in loud unison, "Yellow, yellow, yellow."[5]

It was pleasant to be on a troop train and border-bound again, equipment swinging back and forth on hooks in an atmosphere of cigarette smoke as the train jolted along, and with volunteer quartets carolling forth their joy at being alive and going places. Carranzista troops had shot up two troops of the 10th U.S. Cavalry at Carrizal, Chihuahua, a short time previously and the war fever was running high.[6] There was

Map of Laredo, Texas, c. 1890. Schrantz marked the locations of Indian Ford on the Rio Grande and "Camp Ground 1916."

a cheering reception at many of the towns through which we passed and I recall particularly that at Enid, Okla., where groups of women served ice cream to all personnel, there being a delay there which permitted the troops to be detrained in front of their cars for that purpose. But as we neared San Antonio those of us who had served before told our comrades sagely: "You will get no reception here. San Antone is an army town and army towns are not enthusiastic about soldiers." But as soon as our train drew into the station, ladies were passing along the cars handing up boxes of food and candy through the windows.[7]

South of San Antonio the country took on a warlike aspect, quite different from what it had appeared when I traveled that road a few months before. Bridges and culverts were guarded by squads of troops with red hat-cords—coast artillerymen with bulging cartridge belts temporarily serving as infantry—standing beside sand-bagged trenches. In the small towns a number of citizens were seen wearing revolvers—picturesque old frontier models many of them. Near Webb was pointed out a wooden cross marking the grave of a Carranza colonel, killed some time before

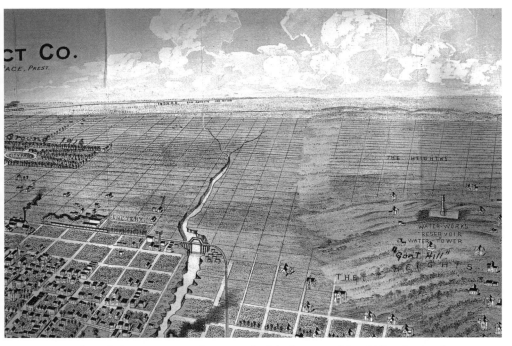

Map of Laredo, Texas, c. 1890. Schrantz marked the location of Goat Hill at the site of the water works, reservoir, and water tower on the right.

in a raid meant to cut the railway. Moving northward on the roads were groups of Mexican men, women and children in burro-drawn vehicles or trudging along on foot, presumably seeking safety from the storm they imagined about to break over the border country.

We arrived at Laredo the night of July 7 and established camp north of the town the following day. There were at Laredo at the time, the 9th Infantry, the 14th Cavalry (less units on border patrol up or down the Rio Grande), the provisional regiment of coast artillerymen less those on railway or border guard, and a battalion of the Third field artillery. Within a few days there was the entire Missouri National Guard, totaling some 5,000 men, the 2nd Maine Infantry, the 1st New Hampshire and I believe a Vermont regiment. Later the 2nd Florida also was to come. Perhaps there was a total of 9[,]ooo or 10[,]ooo men.

The principal concentrations of troops were in the Brownsville District, El Paso and at Douglas, Ariz—the bases from which an invasion of Mexico would be launched if war came. The troops at Laredo, I have since learned, were to move on Monterey, uniting with those coming from Brownsville.

But the concentration of the national guard on the border brought a prompt return of peaceful conditions. To the Mexicans it must have appeared a considerable army. Raids ceased. There was no need for the president to draft the national guard into the federal army under the new defense law and it served throughout under the call under which it could have been used only to "repel invasion."

The Maine regiment relieved the coast artillerymen on the border and on the railway guard, so long as this latter was maintained, other units furnished occasional details to guard fords or bridges about Laredo or public utility plants therein and for the rest the time was devoted to training which no doubt was badly needed. The only danger was from careless handling of ball ammunition which had been issued on arrival, and every few days there was a crack of a rifle bullet as someone accidentally discharged a piece, yet I heard of no one injured thereby.

The days of careless border guard that I had known with the 22d Infantry in El Paso in late 1912 and early 1913 were no more—ended by the Columbus, N.M., and other raids. The 14th Cavalry detachment at San Ygnacio, Texas, some 40 miles below Laredo had been attacked by Luis de la Rosa on June 15 and suffered a number of casualties in killed and wounded before routing their assailants.[8] With these lessons in mind extreme care was taken—some of it possibly due to the newness of our own officers. In our regiment one full company went on guard nightly; another company remained in its company area clothed and armed, and a third was held in readiness to respond immediately in case of an alarm. Nervous sentries made life dangerous for wanderers.[9]

It was told at the time—with how much accuracy I do not know—that Brig. General H. C. Clark, commander of the Missouri troops, was riding through the Missouri camp one night looking over the situation rather hurriedly when a sentry stopped him with the usual "Halt! Dismount!" Not wishing to be delayed, the general explained from his saddle that he was the commanding general checking up on the guard. Not to be cozened the sentry replied threateningly: "Don't you fool with me, mister. This thing[']s loaded. Dismount!" Whereupon the general wisely

Members of Company A, Second Missouri Infantry, at Indian Ford, Laredo, Texas, 1916

dismounted and waited quietly until the arrival of the corporal of the guard to check up on his credentials.[10]

The nervous stage of the camp guard soon passed, and either because the situation was deemed to be less threatening, or because our national guard commanders became acclimated to border conditions, a simple one-company guard was deemed adequate.

My own first tour of border guard was when I commanded an eight-man outpost for 24 hours at Indian Ford northwest of Laredo—a crossing which angled across the river and naturally needed to be watched. With each man carrying 100 rounds of ammunition in his belt and wearing two extra bandoleers each containing 60 rounds more, we were in position to carry on a little war of our own in our isolated position if necessary. Across the river was a similar squad of Carranzista soldiers, stationed not at the fort [sic] but at a house nearby, around which a trench

Ward Schrantz on the Rio Grande with the Second Missouri Infantry, Indian Ford, Laredo, Texas, 1916

had been dug. An occasional Carranzista mounted patrol passed up or down the river, pausing at the Mexican side of the ford to water their horses. The only excitement of our tour happened to a patrol I sent up our own side of the river. These two or three men, hearing voices beyond a thicket, stalked them and burst out on the river bank with rifles at the ready—disturbing a bevy of Mexican women bathing. They retreated in haste at the same voices raised in angry expostulation. At least that was their report to me.

Our camp of pyramidal tents which we had pitched at the north edge of Laredo gradually began to take on a more permanent air. Some frame tables were built in the company street near the kitchen tent and fly, and we ate sitting at these instead of on the ground. Next cots arrived, replacing the hollows we had scooped in the sand for sleeping. Finally a mess hall was built and screened.

The weather varied the monotony of drill, hike and minor maneuvers a little. Dust storms occasionally filled the air so that it was difficult to see across the company streets. The tail of a hurricane caught us one night, flattening three fourths of our regimental camp and submerging with rain water those tent sites on low ground or in gulleys [sic].[11]

A morale factor developed in the national guard troops on the border. While it is known now that relations with the Mexican de facto government remained unsatisfactory and were several times near the point of war, there was no outward evidence of this and the true situation was unknown to the troops or to the public. It all looked peaceful enough and homesick guardsmen and their families wondered why they were kept there. Some had left families, and could not support them on the $15.00 a month pay of the private soldier. Congress soon took care of this by making allowances or authorizing discharges for men with dependents.[12]

In my own company, morale was good enough, due probably to the fact that the noncommissioned officers affected an old-soldier air and derided as weaklings anyone who complained. We looked down with lofty scorn on some neighboring companies where even some sergeants whined about wanting to go home. We made a point of pride in being punctiliously military with our officers, however well we had known them at home. We had, in fact, a very good opinion of ourselves.[13]

My own pride was deflated somewhat however by an incident which occurred when I was sergeant of the regimental guard. The guardhouses consisted of three pyramidal tents and we had 16 garrison prisoners therein who worked around the camp under guard during the day and whose security at night was looked after by two sentries, one of whom walked in front of the tents and one who walked behind them. There was a dense dust storm that evening and when the guard was changed at 10 P.M. two of the prisoners were missing. I was in a fury, "jerked the belts" of the luckless sentries, placed them under confinement too and talked the officer of the guard into leaving them there.

Word of the escapes had gone to the company and as I went over to breakfast I encountered grins on the faces of my fellow sergeants. "How many prisoners did you have last night?" one of them, an ex-Marine, asked me. "Sixteen," I snarled in reply. "And how many do you have this morning?" he smiled. "Sixteen," I snarled again. All looked at me in surprise at this. Evidently their information was incomplete. And I let them stare blankly for a moment before I grudgingly explained: "Yes, I lost two, but I used my Numbers 1 and 2 sentries to fill the vacant ranks."

This reestablished my prestige a little but it didn't last. When I returned to the guard house I found 17 prisoners. One of the two who had escaped had come back during the night and, entirely unseen by another pair of sentries, had slipped back into the prison tent and went to sleep. This was the crowning shame and I could think of no answer to the subsequent good-natured jeers of my associates on this one. But since the provost guard picked the remaining missing prisoner up down town and since the officer of the day released the two sentries I had confined, I at least turned over to the new guard on my relief the same 16 that I had received.[14]

There were strict and, under the circumstances, quite proper orders against soldiers visiting Nuevo Laredo on the Mexican side, but the place being across the river had a fascination, though I had been over there as a civilian a few months before, so twice I borrowed civilian clothes and went over again just for the walk on unfriendly territory.[15] The first time I was accompanied by the first sergeant. He was a slender man who wore glasses and neither of us probably looked very military in civilian clothes and we had no trouble. The next time I went with the ex-Marine who had something of a belligerent countenance and bellicose air and whose borrowed civilian clothes looked like they had been built for someone else.

At the Mexican end of the bridge a Carranzista captain[,] with a group of nondescript Carranza soldiers lounging nearby, glared at us directly and with offensive hostility. The situation looked like the inside of a jail to me but the officer let us pass, though he watched us up the street. Glancing at my companion I noted that his lower jaw was thrust forward and he had cocked his hat forward over his eyes. "Put your hat on the back of your head and try to look like a tourist," I whispered. He complied, but at each unfriendly look we received—and there were many—he would reach up behind and shove his hat forward again.

We did not stay in Nuevo Laredo long. We sat in the first plaza a few moments to see if we had been followed from the bridge but apparently had not been. Then we wandered to the next in front of a building which had been prepared for defense, around which trenches ran, and where, naturally, many Carranzista soldiers lounged. Trying to appear nonchalant we sat on a bench with our backs to the enemy. Then an unpleasant-looking Negro approached us and grinned as he looked at us and then at the Mexican soldiers. He said he had seen us in uniform in Laredo, and here he was in Nuevo Laredo and broke, he said. He thought we might want to buy an old watch he had for a dollar. We looked at it silently. It was indeed an old watch. Once it had been a dollar Ingersoll but it had long since stopped running. A one-dollar blackmail—cheap but humiliating. Our thoughts were murder but we could hardly afford crime under the circumstances. We bought the watch and studied him so that we might remember him. He grinned and ambled off toward a cantina. We later prowled Laredo a number of times looking for this man but never saw him.

We started back to the bridge and passed the Mexican guards unchallenged. I breathed a deep sigh of relief. But on the American side the immigration guard asked us to step in a little room in the bridge shack. He grinned at us and asked to see our vaccination marks. This, we knew, was exposure.

Back at Camp Clark when our regiment had been vaccinated, each man had been scratched in three separate spots, in a triangle. I suppose that someone had given instructions that each man should be vaccinated three times, meaning that the process should be continued this often if the first one did not take, but that the surgeon had misunderstood and made it three times at once. In any event three vaccination scars in a triangle was as identifying as the tattooed name of our state.

"You boys are from the Missouri camp, are you not?" said the immigration guard, grinning again.

"Oh no," we lied hopefully, surmising that the immigration man's orders were to turn persons such as us over to the American army bridge guard outside. There were a few such malefactors already in our own guardhouse. "We are from Missouri," we admitted, "but we are just down here looking around." "In that case you can go ahead," he smiled once more and waved us on.

This was the last time I visited Nuevo Laredo.

In the latter part of August there was considerable talk of an impending nationwide railway strike and our organization, and I suppose all other troops, were polled to find and list men with railway experience, presumably for railway service if the government found it necessary to operate trains. There was some speculation in camp as to how order would be maintained with practically all of the regular army and national guard on the border.

About the 25th my own regiment marched east of Laredo some distance for target practice, missing a visit by Maj. Gen. Frederick Funston, my favorite military hero, before whom all troops at Laredo were passed in review.[16]

Back in the Laredo camp on Sept. 3, we found the camps of the 1st and 3d Missouri regiments empty. They had started back to Missouri on September 2, presumably in order to be available in the event of disorders in connection with the impending strike. Many other regiments were sent home about the same time. The strike not developing, they were mustered out of service several weeks later. A Presidential election campaign was in progress at that time and it is perhaps possible that a return of a part of the national guard might have had some political aspects since President Wilson's supporters were stressing the "he-kept-us-out-of-war" slogan. In any event since no evil effects appeared on the border as a result of their departure it is evident that their services could be spared.

As for my own regiment, it received orders to relieve the 2d Maine Infantry on the Rio Grande where it was patrolling about a 100 mile front from 67 miles below Laredo to 32 or 33 miles above. My own battalion, the first, was to occupy the southern sector with headquarters at Zapata.[17]

Ramireño

THE 49-MILE MARCH from Laredo to Ramireño in Zapata County, which my own company was to garrison, was something of a military idyll. After the first 15 or 20 miles the region was sparsely inhabited and with the border road a trail rather than a highway, shifting whenever ruts on an old route suggested another would be better. Now and then there was a gate through which to pass, marking the boundary of some great ranch. The second night's camp was on a stream known as Dolores Creek, among eroded earth canyons. The coyotes howled about in an unbroken circle. The nights were clear and balmy and our camps were a sort of bivouac-de-luxe—each man unloading his cot from the company escort wagon and sleeping under the stars which in this section of Texas seem brighter than any place from which I have ever seen them.

Yet, not so long before, some of the nights in this section had not been safe ones. At a little store and a few houses called La Perla, some distance south of Dolores Creek, there was a small detachment of troops, their camp surrounded by a wall of earth held in place by a brushwork revetment on each side. The proprietor of the store, a white American, wore a heavy revolver and a dirk, while a Winchester carbine hung on the wall just behind him as he stood at the counter.

At San Ygnacio, further to the south, there was a long parapet about 3½ feet high with a one-foot trench behind it, guarding the front of the camp of the two companies of infantry and a troop of cavalry which formed its garrison. This defense had not been there on the night of

June 14 when Luis de la Rosa and his bandits had attacked the 24 caval-rymen who had then formed the garrison of the place. Three of the cav-alrymen were killed, some while sleeping on their bunks, we were told, and it might have gone badly for the rest except that a full troop, travel-ling down the river, had reached San Ygnacio that night after dark and encamped nearer the river. They entered the fight almost immediately as a surprise to the assailants, who fled forthwith, the Americans in pursuit. Some 15 of the raiders were killed and five captured. These latter, I knew were in jail at Laredo, and I believe were eventually hanged. Many of the houses in the town were bullet-marked. An old American doctor living there—the only non-Mexican American in the town, I think—described vividly to the first sergeant and I who visited him, the events of the night. He had been active in treating the wounded and was quite bitter against the local druggist who he said had barricaded his doors when the attack started and apparently had been most reluctant to open them again badly needed as his medical supplies were for the wounded.[1]

The border road swung away from the river at San Ygnacio, and late that afternoon, some six miles further on, my own company turned to the right down a side trail and after a mile or two came into the friendly Mexican village of Ramireño near the river bank.

Ramireño had not been garrisoned previously and the placing of a garrison there now was said to have been at the request of the Ramirez family who owned the region about it and who were the employers of all who lived in the village. There were a good many cattle and horses, some of the latter very fine ones, and while the Ramirez family lived humbly enough in a vine-covered cottage, I have no doubt that they were people of considerable wealth who profitably might have been held for ransom. Isolated as it was, the place would have been an easy objective for a raid before it was garrisoned. The land beyond the river on the Mexican side also belonged to this family, as I recall it, but it was seldom used and I believe the cattle and horses from it had been brought to the American side—or perhaps stolen. I saw no signs of any activity over there except an occasional Mexican patrol.

Our arrival that evening was something of an event. The whole male population turned out to greet us. They filed by our officers, each man shaking hands with them. Knowing a few words of Spanish[,] I had been called upon to attempt to act interpreter for the captain and as such shared in the hand-shaking. Afterwards I think that most of them shook hands with everyone in the company. That night the local singers (masculine) gathered at the bivouac and sang and strummed on guitars until taps were sounded—whereupon they rose promptly, knowing the call as "silencio," and quickly faded away.[2]

For six weeks we were in this village and mingled with the inhabitants (male again) with all friendliness and no untoward events. The local girls were evidently under orders, scrupulously obeyed so far as I know, not to fraternize and no doubt that wise precaution was a factor in the maintenance of cordial relations.

For some reason our camp was pitched on a flat open space practically as part of the village itself—two rows of pyramidal tents facing each other with the two A-tents meant for the officers pitched at the village end and looking down the street. Still closer to the village and close to the village grocery was the kitchen tent. The officers['] tents were actually occupied by the first sergeant and supply sergeant, the two officers with us occupying a house in the village adjacent to the camp.

The fortification of the camp under such circumstances was something of a problem. Now without any intent to boast and regardless of my humble rank as sergeant I can fairly say that I knew more of that subject of fortification than anyone else in the organization, including the officers. Not only had I had such practical training as was given to soldiers in the regular army and national guard, but I had carefully studied the book on field fortifications issued by the Fort Leavenworth school. In addition, as an amusement, I had studied older systems of fortifications, which were more to the point since there was no danger of artillery being used in any attack on our camp—only small arms. Any attack would be a surprise one and we needed something that would give men a measure of protection from short range fire while asleep on their bunks. The enclosure we saw at the post at La Perla and the long parapet at San Ygnacio were probably both developments meant to meet such need based on the fact that in the San Ygnacio attack men had been killed while still on their cots.

I went to the captain and explained my idea. He approved it and directed me to carry it into effect. The plan was simple enough. Basically it provided for a parapet three-and-a-half foot above the ground level, revetted at the back [?] with brush and with a broad one-foot-deep trench behind it which enabled a man to fire easily over the parapet from a standing position. Additional earth needed for the parapet was obtained by digging a sloping excavation in front, which, when completed, was deep enough that a man in it could not even see over the top of the parapet. In order to prevent an attacker from using the parapet there was a bastion at each lower end, flanking both the long stretches and the entrance to the back of the camp. A field of fire, except toward the houses, was provided by clearing away the mesquite brush on the flat around the camp. The revetment was provided mainly by slender brush obtained along the river and the cut-off mesquite was used partly to block an arroyo which afforded a possible means of hostile approach to the lower end of the camp and partly to provide an obstacle in the ditch in front of the parapet.

This work was given priority above everything else and flowed along smoothly, the more so since the first sergeant was an engineer in civil life and three of our non-commissioned officers had been in the engineer corps of the regular army in a past enlistment. The one-foot trench to provide shelter for a man in a prone position was dug first so there would be some immediate cover available, the clearing of the foreground proceeding at the same time. The officers['] quarters, the kitchens and the latrines were all outside but there was no anticipation of any need of standing siege—only to beat off a first rush. It must be admitted that the officers sleeping outside was a weak point as regarded their personal safety—but that was their worry. So far as carrying on an action was concerned we did not feel that we needed them particularly.

This work pleased me immensely since I had devised it and even the local citizenry commented that it was a "buen fortín"—a good fort. They further suggested that after we were gone they would use it for a goat corral, which I have no doubt they did. Of course it was never attacked. So far as I know no fortified place on the border had ever been attacked. Raiders looked for weak spots, not strong points.[3]

There was one alarm.

At 1 o'clock on the morning of September 29, several rifle shots from the lower end of the camp snapped us out of our slumbers. I snatched

Ward Schrantz on the Rio Grande with the Second Missouri Infantry, September 21, 1916

my rifle which was suspended from my cot, took my cartridge belt from the tent pole and buckled it around my underwear, then sat down on the cot to put on my shoes. Just at that unhappy moment some one directly behind my tent fired twice. I sallied out of the tent barefooted to take part in the war. The hub-bub still seemed to be at the lower end of the camp and noting that all hands were scrambling out and manning the parapet

CHAPTER 9

I started toward the apparent center of activities. Then I stepped on a prickly pear cactus, extracted it with oaths and went back into the tent and put on my shoes.

Down at the end of the camp the sentries were explaining rather vaguely that they had "seen something" to the northeast. It sounded rather silly as an explanation for that much firing but at the direction of the first sergeant I went back and dressed and took out a patrol, finding nothing. Later the guard confessed that they had fired the shots at the directions of the captain who wanted to see how quick the men could get into the trenches.

Being mindful of the effect that this sort of thing would have on our prestige with the local citizens, I was perhaps unduly annoyed. I could have been court-martialed for my thoughts, if expressed, and perhaps I did express them. It turned out rather happily in fact that I had. Being deemed by my words to be one of the party of resentful malcontents that this incident created, I was taken into a private-soldier plot a few nights later which had as its design "getting even" with the captain for wrecking the unit's reputation of not having any false alarms—a thing which previously added to unit esprit. The plot was to stage another false alarm that night, firing a few rifle bullets through the roof of the captain's house to see how quickly he could emerge therefrom and get to his post of duty in the trenches. I explained the folly of such a proceeding to them and the plot was dropped. In some ways, I reflected privately, it was rather a bright and tempting idea at that.[4]

The six weeks or so my company spent at Ramerino [sic] was in general about as happy and carefree a period as any I have ever spent in the military service. Outside of guard, which came every third night, there was little duty once the parapet was completed and with a natural propensity to ramble about on foot in new territory, I spent much of my own time in long walks up or down the river or into the wild hills roundabout in company with one or two kindred spirits with similar inclinations. Since we carried rifles and wore our full cartridge belts on such occasions, these jaunts probably also served the purpose of voluntary patrols.

Perhaps most of these jaunts were made with Cecil R. Stemmons, a corporal, whose family had about as complete a Civil War record for all male members as anyone I have ever known. Of his six uncles, four had been in the Union forces engaged in the guerrilla warfare of Southwest Missouri and two had gone into the Confederate army—one attaining some modest note in the southern forces. His grandfather had been killed by Confederate guerrillas one night when his house was attacked and burned while he was organizing a militia company with men he had assembled at his house. When I became a national guard captain some six or seven months after the Ramireño sojourn it was my pleasure to include Stemmons as one of two men I sent to the first officers' training camp of World War I and he served as [an] infantry officer during that war. I was associated with him for a time in the trenches of the Sommedieue sector southwest of Verdun in October 1918 until he was sent to the rear sick, having caught the measles somehow. This deeply chagrined him. So many things might happen to a man when his unit was in contact with the enemy—and what happened to him was measles.

Some jaunts also were made with Guy A. Roos, the first sergeant frequently heretofore mentioned, and John M. Curlee[,] a duty sergeant. Roos, like myself, was a chronic citizen soldier and was always in some military unit when there was any around, and without caring much about what rank he held. He had been a second lieutenant back in 1912 but lost his commission when he temporarily changed residence and had since been serving as an enlisted man. Some eye trouble caused him to fail to pass the physical examination at the beginning of World War I but [he] later managed to get into a hospital unit in which he served. After the war he was alternately officer and enlisted man in the national guard, attaining the rank of captain once, then losing it when his wandering engineering life led him elsewhere, only to reenlist as a private when he returned. He eventually became a reserve officer, served with the Civilian Conservation Corps during most of its life, went into the active army early in the emergency preceding our entry into World War II and emerged therefrom a major, promptly going back into the reserve again. His father was German-born and in the first war he had a number of uncles in the German army. When I was in France in 1918, he still being in the states, he wrote me a letter in which he said: "If you see any of my square-headed relatives over there, take a crack at them for me."[5]

Curlee, a competent and enthusiastic soldier, did not go into World

War I for some family reason, working as a captain of guards at a plant making explosives. He became a national guard captain between the wars but was out when World War II came along. He could not get a commission because of his lack of World War I service, nor enlist because of his age. He served as a full time state guard officer during the second war, being my own adjutant while I commanded such a regiment before being called to active duty under my reserve commission.[6]

I mention these three men in detail as indicative of the type of national guardsmen of the period preceding the first war.

Once Curlee and I invaded Mexico naked.

With him and Roos, I had wandered up to a place called San Ygnacio Viejo, the site of the first San Ygnacio which seems to have been one of the original Spanish settlements.[7] There were only a few tumbled walls there and some fragments of pottery. The Rio Grande was running rather high and Curlee and I fell into a discussion about swimming it to see what we could see from the bank on the other side. Leaving Roos to guard our clothes and rifles we waded out into the stream but by the time it was waist deep it was so swift that we could hardly keep our feet. We decided to start swimming. Immediately we were swept down the stream at what seemed to me a terrific rate, and for a moment of panic I fought against the current, then more sensibly let it help me. Curlee was right beside me so I suspect his mental reactions were similar. After that we had no trouble, landing on the Mexican side, well down stream. Our path to the top of the bank was over beds of sand burrs not at all pleasant to bare feet. And at the top all that confronted us was dense thickets of mesquite. We could see much more of Mexico from the American hills. We decided to return to the United States and did so, our back swim being easy enough now that we knew how, but there was a long trudge unclothed up stream before we could get back to where we had left our garments and guns.

Once Sergeant Roos and I accompanied the captain on a ride on hired Mexican horses down to Zapata, 17 miles below[,] to visit battalion headquarters there. Thirty-four miles in one day is considerable for one who has not been on a horse for some years. I had no interest whatever in horseback riding for a time after that.

On the evening of October 15, Company H, Fourth Missouri Infantry, hiked wearily into town to relieve us, and the next morning we started the long march back to Laredo. I left rather regretfully, being by nature a lazy man who enjoyed a life like that we were leaving, but I suspect my sentiments were not shared by the majority of my associates. The column broke into song, singing many songs of many verses, and including, I recall, a parady [sic] of some religious one:

"In heaven above, where all is love, There'll be no non-coms there."

After a 21-mile march we reached Dolores Creek, somewhat weary, and paused while the captain considered whether to camp on the south bank where we had before, or on the north. He chose the north, which was just as well for Dolores Creek[,] which was then ankle deep[,] was a roaring torrent before morning and not fordable for days.

It was the usual balmy evening as we bivouacked. Our cots were unloaded and we went to sleep on them under the open sky. During the night, Roos, who slept next to me, woke me up and said hesitatingly: "Schrantz, there is a cloud in the north, and some lightning." Indeed there was—just a spot of cloud vividly illuminated from time to time. Texas storms come up rapidly. We buttoned our shelter tents together to form a tent and shouted for others to do likewise. By then the cloud was almost above us. Men were sitting up looking around drowsily as we feverishly ditched our tent. "Let it rain," said some of them, pulling their shelter tents or ponchos over their blankets. It did—and immediately. Roos and I dived for shelter and lay snug in the only tent up, hearing the muttering and oaths of misery about us. The "let-it-rain" boys on their cots did not do very well. Their ponchos or shelter halves protected them from the direct torrents but the water caught on the end of the bunks and ran down into the depressions caused by their bodies, forming little lakes. They sought shelter elsewhere—and in vain. Dolores Creek rose rapidly for before long we could hear huge segments of undercut banks sliding into the torrent with sounds like explosions. I think the first sergeant and I were the only dry men in the company the next morning, except perhaps some who had been first in the rush to get into the covered escort wagon.

I have mentioned ponchos. So far as I know this border disturbance was the last campaign for these as an article of issue. Our entry into the First World War brought the raincoat as an inferior substitute, I presume because of the introduction of gas into warfare. A gas mask could be worn over a raincoat. Underneath a poncho it would hardly have been accessible.

The next day's march was a long and trying one, the first few miles through the mud. After a 28 mile hike we reached Laredo after dark, tired and footsore.[8] During the day we passed a group of men of the Fourth Missouri, baseball players who had lingered to play a game and now were trudging south to join their companies. Among them was an acquaintance from our own town, Sergeant Marcus O. Bell of the Columbia company which contained many men from the University of Missouri. Bell was commissioned in the regular army soon thereafter and in the Second World War became a brigadier general, assistant division commander of the 81st Division.[9]

The End of Border Service

BACK IN THE Laredo camp the usual routine of drill and maneuver was resumed, to which was added a weekly parade at Fort McIntosh. There were only four infantry regiments now at Laredo, including our own—the regiments numbering about 1,000 men each. Besides us there was the 9th U.S. Infantry, the 1st New Hampshire and the 2nd Florida. There were rumors of impending trouble but I saw no evidences of any change myself. The 1916 election was near and on October 25 the Secretary of War issued a statement that Mexicans might raid border posts before election day in order to discredit President Woodrow Wilson, who, it will be remembered, was being supported for reelection on a "he-kept-us-out-of-war" platform.

Along about October 30 there was a little flurry of interest. Troops were moved down into Laredo. Machine guns were set up in Martin Plaza. Full companies were at the light plant, at the post-office and at Indian ford and detachments of one sort or another were placed at other strategic points. Since we of the Second Missouri had returned so recently from border patrol, we were left in our camps, presumably as a reserve. The occasion for all these precautions I have never learned. Some weeks later, after the election was well over, there were some other alerts of a minor nature, but no actual trouble.[1]

Non-mounted infantry officers were usually not good horsemen and an incident resulting from this fact amused us at one of our regimental parades at Fort McIntosh. For the parades the regiment was always

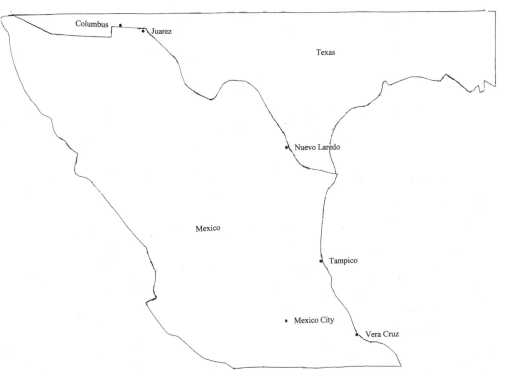

Sites associated with the Mexican Revolution and U.S. intervention, 1910–16

formed with battalions in order of the rank of their commanding officer. Our major was the senior in the regiment and hence our battalion was always on the right in the formation. But he went home on leave and on the occasion of this parade the battalion was commanded by the senior captain who inherited the major's horse during the period of his temporary command. He being the junior battalion commander present, our battalion this time was formed on the left. Obviously ill at ease on the horse, the captain still successfully managed that part of the ceremony where at the command "Officers Center" the commanders of the flank battalions and their staffs closed on the commander of the center battalion and rode forward to a position in front of the colonel. But at the colonel's command "Officers, Posts, March," when battalion commanders were to return to the front of their battalions, by the most direct route, the captain had trouble. His horse on many such occasions had gone through this ceremony and then returned to the right. He did this now, and the captain's vain efforts to guide him to the left were without avail. The horse knew where he belonged, or thought he did, and took the embarrassed captain to the right of the regiment and not until he had completed this accustomed path would he permit himself to be directed over to the left flank. It was most amusing for everyone except that captain, and maybe the horse. The latter's mouth must have suffered from the jerking on the bits, and his sides must have been sore from being violently prodded with the rowelless spurs.

Despite the occasional rumors of further trouble on the border, there was an occasional national guard regiment being moved out for home and muster-out. It appeared that the tour of border duty was drawing to a close but in the meanwhile the customary routine went on.[2] The 1st New Hampshire relieved the 4th Missouri on river guard, and a month later was relieved in turn by the 2nd Florida.

Just after Christmas the 2nd Missouri received orders to return north. We left Laredo on December 28, were mustered out at Fort Riley, Kans., January 13, 1917, and my own company arrived in Carthage, our home station, the following day—reverting back to state control as a national guard unit.

Personally I would have been pleased to stay on the border since there was no interest now to draw me homeward and there still seemed some possibility of more active service in connection with the Mexican troubles, but in truth I was an exception. Most of the national guardsmen were well sick of the border and felt that they served no useful purpose there.

Looking backward, it would seem to have been folly from a national standpoint to have broken up these units which had at least had some training in the field. In theory the units could be called again if needed and while this was so in fact it did not apply to the personnel. Men scattered everywhere in search of employment. It was a partial demo-bilization of our armed forces and I have wondered sometimes if the muster-out of the national guard from federal service might have been a factor in causing Germany to start her unrestricted submarine campaign in February.

In any event, within less than three months after the return of my own company to civil life, the United States was at war with Germany.

Editor's Postscript

ON APRIL 13, 1917, a week after the United States declared war on Germany, Schrantz's hard work with the National Guard paid off with his election as captain of the Carthage Light Guard. The company did not immediately enter federal service. It was not until August 5 that the Second Missouri Infantry was officially drafted, and on August 17 the regiment assembled on the now familiar grounds of Camp Clark, near Nevada, Missouri. After a quick round of physical examinations and inoculations, Schrantz's Company A was designated the "advance detail" and ordered to travel to Camp Doniphan, near Fort Sill, Oklahoma, where the new Thirty-fifth Division was being organized. On August 23, Schrantz and the other Carthage men left for Camp Doniphan, arriving the next day. There they served as a fatigue party and camp guards until the rest of the division arrived. On October 1, 1917, the Carthage Light Guard, Company A, Second Missouri Infantry, passed into history, as Schrantz and his fellow Carthaginians became Company A, 128th Machine Gun Battalion.[1]

The Thirty-fifth Division trained at Camp Doniphan through the winter, and on April 17, 1918, Schrantz's company left Oklahoma for Camp Mills, New York. Eight days later, the 128th Machine Gun Battalion left the United States on the SS *Caronia,* bound for Europe. After a short stay in England, the Missourians arrived in France on May 16.

So that they might become familiar with the Western Front, the Carthage company was initially ordered to train with the British in

Picardy, but in June Schrantz and his men were ordered to move and serve with the French army. They spent the next several weeks in a relatively "quiet" area in the Vosges Mountains of eastern France (near the German border) with the Thirty-third Corps of the French Seventh Army, gradually learning the art of war against their experienced European enemy. Finally, in mid-September, the battalion joined the American First Army for the reduction of the St. Mihiel salient. Although held in reserve during the great offensive, Schrantz and his men admitted that it was better to be in reserve than to miss the operation entirely.

Almost immediately after the successful conclusion of the St. Mihiel operation, the American commander, General John J. Pershing, ordered his First Army to conduct a larger and more difficult offensive. This time the Thirty-fifth Division was ordered into action and would play an active part in the assault on the formidable German defenses in the Meuse-Argonne region. On the morning of September 26, the offensive began, and the green Missourians and Kansans in the division moved to attack. Before being withdrawn on October 1, the Thirty-fifth Division suffered more than six thousand casualties. The intense fighting cost Schrantz's company five enlisted men killed (plus one attached ammunition carrier), with two officers and thirty-two enlisted men and twelve or thirteen attached ammunition carriers wounded.

The Meuse-Argonne offensive was the Carthage company's only major operation. Following that bloodletting, the 128th Machine Gun Battalion moved to the area around Verdun and did not see significant combat for the remainder of the war. The battalion remained in France through the spring of 1919. On March 23, 1919, Ward Schrantz was promoted to major and transferred away from his beloved Company A to command of the 130th Machine Gun Battalion.

On April 24, exactly a year after they entered foreign service, the Carthage men sailed into Newport News, Virginia. They were discharged at Camp Funston, Kansas, on May 7. In twenty-one months of service, the old Carthage Light Guard had lost five men killed in action, one dead of exhaustion, and two from disease.

After his return to Missouri, Schrantz continued to work for the *Carthage Evening Press* newspaper. In 1942, he reentered the army as a colonel and commanded troop transports, making numerous successful

Ward Schrantz, after his return from the border and promotion to captain in the Missouri National Guard, 1917

trips overseas delivering men and materiel. In January 1946, he returned to the *Evening Press* as editor and was still working at the newspaper when he died of a heart attack on July 3, 1958, at the age of sixty-seven. Ward Schrantz was well respected and loved by his fellow citizens, who admired his service to the nation and his community. An editorial in the *Press* praised Schrantz's patriotism, leadership, dedication, modesty, and devotion to his hometown. Although the people of Carthage, Missouri, suffered an "irreparable loss" with the death of Ward Loren Schrantz, they retained proud memories, especially of his heroic military service, preserved in the reminiscences he compiled and left behind for the benefit of historians.

The U.S. Army, the National Guard, and Mexico

Each potential soldier who, like Ward Schrantz, walked into a recruiting office in the pre–World War I period had a different reason for enlisting. Some were immigrants or native-born men with no prospects for employment in the civilian world, looking for steady work and a career with the possibility of advancement. Some had been soldiers in foreign armies who decided to try their hand in America's army or navy. A number were American veterans of the U.S. military who enjoyed the familiar rhythms of martial life and decided to reenlist. Patriotism was a motivating factor for a number of recruits, along with the hope that there might be a foreign war brewing. Others, like Schrantz, held a romantic view of life in the military. Some simply wanted to escape the law or an unpleasant situation at home, were bored with civilian life, or desired to see the United States and its overseas possessions. Some were quite well educated, while others were barely literate.

U.S. Army regulations gave strict requirements for the enlistment of recruits during this period. Males between twenty-one and thirty-five years old (or eighteen to twenty-one with the permission of a parent or guardian), able bodied, free from disease, with good character and temperate habits, and either a citizen or a person who had legally declared his intention to become one were allowed to enlist. Men with previous service were exempt from the age and citizenship requirements. Insane or intoxicated men, military deserters, former soldiers with bad service records, felons or those who had been incarcerated, men under eighteen years old, and those who could not speak, read, and write English were forbidden to join. The enlistment of married men for "line" units (service branches) was discouraged. New recruits were required to furnish proof of age, if questioned, and evidence (testimonials) of good character.[1]

At the time of Ward Schrantz's enlistment, the army operated 144 recruiting stations. Of these, 59 were main stations, in charge of a recruiting office, while the rest were auxiliary stations. Temporary stations were opened occasionally as well in order to aid recruitment efforts. Schrantz entered the army at the Joplin, Missouri, station. Contrary to popular opinion, and despite the army's need for recruits, army recruiters were not so desperate that they would take any enlistee. In fact, recruiting officers were quite selective about which men they would accept. During the reporting period of June 1912 to June 1913, for instance, a total of 3,145 men presented themselves for enlistment at the Joplin station. Only 375 were accepted, and of those, 48 were later rejected before being sworn into service. This was by no means unusual, as 80 percent of those who applied at all recruiting stations were initially rejected, while a further 14 percent were subsequently rejected as recruits. The reasons for rejection varied. Some potential recruits were too young, others were physically unfit, some were illiterate, and some were aliens. Some even declined to enlist after being accepted, for on November 1, 1912, a new seven-year service agreement went into effect, replacing the old three-year term. This new law required four years of active duty and three in the reserves, although a soldier could apply for transfer to the reserves after three years of active duty. Surprisingly, the net gain in enlistments and reenlistments to the regular army and Philippine Scouts for the year ending June 1913 was just over 25,000 men.

The vast majority of new and reenlisted soldiers were white and native born, although some African Americans, American Indians, and Puerto Ricans were accepted as well. More than 80 percent of the new or reenlisted soldiers entered the infantry, cavalry, or coast artillery branches. The army tried a variety of advertising media ("exhaustive and resourceful efforts," according to the adjutant general) to attract men, but the tried and true methods of recruiting stations, flags, and posters appealed to the most recruits.[2]

New applicants who were examined and found physically, mentally, and morally qualified at recruiting stations were then sent to either recruit depots or depot posts to undergo a physical examination and, if accepted, formal enlistment. The majority were sent to five recruit depots for processing—Fort Slocum (New York harbor), Columbus Barracks (Columbus, Ohio), Jefferson Barracks (St. Louis, Missouri), Fort Logan

(Colorado), and Fort McDowell (California), where they were "retained for instruction" before being distributed to their units. Enlistees could also be sent to one of the nine depot posts (located closer to recruiting stations than recruit depots), where they underwent a physical examination and final enlistment, then were sent off to their assigned units. Soldiers who wished to reenlist already had training and did not need to be sent to recruit depots, so they could be examined at depot posts, their own military posts, or in the field.

Ward Schrantz was sent to Jefferson Barracks, a few miles south of St. Louis. There, recruits were organized into recruit companies, and veteran officers and noncommissioned officers ("permanent parties") began a period of thirty-six working days of basic instruction in order to introduce the civilians to military discipline, although some men were sent from these recruit depots early, depending on the needs of the service. Drills, inspections, sports, parades, fatigue duty, classroom instruction, and other activities filled each day. After the recruit had become somewhat acclimated to army life, he was sent on to his company and regiment, his "family" and "home" for the remainder of his enlistment.[3]

Once a soldier arrived at his regiment's station, he might undergo further specialized training, along with the daily routine of guard duty, drill, and fatigue duty, accompanied by standard military discipline, monotonous rations, and largely stark surroundings. Off duty, soldiers found ways to pass the time, including reading, sporting events, religious services, card playing, gambling, drinking, storytelling, singing, and the many other diversions so common to professional soldiers through the centuries. Army life did not sit well with every soldier, especially in areas with little opportunity for combat, danger, or even excitement. Although Schrantz had an advantage over other soldiers in that he served in a potential "war zone" along the Mexican border where some form of combat was likely to occur, it should be noted that some men ran away from even those stations, and desertion continued to be a problem for the army as a whole during the period.

Despite mediocre pay, poor chances for promotion, and little attention from the population at large, the majority of men, like Ward Schrantz, remained in the ranks and guarded America's interests at home and abroad in the relatively peaceful period from 1912 to 1915. According to one Texas newspaper, "for everyday work the regular is the stand-by of the nation, when it comes to real soldiering," a man who "realizes that he has burned his bridges behind him, and that until the day his discharge is due he would better buckle down and soldier." The advantage the average regular enjoyed, however, was the realization that "every soldier carries the baton of a field marshal in his knapsack." He had gone into the work to stay until his time was out and had no regrets, or if he did, he hid them well. These regulars followed military life "as others would a trade or a profession" and could not understand why anyone would feel pity or sympathy for a soldier. Instead, they pitied the man who never "did his bit."[4] Many compiled excellent service records, while some could boast only of a host of discipline problems and a history of poor soldering. After serving their "hitch" as professional soldiers, many regulars, such as Schrantz, returned to civilian life and quietly went about raising families and becoming useful civilian members of society. Some joined local National Guard units in order to continue the experience of army life, if only for a few weeks each year. Others found army life comfortable, safe, and appealing and continued to reenlist repeatedly in the regular army until death or disability ended their military careers. Many former soldiers returned to the service temporarily when the United States entered the European war against the Central Powers in 1917.[5]

During the early 1900s, the regulars were largely "unknown soldiers," a nameless, faceless mass of men most Americans encountered only in newspapers, magazines, or occasionally on film. On the other hand, civilians frequently encountered fellow citizens who had served as volunteer troops and preferred to celebrate these men who had served for brief periods during wartime, when the fate of the nation was clearly at stake. Ordinary citizens who would otherwise never have considered donning a uniform in peacetime enlisted in great numbers in relatively short-term state units during the Civil and Spanish-American Wars and the Philippine insurrection. These men held unit reunions and were honored for decades by their fellow citizens for their part in saving the republic. The fact that there were comparatively few regular army veterans in the population at large ensured they would be forgotten. Discharged regulars never made up a significant percentage of the American work force and did not become familiar sights in small towns and villages such as

Carthage. In addition, because of their diverse origins (the fact that they had been recruited from many different areas), old regulars were usually not able to gather at frequent reunions the way the volunteer veterans of 1861 and 1898 had. Former servicemen of the regular army for the most part did not come together to renew old acquaintances and recall their heroism. Consequently, they could not give newspaper interviews, promote the records of their units, and be visible reminders to their fellow citizens that they too had contributed significantly to America's victories in wartime, in addition to protecting the nation during times of peace. These factors, combined with a traditional American fear of standing armies and a belief among some that regular soldiers were idle, shiftless men who wasted public money, ensured that, as historian Edward Coffman has written, "most civilians had little knowledge of and less interest in the regulars."[6]

Today, the U.S. Army regulars of the pre–World War I period are largely forgotten. Few Americans can recall the Spanish-American War or even World War I, let alone the "lost" two decades between those major events. Even many military historians focus on the generals, politicians, and diplomats of that period, rather than on the common soldiers in the ranks. But men like Ward Schrantz deserve to be remembered for defending the nation in a time of crisis and maintaining the proud lineage of the professional American soldier. Perhaps cavalryman Frank Tompkins summed up the record of the regulars best when he wrote that the "gallant services" of the officers and men of the "Old Army," "whether in the deserts of Arizona, the snows of the far north, the jungles of Cuba, the rice swamps of the Philippines, or the plateaus and mountains of Mexico, have added many a brilliant page to our National history."[7]

Ward Schrantz and his fellow veterans served in an army that was an interesting hybrid of nineteenth- and twentieth-century military forces. Although the United States had conducted large-scale land operations that had resulted in victories in both the Spanish-American War and the Philippine insurrection, both conflicts had strained America's ability to transport and support field armies and exposed serious shortcomings in army administration. In many ways the regular army at the turn of the twentieth century was still a constabulary force reminiscent of the organization that had fought the American Indian Wars from 1865 to 1890.

Fortunately, as the new century began, officers in the American army instituted a number of reforms to improve its efficiency and attempt to make it the equal of the great armies of Europe. In the words of military historian Clarence Clendenen, this period "marked a transition that amounted almost to a revolution," as the "'Old Army' gave place gradually to the new, without any break or convulsion."[8] Army officers created a chief of staff and general staff in 1903, formed the Army War College and various service schools, established professional journals, published Field Service Regulations, and supplied U.S. soldiers with modern rifles, pistols, machine guns, and artillery.[9] Automobiles and aircraft became part of the country's arsenal, albeit on a limited basis, and able recruits filled the army's ranks. For the most part, Americans who dared to notice could proudly point to the fact that educated and well-trained army officers led intelligent and resourceful enlisted men, all of whom were well armed, clothed, and fed. To those interested citizens of the United States, the soldiers of their army were continuing a venerable and proud tradition dating back to the early days of the republic. A high-ranking general wrote that the regular soldiers had consistently earned "honorable recognition" for themselves, had "maintained the honor of the nation upon innumerable fields of combat," and had shown "tenderness and sympathy in public disaster."[10]

Underneath the veneer of a modern, European-style army, however, lay significant problems. With duties not clearly defined, the chief of staff frequently clashed with the heads of the army bureaus, who fought to keep or increase their power. Conservative officers supported minor reforms but disagreed with more significant changes. Still other officers believed the reforms were not radical enough. Nearly all officers could agree on at least one point, however—that the various positive reforms and obvious advantages enjoyed by their forces were offset by the fact that America had both vast commitments abroad and threats closer to home. The $184 million spent by the War Department in 1912 would have helped modernize the army to a greater degree had troops been required merely to garrison the continental United States and patrol peaceful borders.[11] But soldiers were required to defend various overseas possessions, such as the Philippine Islands, Hawaii, Puerto Rico, Panama, Alaska, and China (with occasional combat against the natives in some of those locales); monitor the hostile U.S. southern border; and prepare for possible war with Mexico after a civil war erupted there. These obligations meant that, in the words of one major general, the army could only "present a bold front at the most important points."[12] According to one estimate, between the end of the Philippine insurrection and the start of World War I, "20 to 30 percent of the small postwar army was serving outside the continental United States."[13]

Concern for America's southern neighbor began in late 1910, when Francisco Madero began directing a revolt against Porfirio Díaz, dictator of Mexico for more than three decades. In early 1911, Madero returned to Mexico from the United States to lead the revolutionary forces in person.

The unstable situation in Mexico was the reason behind the largest U.S. Army expedition mounted between the end of the Philippine insurrection and the time of Ward Schrantz's enlistment in 1912. On March 6–7, 1911, President William Howard Taft ordered thirty thousand troops to assemble near the Mexican border for maneuvers. Most of the men were ordered to San Antonio in case they were needed in Mexico. In order to blunt possible moves by the Mexican navy, the remainder were stationed in Galveston and San Diego. Major General William H. Carter was designated the commander of the thirteen-thousand-person "Maneuver Division."[14]

Over the next several months, Carter's division remained on alert and conducted field problems, giving the officers and enlisted men valuable experience operating with sizable numbers of troops. They used aircraft for reconnaissance and tested the wireless telegraph for communication. But despite these positive aspects of the mobilization, the army was still found to be lacking in several areas. The division was slow to assemble, recruits needed further training, and equipment required standardization. The *Infantry Journal* for May–June 1911 summed up the feelings of army professionals about the Texas experiment when its editors wrote of the "pitiable display" of the army's weakness and declared that the mass of line officers "declared our whole military organization inefficient and our whole military system extravagant and useless," as foreign military attachés "came and saw and laughed."[15] John Palmer, a member of the Maneuver Division, wrote that the "jury-rigged organization" was composed of units that had heretofore played "military solitaire," led by officers with no experience in commanding a brigade or division. As a guide for a visiting German military attaché, Palmer showed the European officer everything and gave him valuable intelligence regarding the state of American arms. Although he did not see the officer's report back to Berlin, Palmer theorized that the attaché pointed out that the American officers had "little or no conception of what a modern army is."[16] Major General Leonard Wood, the army's chief of staff, also admitted that the mobilization "has brought out very forcibly the necessity for proper military organization and preparedness for war."[17] Finally, in late July 1911, units began returning to their stations, and by early August, the Maneuver Division had passed into history.

Unfortunately for the United States, after the Maneuver Division was disbanded the situation in Mexico continued to deteriorate. Following Madero's capture of Ciudad Juárez in May 1911, President Díaz resigned his office and left the country. On November 6, Madero became president of the still deeply divided nation. He was destined to face several threats to his presidency from anti-federal revolutionaries in the following months. General Pascual Orozco Jr., one of Madero's military chiefs in the Ciudad Juárez victory and his commanding general in Chihuahua, led one revolt against the new president in early 1912. Madero sent General Victoriano Huerta to deal with the rebels, and Orozco was decisively defeated that May at the Battle of Rellano. Nevertheless, following the battle, Orozco's army split into smaller guerrilla bands, and their commander fled to the United States. Francisco Villa, another of Madero's subordinates, was also a veteran of his border campaign. In June 1912, Huerta ordered Villa to return a horse he had confiscated during the Orozco campaign. Villa refused and was arrested. Sent to Mexico City, he easily escaped in December and fled northward across the American border to safety, where he plotted his return to his homeland.

The volatile conditions along the U.S.-Mexico border dictated how American troops were deployed and used in the Southwest. The astute Brigadier General Tasker H. Bliss summed up the American position quite well in his report to the War Department in 1913 in which he explained that despite Madero's success and the apparent end of the struggle, some revolutionary leaders still kept their men organized and under arms. These "Red Flaggers," especially members of Orozco's defeated forces still in the field, operated as bandits against Madero's federal army and civilians. Bliss thought that such fighters maintained a state of "armed neutrality," waiting to see if the new government would redistribute land and wealth and reward those who had made the revolution a success. Early in July 1912, it appeared to the Americans that a general movement of rebels northward toward Juárez and the border was taking place. Such conditions hinted at further trouble and encouraged a sense of apprehension, so much so that by February 1913, despite the fact that no new revolution had broken out and Madero was still at least nominally in power, more American troops had been assigned to guard the border.

It was up to the U.S. Army during this period to protect against "incursions by individuals or small raiding parties from Mexico," to prevent violations of the neutrality laws, and to prevent the export of arms and ammunition to Mexico in violation of a munitions ban issued by President Taft on March 14, 1912. The last of those duties was probably the most difficult assignment the army faced. Bliss believed that practically the whole population on the American side of the border sympathized with the rebels, and hardware stores in border towns stocked large amounts of arms and ammunition, even machine guns, and moved them across into Mexico with impunity. The only way to prevent the movement of large arms shipments was to be fortunate enough to intercept them as they crossed the border. Even though the army seized a significant amount of munitions in many small lots, other arms and ammunition were successfully smuggled across by stealth or in the open by being disguised as general merchandise. Although the U.S. troops performed this "locally unpopular and thankless task" of seizing munitions with some success, Bliss explained, it was simply impossible for such small numbers of soldiers to watch a vast border, one that could be crossed at any time, day or night.[18]

Bliss pointed out that the vagueness of President Taft's proclamation caused difficulties for the troops as well. The general believed that in order to do the job properly, the army would have to be allowed "to invade private property or to hold and search the persons of citizens . . . in search of unlawful articles," powers he felt were not likely to be granted to the military during peacetime. This vagueness had caused "much embarrassment and anxiety," and Bliss longed for more definite and detailed instructions. Isolated, small detachments of American soldiers along the border were forced to make quick decisions and take action that could potentially affect the peace of the United States. Nonetheless, Bliss felt sure that Washington would be proud of the soldiers for their performance of "an arduous and disagreeable duty, for their forbearance under irritating conditions, and for their consideration of the just rights of all concerned."[19]

Bliss also correctly wrote that any successful Mexican revolution always prompted a counterrevolution, and peace would come only when a government proved strong enough to thoroughly crush that backlash. "When . . . the established government can occupy and hold its own border towns, normal conditions will be restored and a redistribution of our troops will be possible," Bliss explained.[20]

The counterrevolution Bliss expected occurred on February 9, 1913, when a new revolt against Madero broke out in Mexico City. Once more the president turned to General Huerta for assistance. This time Huerta was not so helpful, as his true sympathies lay with the anti-Madero forces. Ten days of fighting followed (the "Tragic Ten Days"), and the general ordered the arrest of Madero and proclaimed himself president on February 19. The imprisoned Madero was murdered on the night of February 22.[21]

In response to the events in Mexico, President Taft issued orders on February 21 and 24 for another concentration of troops near the border. The provisional "Second Division" was directed to move to Galveston and Texas City under the command of Major General William H. Carter, "with a view to active service beyond the territorial limits of the United States."[22] Private Ward Schrantz and the men of the Twenty-second Infantry received the orders in El Paso on February 24. Troops quickly moved toward the Texas City–Galveston area and began to arrive on February 27. The majority of the division encamped in Texas City, close to roadways so that supplies could be gathered for an advance into Mexico. The city hosted two brigades of infantry (six regiments), a cavalry and artillery regiment, and attached engineers, medical, aviation, and signal corps units. The Fifth Brigade, consisting of four infantry regiments and other units, pitched camp in nearby Galveston. By March 3, more than 11,500 men were in place. Not only did Carter have to worry about supporting a massive number of soldiers but he also had to ensure that more than four thousand necessary animals received care as well.

General Carter soon launched a rigorous training program to prepare his men for duty south of the border. Long marches, target practice, and swimming lessons were all part of his regimen. Carter's troops maintained surprisingly high discipline and order, considering the fact that they were stationed near the temptations of populated areas. Despite the fact that large quantities of watermelon and cantaloupe were raised in the vicinity, the general heard few complaints from the local population about "foraging" soldiers. "Taken as a whole," Carter reported, "the men of this division have shown themselves to be a self-respecting, intelligent, and splendid lot of soldiers . . . upon whom the Nation may rely with perfect confidence in time of emergency."[23]

Once more, as in 1911, the Americans received valuable experience in the concentration of units, tactical exercises, and administration and supply in the field. Morale was high. Foreign observers were impressed by the discipline of the American troops and the layout of their camps. But the Americans again found certain areas where improvement was required, reminiscent of the Maneuver Division of 1911. There was a shortage of field artillery, field hospitals, engineers, transportation, and even regular infantrymen. If the division was needed for active service, argued the *Infantry Journal*, it would need a massive number of recruits but would then be unable to move because it would take time to train them.[24]

Shortly after assuming office upon Madero's assassination, President Huerta, like his predecessor, found himself under attack by several revolutionary leaders. Francisco "Pancho" Villa crossed back over the border from the United States to oppose Huerta and joined Alvaro Obregón and others—all of whom came under the loose leadership of Venustiano Carranza, the self-designated "First Chief" or "Top Chief" of the Constitutionalist Army, and Madero's legal successor. A bitter civil war ensued.

Huerta faced opposition north of the border as well. President Woodrow Wilson, inaugurated just after Madero's murder, was disgusted by the manner in which Huerta had gained the presidency. Huerta's actions throughout 1913, along with his refusal to resign his office, demonstrated to Wilson that the Mexican president was a cruel dictator. Two incidents in 1914 brought Huerta into direct conflict with the Wilson administration and gave the American president an opportunity to force Huerta's removal. On April 9, 1914, Huertista soldiers at Tampico boarded an American whaleboat and arrested its occupants. The Americans were paraded through the streets, then released. Although the Mexican general in command in Tampico apologized to Admiral Henry Mayo, who commanded the American vessels at Tampico, the latter demanded a formal apology and a twenty-one-gun salute. Huerta refused the American demands. A second, more serious crisis occurred on April 21. President Wilson received word that a German ship was about to unload a large cache of machine guns and ammunition for the Huerta government at Veracruz, technically in defiance of the American arms embargo (the weapons had been purchased the previous year, while the embargo was still in effect). Wilson acted quickly, ordering U.S. forces to seize the Veracruz customs house and prevent the landing of the munitions.

Although American sailors and marines were successful in capturing the customs house, Mexican citizens opened fire on the landing party and caused numerous casualties. U.S. reinforcements soon arrived, and fighting flared again the next day. By the end of April 22, the Americans controlled Veracruz, but the cost was high—17 Americans dead and 63 wounded, and at least 126 Mexicans killed and 195 wounded.[25]

Due to the fighting in Veracruz, a portion of Carter's Second Division was destined to see service on Mexican soil. On April 24, the four infantry regiments in the Fifth Brigade, plus a company of engineers and a field hospital unit, just over thirty-two hundred men in all, sailed from Galveston for Veracruz. Led by Philippine insurrection hero Brigadier General Frederick Funston, the task force arrived in Veracruz four days later. On April 30, Funston took over command of the city from the navy, and a U.S. Marine Corps brigade was attached to his command, giving him a total force of more than seven thousand men.[26]

Funston then assumed the role of military governor of Veracruz, charged with not only preparing for an expected Mexican attack but also establishing provost courts and cleaning the city to reduce the chances of a disease outbreak crippling his small force. Although his men were trained and ready to do battle with the Mexicans again, no combat followed, and the Americans quickly became bored with occupation duty. In the words of historian Jack Sweetman, during the "seven singularly dull months" Funston and his men spent in the city, "the only action in which the members of the army of occupation would engage was at the end of a shovel."[27]

Pressured by opposition forces and unable to expel the Americans from Veracruz, President Huerta submitted his resignation to the Mexican congress on July 15, 1914, and fled to Europe. After assurances from "First Chief" Carranza that there would be no retaliation against those who had cooperated with the Americans, Wilson directed Funston to withdraw his forces. On November 20, Funston received orders to evacuate Veracruz, and three days later the army force sailed for Galveston. The Marine Corps brigade left the same day, formally ending the U.S. occupation of the city.[28]

The Second Division remained in Texas even after the Veracruz incident, however. Although the Sixth Brigade was detached from the division and transferred to Arizona in December 1914, Carter still kept 338 officers and 9,100 enlisted men on duty guarding that section of the border. Finally, the Second Division was ordered disbanded on October 18, 1915, and its components were dispersed for border duty in the Southern Department.

Secretary of War Lindley M. Garrison summed up the experiences of the nearly fifteen thousand men serving on or near the Mexican border in his annual report in November 1915: "Those along the border have not suffered themselves to be provoked into retaliation, but under conditions calculated to test a soldier's mettle they have shown poise and self-restraint, and with tact, patience and a high order of intelligence have overcome every obstacle confronted in the discharge of the difficult and delicate duties entrusted to them." Major General Hugh Lenox Scott, chief of staff, agreed, noting that "this is the hardest kind of service, and only troops in the highest state of discipline would stand such a test. The work along the whole Mexican border has been of the most difficult character for the last three years. The troops have been scattered at many places, sometimes in small detachments and sometimes in larger, for nearly 2,000 miles. They have been separated from their families and put individually at great expense, but no complaint has been made and no overt action has been taken. This evidences a discipline of the highest order."[29]

The Americans had good reason to keep the Second Division intact through 1915. Despite the fall of the Huerta regime and the rise of "First Chief" Venustiano Carranza in the summer of 1914, peace did not return to Mexico. Clashing personalities and old rivalries (particularly between Villa and Carranza) soon led to the resumption of violence. The various revolutionary leaders agreed to meet and appoint a new president, and in early November, the Convention of Aguascalientes chose Eulalio Gutierrez and called on Carranza to resign. The new president named Villa commander of the Army of the Convention. Nevertheless, Carranza refused to resign as first chief, requiring, among other demands, the exile of both Villa and revolutionary commander Emiliano Zapata.

The prominent revolutionary leaders now chose sides. Obregón allied himself with Carranza and the Constitutionalists, while Villa, Zapata, and other pro-Convention leaders joined forces against them. In early December, Villa and Zapata led the Convention forces in triumph into Mexico City, but it was to be only a temporary success. In the spring of 1915, Obregón's forces defeated Villa on several occasions, and Zapata likewise met defeat and was on the defensive (although neither leader was captured nor their armies totally eliminated). By summer, Carranza had captured the last Convention president, and that August his men entered Mexico City. The Wilson administration initially did not recognize either warring faction, but in October 1915, as the opposition forces seemed to be on the decline, the Americans decided to recognize Carranza as the de facto chief executive.[30] The Wilson administration even allowed him to move his troops through U.S. territory to reinforce the town of Agua Prieta. The still dangerous Villa launched an assault on that city but was defeated with heavy losses.

Villa, angered by his fading fortunes, by Wilson's recognition of the Carranza government, and by the fact that the Americans had even given his enemy a decided advantage, began to look for an opportunity to strike a blow at the United States. The revolutionary was motivated by revenge, a desire to regain his prestige, a need to capture arms and equipment with little loss, and perhaps even a belief that another foreign invasion would unite his countrymen. His chance came on March 9, 1916, with an attack on the military garrison and civilian population of Columbus, New Mexico. The pre-dawn strike by about four hundred Villistas resulted in fifteen American soldiers and civilians killed and nine wounded, but the Americans claimed that Villa lost sixty-seven men killed and seven wounded and captured in the fighting, with an additional seventy to one hundred more dispatched in the subsequent American pursuit.

The American response was immediate and impressive. Ultimately, more than ten thousand U.S. regulars under Brigadier General John J. Pershing drove deep into northern Mexico in pursuit of Villa, in what became known as the Punitive Expedition. With more than two-thirds of the domestic regular army on the border or with Pershing and Mexicans threatening to attack Pershing's force, National Guard troops were mobilized in large numbers to help protect the border. Despite their best efforts, the Americans failed to capture Villa or completely eliminate bandit incursions into the United States. The regulars withdrew across the border and the National Guardsmen returned home by February 1917. The Punitive Expedition and the associated National Guard mobilization ended large-scale American military involvement in the affairs of Mexico.

Despite their inability to destroy Villa, the actions of Pershing and his troops showed the strong resolve of the United States to deal with Mexican attacks on American soil and prevented at least some bandit attacks. The border campaign also highlighted the strengths and abilities of "Black Jack" Pershing and a number of his officers and gave both regulars and National Guardsmen valuable experience that would be applied only a few months later against a far more formidable foe across the Atlantic.

It was during the Punitive Expedition that Ward Schrantz returned to the Mexican border, this time as part of the Missouri National Guard. Although the regular army was considered the American "first line of defense" during the early 1900s, state National Guard units were theoretically organized and trained as a reserve force to support the regulars.

The first major legislation of the twentieth century affecting the National Guard was the Dick Act of 1903, named for Representative Charles W. F. Dick of Ohio. Under this act (and subsequent amendments in 1908), two organizations were established—the Organized Militia (the National Guard), and the Reserve Militia (able-bodied men aged eighteen to forty-five). The Guard could be called upon to repel invasion, maintain domestic order, and enforce federal law. Although initially guardsmen could not be required to serve outside the continental United States or to serve more than nine months, both stipulations were dropped in 1908 (although the former provision was reinstated in 1912).[31] Members of the Guard could also volunteer for service in time of war before any volunteer units were organized. In return, guardsmen were required to attend drill sessions and summer camp, and Guard units were required to undergo inspections by regular officers. Most importantly, if National Guard units maintained certain numbers and met certain standards, the federal government would provide much-needed arms, equipment, supplies, and instruction.

The Dick Act forged a permanent bond between the National Guard and the regular army, but the relationship was never without acrimony in the pre–World War I period.[32] Although regular officers knew that the Guard would be required in future wars, many were disappointed in their lack of training and professionalism and their allegiance to state organizations rather than to the concept of a unified National Guard, in essence creating a force of forty-eight separate armies rather than one.

Regular officers were also dismayed by the fact that men did not flock to the Guard or generally want to stay once they joined. Recruitment and retention were always difficult during this period, as National Guard numbers rose from 116,000 in 1903 to only 132,000 in 1916 (as the possibility of war in Europe or Mexico spurred recruitment). Some regulars (like Major General Leonard Wood) even argued that the National Guard would never be sufficient as a reserve force, and he pushed for the creation of a separate reserve.

On the other side, although some welcomed the guidance of the War Department, many guardsmen resented that agency's attempts to control them, establish policies without their input, and interfere in what they considered to be a state affair. Guardsmen resented overbearing and demanding regular troops, bristled at the contempt exhibited by some regular officers toward Guard units, and were angry that some regulars failed to recognize the professional progress made by guardsmen. The guardsmen also knew that War Department officers could simply withhold recognition of units and federal funds in order to gain acceptance of their policies and force an increase in company strengths and drill attendance.

APPENDIX A

In addition, Guard members could also point to the fact that although federal aid to National Guard organizations was substantial, it did not increase as the Guard grew in strength, was not in the form of cash, and was sometimes not delivered in a timely manner. Of course, this meant that individual states were required to try to meet the shortfall and fund the improvements required by the War Department.[33] Some states allocated funds and maintained their Guard forces reasonably well, but many did not. Many National Guard units were forced to rely on funds raised at the local level by the community, individuals, or even by the guardsmen themselves.

The nature of the regular army–National Guard relationship changed profoundly with the passage of the National Defense Act of 1916 (NDA). Under the strict provisions of the act, commissioned officers in the Guard were required to pass physical and professional fitness tests (to remove unqualified officers elected by the men). Summer training and drill periods were extended, troops were required to swear separate oaths to the state and the president and enlist for a uniform term, and the president was allowed, with the approval of Congress, to draft guardsmen into federal service and send them outside the continental United States. The War Department could also stipulate the type and number of Guard units (the National Guard was overwhelmingly composed of infantry units). In return, the Guard received massive financial aid from the federal government to pay men for both drills and summer camps (previously they had been paid just for the latter) and fund necessary improvements in Guard operations. Guardsmen could again be required to serve overseas for indefinite periods as part of their state units. Although some guardsmen viewed the National Defense Act as a significant victory in that they were truly recognized as the nation's reserve force, in reality the legislation allowed the federal government to finally exert complete control over the National Guard and eliminate the strictly autonomous, state-run organizations. Once again, funding could be withheld from those units that did not meet the regulations. In addition, the anti-Guard faction that supported a reserve force scored a victory with NDA provisions for the creation of both the Officers' and Enlisted Reserve Corps and the Reserve Officers' Training Corps (ROTC).

The first serious test of the National Defense Act came a mere fifteen days after its passage. In June 1916, following Pancho Villa's raid on Columbus, President Wilson realized "the possibility of further aggression upon the territory of the United States from Mexico" and tasked the guardsmen with "the proper protection of that frontier" through a massive mobilization for federal service in time of peace. Ultimately, more than 100,000 guardsmen went to the Mexican border in the largest mobilization of the National Guard since 1898.[34]

The call-up again exposed weaknesses in the National Guard. Officers and men were not sufficiently trained in regimental and battalion maneuvers, officers were not prepared to meet the needs of their troops for such extended periods of field service, and equipment was found to be in short supply. Many Guard units were under authorized strength because desperate officers had recruited men who were not able to meet federal physical standards. Other recruits included men who had family or business commitments that would interfere with actual service and who had therefore requested discharges. Still others refused to take the new separate oaths to state and president, while some men did not even bother to appear at the mobilization sites. In the enthusiastic rush to get troops to the border, some of the most efficient units were not mobilized, while others with less combat readiness found their way to Texas.

Once on the border, the stark reality of guard duty hampered the effectiveness of the National Guard. The likelihood of seeing actual combat was remote, conditions were poor (with heat, insects, and sand in abundance), and with the possibility of long periods of dull training by regular army officers seemingly obsessed with discipline and paperwork, it was difficult to recruit Guard units to full strength. Many dedicated soldiers in the ranks longed to leave the border, believing that the danger had passed and that they were being held in the service unfairly. These men forgot, as the chief of the militia bureau wrote, that the duty of a soldier "is to perform the task that is set before him, whatever it may be" and that results were frequently obtained by the show of, rather than the actual application of, force.[35] Back at home, state politicians pushed to have their men released from service. In an official report on the border mobilization, the National Guard was likened to a volunteer fire department—dedicated, patriotic, willing to suffer inconvenience, but often arriving too late to save the structure, despite their best efforts. The regulars were the paid professional firefighters—always ready, well trained, with the latest equipment, and ready to respond with the least possible delay.[36]

Nevertheless, an objective evaluation of the performance of the National Guard must recognize other facts. Guardsmen such as Ward Schrantz responded quickly for service and performed their mission of protecting the border. In reality, the regular army could not have been reinforced in any other way. The guardsmen were never intended to serve as combat troops, and even the regulars themselves had been unable to capture or kill Pancho Villa. Some regular officers held the guardsmen to high standards that even they could not have met. In addition, the movement of such a large number of troops exposed deficiencies in the regular army's operations as well, and it strained their ability to muster the guardsmen into service and supply them.

Several positive aspects of the mobilization are noteworthy as well. Despite the clashes between regulars and guardsmen and the fact that the latter had been mobilized for guard duty, not for training, the mobilization gave the regulars an opportunity to instruct the Guard in much-needed company, regimental, and brigade maneuvers. Officers who had heretofore solved theoretical problems on paper were required to make plans and care for their men for extended periods. Officers and enlisted men in both organizations were given practical training under actual field conditions. Thanks to the mobilization of 1916, members of the National Guard were able to learn what deficiencies still needed to be resolved. In addition, unlike during the Spanish-American War, when many National Guard troops were felled by poor sanitation and disease, the large number of men on the border—hurriedly rushed from cities and farms to the unique climate of southern Texas—were extremely healthy and suffered few losses.[37]

Both officers who served on the border and later historians believed that the border campaign was a worthwhile experience, an endeavor that prevented the spilling of even more Mexican and American blood and helped prepare the American soldier for service in Europe in 1917. Brigadier General Henry J. Reilly Jr., a participant in the Punitive Expedition, believed that "both the National Guard and the Regulars learned to transport, train, supply and in all other ways handle bodies of troops in the field."[38] Brigadier General W. A. Mann, chief of the Militia Bureau, wrote that "the mobilization of the National Guard and its dispatch to the border was a great accomplishment. . . . Whatever mistakes were made were those of judgment and not of purpose. . . . [T]he knowledge and experience gained from the mobilization are incidental advantages worth the cost."[39] Mann argued that although the guardsmen had longed for active service, the "serious and extended course of training" and the routine of a soldier's life, along with dust storms and marches, grated on the guardsmen and prompted complaints, criticism, and calls to go home. Although many men became "completely disillusioned as to the romantic side of soldiering," they had "rendered really more valuable service to their country by preventing war than by making it."[40] Historian Clarence Clendenen echoed this sentiment when he wrote that although the United States was woefully unprepared for war against Germany in 1917, it was "not nearly as poorly prepared as it would have been had not the Punitive Expedition of 1916 brought about the first nationwide mobilization of the National Guard."[41]

Overall, the National Guard in the pre–World War I period made great strides toward becoming a true reserve force. Men like Ward Schrantz clearly recognized that changes were necessary and worked hard to increase the combat-readiness of individual units. Increased funding, training, and drill pay and tighter federal controls all helped increase the professionalism of the Guard. Nevertheless, the National Guard still remained, to a certain extent, a collection of units with strong ties to their individual states and communities and lacking experience in operating as part of large units. Guard units struggled to fund all the tools of war needed for active operations and had difficulty keeping units at adequate strength, let alone increasing in numbers. Citizen-soldiers like Ward Schrantz should be admired for their ability to accept their lack of modern equipment, funding, training, and public support and yet to maintain a determination and drive to become professional soldiers.[42]

By the spring of 1917, with relations rapidly deteriorating between the United States and Imperial Germany, guardsmen and regulars like Schrantz must have realized that another far more serious mobilization was quite likely. Although neither group would be completely prepared for the harsh combat they would face in France, and although the loss of life would be heavy, Schrantz and his comrades recognized that their many years of struggle to improve the effectiveness of their organizations would ultimately serve them well and improve their chances for victory against the Central Powers in the fall of 1918.

Schrantz's Letters to the *Carthage Evening Press*

Carthage Boy in Army—Ward Schrantz Writes of Conditions on
Mexican Border—Likes Army Life Among the Regulars—He Believes
Warfare in Mexico Will Drag Along For Years

Special Correspondence of the Press

El Paso, Texas, Jan. 4[, 1913]—
There is a good deal of popular misconception regarding the United
States army and to a large extent the prejudice which exists against
the uniform of the regular service is due to the misunderstanding regarding the real character of the organization. The enlisted men of the
army as a class will compare very favorably with the same number of able
bodied men drawn anywhere from civilian life and if a man has a taste for
military things, knows something about the army and carefully considers
the matter before he enlists there seems to be no reason why he should
ever regret his step. For instance a national guardsman from his own
experience at maneuvers and from what he sees of the regulars there generally has a pretty correct idea of what life in the army is. Field service in
the regular army does not differ much from field service in the guard except in the one point that the regular soldier usually gets enough to eat.

Joining Uncle Sam's military organization in haste however resembles
getting married in haste in that there is ample time to repent at leisure. It
is astounding how many young men join the army on some sudden im-
pulse or whim with no more knowledge of what they are getting into than
is conveyed in the sometimes misleading pictures used by the recruiting
service. Under these circumstances it is inevitable that many men enter
the service who no sooner find themselves in than they straightway [*sic*]
wish themselves out. Most of these men gamely stay with their contract

with the government until their time expires but a certain per cent of them become reckless, take to drink and do things they would not do when sober. Light offenses are heavily punished in the army and after these men have gone up before the summary court and done time in the guardhouse a few times, many of them eventually "go over the hill" which is army slang for deserting. Over 90 per cent of the desertions are the result of men "getting in bad" on account of whiskey.

Life in the army varies of course according to the locality where the different organizations are stationed, but there is probably no more interesting place to a soldier in the United States than on the Mexican border, only the border guard does anything but "soldier," in the slang sense of the word. President Taft's proclamation issued last spring forbidding the shipment of arms, munitions of war or supplies into Mexico still holds good and every day and every night since that proclamation was issued the international line has been dilligently [sic] patrolled and outposts keep constant watch at the fords and bridges on the Rio Grande.

The larger part of the troops which are for convenience classified as at Fort Bliss are scattered along the international line for many miles. This company, F of the 22nd Infantry, is stationed in the eastern outskirts of El Paso and patrols about three miles of the international line which at this point is a dry former channel of the Rio Grande. At present single sentries walk the posts in day time and double sentries after nightfall. The border guard in El Paso and for some miles east is in charge of Captain W. M. Kassett, whom Carthage guardsmen will remember as having inspected Company A in the spring of 1910.[1]

The progress of the Mexican war in northern Chihuahua viewed at close range would be amusing if it was not disgusting. A more weak and irresolute campaign can hardly be conceived than that which the federals are carrying on against the bands of Red Flaggers. The guerrillas, who are familiar with the country, evade with ease the occasional spiritless expeditions sent out against them. The cold nights have driven most of the insurrestoes [sic] to paths of peace and since those that remain in the field are not strong enough to gather to a head the situation in northern Mexico is not likely to become critical for several months yet.

The veriest novice in the military game can see however that there will be bullets flying along the border in the spring and unless Mexico hires some fighting mercenaries, or some nation intervenes there seems to be no reason why the same conditions should not prevail the next spring and the next and so on ad infinitum.

Meanwhile the United States troops along the Rio Grande are resting on their arms and awaiting developments.

WARD SCHRANTZ

Carthage Evening Press, January 7, 1913

WITH UNCLE SAM'S ARMY — Ward Schrantz Writes of Conditions on Mexican Border — Soldiers not Expecting War, but are Hoping for it — "Just Waiting for What is Next."

Texas City, Tex., March 9[, 1913] —

For five miles north of Texas City stretches a low, flat, treeless, grass covered plain, bounded on the north and east by the bay and it is on this ground that the second division of the United States army has pitched its thousands of khaki pyramidal squad tents and is waiting for whatever is coming next; intervention in Mexico, a summer's maneuvers or orders for the different regiments to return again to their home stations. The one brigade of the division not present is camped at Fort Crockett just across the bay.

This regiment, the twenty-second infantry, received the order to leave El Paso on the morning of the 25th of last month and after waiting for transportation 24 hours after everything was packed, left on the evening of the 26th.

Hysterical El Paso is now protected by the second cavalry which is easily able to defeat all the Mexican soldiers in Chihuahua but the excitable citizens of the border town think they are in the greatest peril if less than three or four regiments are watching the border there.

The army as is natural, always welcomes war, because it means experience and promotion and a chance to demonstrate to the public that Uncle Sam is spending his good hard dollars on an army that is able to deliver the goods when the time comes to strike. In this case however not one soldier in ten expects that anything but maneuvers will result from the assembly of this huge expeditionary force within hitting distance of Vera Cruz.

The civilian idea along the border is different however and from El Paso to the gulf, the war fever is at its height and seemingly the people regard hostilities within the next few months as certain as if war was already declared. This feeling is especially strong between Sanderson and Del Rio and at every station the troop train stopped the cowboys and other depot loungers would come down to the car windows to wish us good luck and on one occasion to tell of a proposed foray into the neighboring state of Coahuila in case war was declared.

Of the many Mexican section crews that the train passed a few even cheered lustily and waved their hats. Now that a traitor and alleged murderer is at the head of the troubled republic the dislike for the United States uniform is not near as marked as it was among the Spanish Americans on this side of the line.

There is quite a difference in the appearance of the various regiments of the division here, which plainly shows the widely separated localities from which they come and the different duties on which they have been engaged. This is especially true in the case of the bronzed border guards, who, with their faded hat cords, weather-beaten appearance and, it must be admitted, with discipline just a trifle slack, form quite a contrast to the regiments whose white faces, bright new hat cords, neatly pressed clothing and carefully polished shoes all proclaim that they are fresh from quarters in the north.

There are many fine jack rabbits in the grass country west of camp, where the drills and smaller maneuvers are being held and almost every day they occasion much amusement. One will be aroused by a galloping troop of cavalry and when its headlong flight is checked by an infantry column, it will double on its trail, only to run against a regiment of artillery. Usually it eventually makes its escape, but occasionally it is dragged down by the dozen or more fat, overfed, canine mascots.

Texas City is a small town which is almost, but not quite, a suburb of Galveston. The natural result is that the large Galveston papers often ignore the existence of Texas City and speak as though the maneuver camp was at Galveston. This much angers the small but venomous Texas City daily whose editorial columns are full of fierce and vindictive articles against their more powerful contemporaries.

It is a little too early to tell just what the program of this camp will be, but is rumored that a number of long hikes will be taken, one it is said, as far west as San Antonio. However that may be, some change is contemplated for the word has been passed around not to ditch the tents too deep, not to level off the streets and not to do a dozen different things because "This is only a temporary camp."

Meanwhile every enlisted man from the newest recruit to the old soldier who is ready to be retired, is eagerly scanning the newspapers for news of the Mexican war and President Wilson's attitude on the concentration camp and between drills are arguing about "what next."

WARD SCHRANTZ
Carthage Evening Press, March 11, 1913

WITH UNCLE SAM'S BOYS.—Ward Schrantz Writes Another of His Interesting Articles—Soldiers Encamped at Texas City, Texas, Get Practical Lessons in Digging of "Small Canals."

Special Correspondence of the Press

Texas City, Tex., July 22[, 1913]—

The encampment of the second division at Texas City and Galveston has now lasted about four months and it is not likely that ever before in the United States has there been a camp more sanitarily arranged or with less disease.

When the troops arrived at Texas City the camping place was some distance back from the water front in about as swampy and disagreeable a place as could be picked out from all the many swampy and disagreeable places in this section of the country.

Before long, however, a new camp was laid out at the very edge of the beach some distance east of the old camp and an elaborate and intricate system of ditches was laid out by the engineers and completed, of course, by the infantry. The original plans called for about 17,000 feet of ditches to be constructed by each regiment, but after the camp had been moved it was found that much additional ditching was necessary before perfect drainage was established.

Roads of mud, shell and sea sand were then built not only in the camp, but leading to the various depots and warehouses. Drill was almost entirely suspended while all of this road making and ditch digging was going on, and it was about this time that a camp song to the tune of "Just Before the Battle, Mother" reached its greatest popularity. One of the few verses that will permit of publication runs something as follows:

> The captain says my gun is rusty,
> And I guess he must be right;
> If he inspects my pick and shovel,
> He'll find them shining and bright.

Now, however, this is all forgotten and the present condition of the camp shows that all the work put in was well worth while.

Everything possible has been done to make life here as pleasant as possible. Some of the squad tents have wooden floors and such of them as have not, have smooth floors of mud baked by the sun until they are almost as hard as cement. In every tent are electric lights which are paid for by the squad. Screened mess halls used in the evening for reading and writing are a further much appreciated convenience.

At present there are but few large maneuvers on account of the intense heat. Usually each brigade holds one now once a week. The problems solved vary to cover every conceivable situation that might arise in war. The one worked out by the Sixth Brigade last week is a fair sample:

The assumed situation was that a force of the enemy, consisting of about a regiment, held a defile, which it was imperative that the brigade, formed by the Eighteenth, Eleventh and Twenty Second infantry, capture. Now there is nothing for miles around that even remotely resembles a defile so an imaginary defile about two hundred yards wide was marked off by a long line of white signal flags.

Into this marked off space the attack was launched. Thick lines of skirmishers advanced by rushes keeping up a continual fire. Behind them came the support and reserve pushing up to fill the gaps in the lines caused by the dropping out of the men detailed as "casualties." In the rear waited the ambulances, for this attack with imaginary ammunition upon an imaginary enemy holding an imaginary defile was a bloody affair, that is of course, bloody with imaginary blood. The hospital corps followed the battle, binding up imaginary hurts and shortly after the fight opened a line of "wounded" began to trickle back to the ambulances which, being filled, galloped with their loads to the first aid stations and, empty, galloped back for more.

Now there are some curious things about the wounds received in this fight which speaks much for the tact of the hospital corps men. All of the men wounded seem to have their wounds in the arms or head and none at all receive bullets through the body or legs. Thus all were able to walk to the ambulances. If the hospital corps men had located the wounds in such a position that, had they been real, the injured ones would have been unable to walk, it would have been necessary for said hospital corps men to have carried the wounded to the ambulance on a stretcher. And although many things in these maneuvers are imaginary, the weight of a husky American soldier and the heat of a mid-summer Texas day are not among them. It is a noticeable fact however that on the occasions when the members of the regimental bands act as stretcher bearers and the hospital corps men do nothing but the bandaging that most of the wounds turn out to be broken legs or something similar.

Another curious thing about this fight is that the killed or wounded give their comrades the laugh as they drop from the lines and the sooner they receive their wound the better they like it. When the charge is sounded a mile or so farther on and the sweating survivors rush forward with fixed bayonets, through the dust, cursing the heat in the mixed jumble of English and Spanish which forms army profanity, the "casualties" are grouped away back in the rear congratulating each other on their good fortune.

In the earlier maneuvers the aviation corps took part, acting mostly as scouts or messengers. When an aeroplane belonging to the opposing side is circling around out of rifle range watching every move, it is easy for men to understand how disconcerting this would be in real war.

A month or more ago all the air machines except three were taken to San Diego, California to the aviation school there. Of the three remaining, one was destroyed in the accident of July 8 in which Lieutenant Call was killed. The other two have not made a flight since the accident for the reason probably that they will be needed if the division goes to Vera Cruz. Certainly no one can accuse the aviators of having "cold feet." Their constant flights during the rest of the encampment have too emphatically demonstrated otherwise.

The possibility of intervention in Mexico is one of never failing interest to the troops here and every new move in that country is eagerly discussed. Of course no one knows anything about it except what is published in the newspapers, unless perhaps it is General Carter, so a soldier has no more ground on which to base his opinions about intervention than has a civilian.

Meanwhile constant rumors are going about to the effect that the camp is to be broken up. A new impetus has been given to these by a "maybe so article" which has just appeared in the *Army and Navy Journal,* but it is quite likely that tomorrow some other article or happening will start new contrary rumors. Everyone however is agreed that something definite will be done in the next few months.

WARD SCHRANTZ
Carthage Evening Press, July 24, 1913

HOW WAR GAME IS PLAYED—Corporal Ward Schrantz Writes Interesting Letter to "Press"—Work of Troops on the Texas Border—Tales of Mexican Refugees—Permanence of Camp

Special Correspondence of the Press

Texas City, Tex., Feb. 1[, 1914]—

Next to the final test of a war itself the surest test of the battle efficiency of a body of troops is a combination of a maneuver and target practice known as a field firing problem. It is the working out of these problems that forms the most important occupation of the second division at the present time.

A field firing problem is a maneuver in which ball cartridges are used and in which the enemy is represented by lines of small olive drab targets the same size and shape as the head and shoulders of a man and occupying the position where the hostile forces are supposed to be. The field firing range at Texas City lies on the prairie northwest of the camp. The range occupies several square miles and scattered over it are concealed trenches where the lines of targets are kept and where the men operating them are safe from rifle fire. The location of these pits is unknown to the officers and men participating in the firing.

When the battalion whose efficiency is being tested moues [moves] out on this prairie the country is apparently uninhabited and presents no different appearance from the rest of the country which stretches for miles west of the camp.

The battalion moves across the country in the same formation it would use if it was in an enemy's territory—advance guard in front and patrols on the flanks. Suddenly some seven or eight hundred yards in front of the head of the advance guard, known as the point, a line of olive drab figures appear above the long grass. The point at once opens fire. If the figures disappear it means that the enemy has fallen back and that the battalion may continue its advance. If, however, the figures stay up and others appear it signifies that the enemy has been encountered in some force and that the battalion must fight. The column deploys into skirmish lines and advances on the enemy, one portion of the line rushing forward while the other portion covers its rush with a hot fire. The range is at first not known for certain but the dozens of dust spurts where the bullets are kicking dirt above the grass indicate whether or not the distance has been estimated properly and, if not, it is soon corrected.

Umpires detailed by the division commander follow behind the lines and if the men neglected to take proper shelter, or the time the targets remain up show that the fire is not accurate, various men are detailed as casualties. These men must fall out and take no further part in the combat. As each one is "killed," his comrades on either side of him quickly take all of the ammunition out of the "dead" man's belt and put it in their own.

Whether the battalion working out the problem defeats the enemy or is itself defeated and forced back is decided by the accuracy of their fire and the tactical disposition of the troops. Five or six hundred yards in rear of the firing line is a signal station connected with the different pits by means of telephone wires running through the grass and messages are received here all during the action telling whether the fire is accurate or whether the bullets are going wild. These messages are given to mounted orderlies who gallop with them to the umpires who are thus able to make intelligent and just decisions.

An attempt is made to have these field firing exercises resemble real war as near as possible so that the maximum benefit may be obtained therefrom. However, the performances of various men who get excited and whose marksmanship, consequently, is more disconcerting to their comrades than it is dangerous to the enemy, sometimes add a realistic tinge that is entirely unintended and which would be gladly dispensed with by most of us.

For the most part the life of a soldier in Texas City is monotonous and uneventful. The water front, however, gives the town a certain interest that an inland town would not possess. There is a steamship line from Texas City to Tampico and Vera Cruz and frequently these boats bring in numbers of refugees who had found life in Mexico intolerable. They tell many stories of their experiences in that country some of which are not of a character to make a person feel any kinder toward Mexicans in general.

It may be remarked, however, that no two refugees agree in their stories, which suggests the thought that the average American soldier is an appreciative listener and they magnify their tales accordingly. Among these refugees are men who went to Mexico years ago, married women of that country and apparently forgot all about their own race until the growing hostility toward the Gringo reminded them that the United States is not such a bad place after all. I met one American who was accompanied by his wife and 15-year-old son, neither of whom could speak a word of English.

But the boats from Mexico bring more dejected and unhappy passengers than the refugees. These are the long horned Mexican cattle which are imported by hundreds as deck cargo on the coasting steamers. Huddled close together, their heads tied closely to ropes run inside the bulwarks and their feet slipping about on the iron decks as they move, they are miserable enough when the vessel is tied up to the dock waiting to be unloaded. Their condition when the ship is traveling in the choppy gulf of Mexico can better be imagined than described.

The duration of the Second Division camp in Texas City is a subject which is no longer discussed here. Many officers are replacing their tents by small wooden shacks, frame buildings are erected to take the place of the various amusement tents and enlisted men's clubs, frame stables are being built for the horses and there is even some talk of turning the camp into a regular cantonment by building bunk houses for the men. If the camp is to last another year this would probably save the government since every pyramidal tent, which houses eight men, costs forty dollars and does not last many months in this damp climate. There are over fifteen hundred tents of this style alone in use so it can be seen that their wear is a considerable item of expense.

WARD SCHRANTZ

Carthage Evening Press, February 6, 1914

TELLS OF WAR PREPARATIONS—Ward Schrantz, Carthage Boy, is in U.S. Army at Texas City

Mrs. Kate Monnett, of Carthage, has just received a letter from her son, Ward Schrantz, who is a corporal in the United States army, stationed at Texas City, Texas, in which he tells of the preparations being made for a possible war with Mexico. He was a member of the company of soldiers which was on a long hike to Houston, Texas, when the situation became so acute. The company was at once ordered back to camp and the return trip was made with all the haste possible. Schrantz writes that the soldiers as a whole are anxious for an opportunity to war a little with the soldiers of the southern Republic.

Carthage Evening Press, April 24, 1914

U.S. TROOPS HOPE FOR WAR—Ward Schrantz Writes of Preparations For War With Mexico—Carthage Boy Stationed at Texas City Expects That His Company Will Be Ordered to Vera Cruz

Special Correspondence of the Press

Texas City, Tex., May 1[, 1914]—

It is entirely possible that before this letter appears in print the entire second division of the army may be at Vera Cruz or at least on the way there, but at the present time the two brigades of infantry, ten troops and three batteries of artillery left at Texas City are impatiently awaiting for the sailing orders that were expected a week ago.

No one here puts any faith in the success of the peace plans of the South American republics nor thinks that such plans can delay war more than a few weeks, if indeed that long.[2] All men on furlough have been called in; all clothing and equipage not to be taken along have been packed in boxes and stored with the depot quartermaster; detailed instructions have been posted regarding embarkation and the routine on shipboard, and instead of the regular drills and maneuvers we are being given lectures on yellow fever and other diseases of the tropics. Everybody and everything is ready for the expected campaign, so it is not surprising that everyone is impatient and not much in favor of peace plans that can only delay a war that cannot be averted.

Jubilant at War Prospects

At noon on the nineteenth of last month, the day that the time allowed for Huerta to salute the United States flag expired, the division finished a four days march and camped in Magnolia park in the southern part of Houston, expecting to rest the following day and to parade through the streets of the city on San Jacinto day, which was the twenty first.

Needless to say there was a good deal of speculation as to what General Huerta's answer to the United States would be. About 8 o'clock newsboys invaded the camp of the 23rd infantry which was stationed nearest the city with extra editions of the Houston papers and in a few minutes that regiment's jubilant cheering notified the rest of the camp that Huerta had failed to salute.

Regiment after regiment took up the shouting until the whole division was giving voice to it's [sic] delight that the period of waiting seemed over and the opportunity for active service near at hand.

First call for reveille was sounded at 3:30 the next morning and the word was passed around that the San Jacinto day parade in Houston had been abandoned and that the division was to return at once to the camps at Texas City and Galveston.

"We march in one hour" was the information given out, "Hurry up! Hurry up!"

Hurry Causes Confusion

When it is remembered that it was necessary in that hour to prepare and eat breakfast, to strike camp and to load the wagons it will be seen what a wild scramble in the darkness resulted. In a few minutes, thousands of lights and scores of camp fires were burning in the pine woods where the camp was located. Meager breakfasts were hastily swallowed; shelter tents hurriedly struck and packs rolled; five or six regimental bands in different places struck up patriotic airs; cursing teamsters, cutting through fences—a measure prohibited in ordinary times of peace—trotted their wagons to the various companies for loading; and all the time there continued the constantly reiterated command to make haste. It was a scene of stirring activity, this breaking of camp by ten thousand men who thought that they were to be hurried off to war with all speed. Incidentally there was some confusion and a little excitement. One man who had slept in a tent next to mine became excited and when rolling his pack threw in everything, within reach including my bayonet and most of my other belongings. I promptly claimed my bayonet but since he had seemed so anxious said nothing about the rest but permitted him to carry it for me the fourteen miles that we marched that day. He probably will be calmer and more careful the next time that he breaks camp in a hurry.

Hike Back to Headquarters

At 4:30 the column was ready to march but no orders to move were given. There was nothing to do but wait. At daybreak the Fifth brigade swung by on their way to the trains which had been rushed up to receive them, for ever since the division has been mobilized they have been scheduled for the honor of being the first to go to Mexico.

It was 8 o'clock before the rest of the division started on it's march back to Texas City. Many civilians lined the road as the division moved out of Houston and numerous small boys, apparently infected by the war fever, fell in alongside the column and accompanied it for a mile or two outside the city limits.

About 10 o'clock as we plodded southward along the blazing asphalt road six or seven miles out of Houston, the last regiment of the Fifth brigade, which had been delayed by loading, came by on the railway running parallel to the road. There was a chorus of shouted banter and friendly jeering as the trains passed by, the men on the cars mockingly signaling "double time" to the slow moving, perspiring column on the road and throwing off to us the latest extra papers from Houston proclaiming, what afterwards proved to be untrue, that the Fifth brigade was to sail for Vera Cruz immediately upon its arrival at Galveston.

A Three Days' March

It was a three days march from Houston to Texas City and as soon as we arrived here, and without waiting for orders, every man began packing his personal property, burning letters, and buying as much smoking tobacco as a soldier on active service can conveniently carry. These three steps constitute the average soldier's individual preparations for war. Later orders were issued for all company property to be boxed up for storage or shipment and since then we have been waiting for orders.

The last of the artillery and cavalry for the reinforced brigade at Vera Cruz left Texas City on the *San Marcos* the day before yesterday. Every time any troops leave, a crowd of their envying comrades turn out to see them off but so many of the officers and the older non-commissioned officers have their wives and families here that there cannot be said to be much cheerfulness to the occasion no matter how much it has been looked forward to. The scenes at the departure of a transport are not hard to imagine—crying women and a cheering crowd on the docks; soldiers trying not to appear self conscious as they mount the gang-plank and failing miserably; fifty-seven varieties of canine mascots trying in vain to get aboard and barking resentfully at their abandonment; and, as the ship casts off her lines and moves out, the inevitable chaffing between the uniformed men on the ship and those on the docks, advice about conduct in battle being replied to with taunting remarks about home guards.

It is generally thought that as soon as the transports get back from

Vera Cruz, today or tomorrow perhaps, that either the fourth or the sixth brigade will be embarked but regarding this there is a difference of opinion. In any case the wait is not expected to be long and meanwhile every soldier in Texas City is hoping for a speedy and unsuccessful conclusion to the peace negotiations.

Carthage Evening Press, May 5, 1914

Notes

Introduction

1. Regular army strength during the period of Schrantz's service was 92,121 officers and men in 1912, 92,756 in 1913, and 98,544 in 1914. Russell F. Weigley, *History of the United States Army* (New York: Macmillan, 1967), 568.

2. One publication described Carthage as "the most beautiful city of its size in America," featuring "surpassing natural attractiveness, handsome residences, stately business blocks, shady avenues, magnificent court house, pretty lawns, and enchanting park." Walter Williams, *The State of Missouri: An Autobiography* (Columbia, Mo.: E. W. Stephens, 1904), 309–10. An extensive profile of the town at the turn of the century may be found in Howard L. Conard, ed., *Encyclopedia of the History of Missouri*, 6 vols. (New York: Southern History, 1901), 1:508–15.

3. Twelfth Census of the United States, 1900, Population Schedule for Carthage, Marion Township, Jasper County, Mo., T623, roll 866; Thirteenth Census of the United States, 1910, Population Schedule for Carthage, Marion Township, Jasper County, Mo., T624, roll 791. Henry Schrantz married Catherine Ream on February 19, 1878. Homer Schrantz, their first child, was born in 1879 but died the following year. The remaining children included Henry H., born in 1881; Lottie, born in 1883; Rachel V., born in 1886; Michael Roy, born in 1888; Ward, born in 1890; and Katie, born in March 1893. Reverend George Witwer and Ananias Clime Witwer, *Witwer Genealogy of America* (South Bend, Ind.: L. P. Hardy, 1909), 151.

4. *Carthage (Missouri) Evening Press,* December 11, 1950.

5. David M. Kennedy, *Over Here: The First World War and American Society* (New York: Oxford University Press, 1980), 178. Kennedy includes a short but valuable examination of the heroic legacy of the Civil War and views of war in the early 1900s. The quotation from Schrantz in this and subsequent text paragraphs all come from the memoir published here.

6. *Carthage Evening Press,* November 13, 1918.

7. Ibid., October 21, 1912.

Chapter 1. The Missouri National Guard

1. Carthage played an important role in the Civil War in Missouri. The Battle of Carthage (July 5, 1861), part of the Wilson's Creek campaign, was arguably the first major land engagement of the war. Guerrilla activity and "revenge" murders plagued the Carthage area during the war, Confederate guerrillas burned the Jasper County Courthouse in October 1863, and guerrillas practically destroyed Carthage on September 22, 1864. Schrantz undoubtedly heard the stories of many local veterans, stories that he would document in newspaper columns and a book. Schrantz quickly realized that it was difficult to categorize one side or the other as entirely noble or despicable. Both Union and Confederate soldiers operating in Missouri exhibited both remarkable kindness and shocking cruelty. For a thorough analysis of the guerrilla war in Missouri, see Michael Fellman, *Inside War: The Guerrilla Conflict in Missouri during the American Civil War* (New York: Oxford University Press, 1989).

2. The Carthage Light Guard was formed on January 8, 1876. State of Missouri, Office of the Adjutant General, *The Service of the Missouri National Guard on the Mexican Border* (Jefferson City, Mo.: Hugh Stephens Printing, 1919), xxxv.

3. Actually, the Second Missouri used the Model 1873 .45–70 Springfield rifle, a single-shot weapon used by the regular army until the early 1890s. National Guard units continued to carry the .45–70 through the end of the decade and even into the first part of the twentieth century. Weigley, *History of the United States Army,* 324.

4. William King Caffee was born in Newark, Ohio, on June 30, 1856. He came to Carthage in 1868, then attended Shattuck Military Academy in Faribault, Minnesota, where he graduated with honors. He then went into the drug business with his uncle. When the Carthage Light Guard was organized in January 1876, Caffee was a sergeant in the outfit. He was promoted to captain about 1880, but the company was disbanded in 1887. When the unit was reorganized two years later, Caffee was elected captain, then became the first colonel of the Second Missouri Infantry in 1890. He led the regiment through the Spanish-American War and retired from military life shortly afterward. Caffee died in Carthage on March 10, 1923, at the age of sixty-six. At the time of his death, he was the director and treasurer of a local business and a bank director. He was buried in Carthage's Park Cemetery with full military honors, and his funeral was probably the most well attended in the history of the town—in fact, Ward Schrantz served as a pallbearer. *Carthage Evening Press,* March 10, 12, 1923. John A. McMillan, born January 31, 1868, came with his family to Carthage in 1872. He graduated from the Carthage Collegiate Institute and enlisted in the Carthage Light Guard in 1887. Promoted to lieutenant in 1892 and captain in 1896, he led the company as captain in the Spanish-American War. Unfortunately, he contracted a cold while serving with the company in Lexington, Kentucky, his eyesight was impaired, and his vision gradually failed until he was totally blind by 1940. He died in Carthage on February 18, 1964, one of the town's oldest and most beloved citizens. He too is buried in Carthage's Park Cemetery. *Carthage Evening Press,* February 19, 1964. The Second Missouri Volunteer Infantry did not see combat during the Spanish-American War. The regiment was mustered into federal service at Jefferson Barracks, near St. Louis, on May 12, 1898. After being stationed at Camp Thomas (Chickamauga, Georgia), at Louisville, Kentucky, and at Albany, Georgia, the Second

was mustered out of service on March 3, 1899. State of Missouri, Office of the Adjutant General, *Service of the Missouri National Guard,* xxxix.

5. Schrantz was unsure of the unit designation. It was actually the Thirty-second U.S. Volunteers. *Carthage Evening Press,* February 25, 1958.

6. George Pentzer Whitsett was born in Jasper County, Missouri, on August 10, 1872. He attended the University of Missouri, then graduated from the University of Michigan law school in 1892. He served as captain of Company G, Fifth Missouri Infantry, during the Spanish-American War. After the war, he became a lawyer in Kansas City but was soon commissioned a first lieutenant in the Thirty-second U.S. Volunteer Infantry for service in the Philippines. He sailed to France with the Thirty-fifth Division in World War I and became judge advocate of the Fifth Corps. Whitsett was cited for "conspicuous performance of duty" during the St. Mihiel offensive and for regulating road traffic at Avocourt on September 26, 1918. Although badly gassed and wounded by shrapnel, Whitsett recovered and returned to the Thirty-fifth Division. He remained in the army following the war, serving in the judge advocate general's office until he died of complications from his wound in Washington, D.C., on August 9, 1924. Major Whitsett is buried at Arlington National Cemetery. James E. Payne, *History of the Fifth Missouri Volunteer Infantry* (privately printed, 1899), 81–83; *Carthage Evening Press,* January 7, 1919; *Washington Post,* August 11, 1924.

7. Although Missouri was never a hotbed of support for the Socialist Party, some residents of the state, like Schrantz, did sympathize with the socialist cause. Eugene Debs obtained 6,139 Missouri votes in his presidential bid of 1900, more than 13,000 in 1904, and more than 15,000 in 1908. In addition, one Socialist Party candidate unsuccessfully ran for a U.S. House of Representatives seat in Missouri in 1906, two did so in 1910, and three in 1912. Congressional Quarterly, Inc., *Guide to U.S. Elections* (Washington, D.C.: Congressional Quarterly, 1975), 17–19, 703, 713–14, 719. The southwestern Missouri town of Liberal elected a socialist mayor in 1913, and a party newspaper (*The Socialist*) was established in nearby Joplin, Missouri, in 1912 (James Weinstein, *The Decline of Socialism in America, 1912–1925* (New Brunswick, N.J.: Rutgers University Press, 1984), 98, 117.

8. The National Guard had been extensively used as a domestic police force before 1898 to deal with labor strikes. Overall, the guard was not used as frequently for such duties in the 1898–1917 period, but it was called up to maintain order during coal strikes in West Virginia and Pennsylvania in 1902, in Utah in 1903, and in Colorado in 1903–1904. John K. Mahon, *The History of the Militia and the National Guard* (New York: Macmillan, 1983), 150; Jerry Cooper, *The Rise of the National Guard: The Evolution of the American Militia, 1865–1920* (Lincoln: University of Nebraska Press, 1997), 146–50.

9. William E. Hiatt was born in Barton County, Missouri, in 1872. He died in Baxter Springs, Kansas, in March 1966, and is buried in Park Cemetery in Carthage. Schrantz was correct about his lengthy National Guard service. He joined Company A, Second Missouri Infantry, as a private in February 1892. He remained with the company and served during the Spanish-American War, first as a sergeant, then as a second lieutenant. Promoted to first lieutenant in 1899 and captain in 1900, he resigned from the company in 1905, then was commissioned captain again in 1907. State of Missouri, Office of the Adjutant General, *Report of the Adjutant General of the State of Missouri for the Years 1907–8* (Jefferson City, Mo.: Hugh Stephens Printing, 1908), 201.

10. One provision of the Militia Act ("Dick Act") of 1903 called for National Guard units to attend state encampments, conduct joint maneuvers with the regular army, and be inspected by regular army officers. Michael D. Doubler, *I Am the Guard: A History of the Army National Guard, 1636–2000* (Washington, D.C.: Government Printing Office, 2001), 144, 149. The Second Missouri attended the camp at the state rifle range near Nevada July 18–25, 1909. State of Missouri, Office of the Adjutant General, *Service of the Missouri National Guard,* xxxvii.

11. The Camp of Instruction for officers, noncommissioned officers, buglers, and cooks was held at the state rifle range July 3–17, 1910. The maneuvers at Fort Riley lasted from September 3 to September 10, 1910. State of Missouri, Office of the Adjutant General, *Service of the Missouri National Guard,* xxxvii; Missouri National Guard, *History of the Missouri National Guard* (n.p., November 1934), 87.

12. Schrantz was appointed corporal on March 18, 1910, sergeant on June 26, 1911, and quartermaster sergeant on July 28. The Second Missouri attended the encampment near Nevada August 20–27, 1911. State of Missouri, Office of the Adjutant General, *Service of the Missouri National Guard,* xxxvii, 122.

13. Although he wrote extensively about all aspects of his hometown's history, Schrantz was particularly fascinated by the Civil War period. His *Jasper County, Missouri, in the Civil War* (Carthage, Mo.: Carthage Press, 1923), a detailed account of that county's important role in Missouri Civil War history, has been reprinted twice since it originally appeared in 1923. The *Carthage Evening Press* described the book as "an important research work for all students of the subject," written by "southwest Missouri's leading historian." The *Press* believed that Schrantz was uniquely qualified to write military history due to his experience as a citizen-soldier. *Carthage Evening Press,* June 28, 1961. In addition, his article "The Battle of Carthage" in the *Missouri Historical Review* (vol. 31, no. 2, January 1937) was the first attempt by anyone who had not participated in the battle to thoroughly document the historic July 5, 1861, fight in a scholarly publication.

14. Unfortunately, a common surname like Johnson makes a positive identification difficult. At least four men with that surname served in the Fifteenth Infantry from 1909 to 1912, but none was in Company A. One likely possibility is Sergeant Arthur C. Johnson of Clinton County, Ohio, who enlisted for the fourth time on March 20, 1911, and was assigned to Company F. Other possibilities include John A. Johnson (presumably a private), born in Perry County, Ohio, who finished his third term of enlistment when he was discharged on June 30, 1911, from Company H; Private Frank Johnson of Company M, who enlisted on October 16, 1909, and was discharged on December 20, 1912; and James H. Johnson (presumably a private) of Company D, who finished his first enlistment on November 30, 1911. Registers of Enlistments in the United States Army, 1798–1914, roll 66, vol. 129, Microfilm M233, Record Group 94, National Archives, Washington, D.C. Julian Foster, a twenty-four-year-old former miner from Belva, West Virginia, reenlisted for the second time on November 28, 1910, at Fort Logan, Colorado, and was assigned to Company I, Fourth U.S. Infantry. He was discharged at Galveston, Texas, on November 27, 1913, as a private. Registers of Enlistments in the United States Army, 1798–1914, roll 66, vol. 128.

15. Daniel Cornman, born in Pennsylvania in 1852, graduated as an infantry lieutenant from West Point in 1873. He remained with the Twenty-first Infantry until 1901, when

he was promoted to lieutenant colonel in the Twenty-fourth Infantry. He advanced to colonel of the Seventh Infantry in 1903 and retired in 1915 after forty years' service. U.S. Adjutant General's Office, *Official Army Register for 1911* (Washington, D.C.: Government Printing Office, 1910), 281; U.S. Adjutant General's Office, *Official Army Register for 1916* (Washington, D.C.: Government Printing Office, 1916), 574. The Second Missouri participated in the practice march and maneuvers from Overland Park, Kansas, to Fort Leavenworth August 17–27, 1912. This was the first time in Missouri National Guard history that the summer training actually incorporated "field conditions of presumed warfare." State of Missouri, Office of the Adjutant General, *Service of the Missouri National Guard,* xxxvii; Missouri National Guard, *History of the Missouri National Guard,* 87.

16. "Long wagon trains picturesque" is written in pencil at the end of this paragraph in Schrantz's typescript, but there is no indication as to where it fits in the narrative.

17. In 1899, the U.S. Army established the Macabebe Scouts, a group of Filipino enlisted men under the command of Lieutenant Matthew Batson. Two years later, the Philippine Scouts were formally established as a U.S.-led native force to operate in the islands. By the time Schrantz considered joining them, the organization was well organized, equipped and trained, and commanded by American regular army officers.

18. Schrantz had reenlisted on February 6, 1912, and was honorably discharged on September 15 of the same year. State of Missouri, Office of the Adjutant General, *Service of the Missouri National Guard,* 122.

Chapter 2. A Civilian Visits Mexico

1. Tracy C. Richardson (1892–1949) was a "soldier of fortune" from Lamar, Missouri. In addition to military service in Nicaragua, Honduras, and Mexico, he saw combat in France during World War I with the Canadian Expeditionary Force. He served in the U.S. Army during World War II and attained the rank of lieutenant colonel. Lee Christmas (1863–1924), a native of Louisiana, became a railroad engineer in Honduras in the mid-1890s. He served as Honduran police chief and in the Honduran-Nicaraguan war of 1907. Perhaps his most famous exploit was his campaign to place the deposed president, Manuel Bonilla, back in power. In December 1910, he sailed from New Orleans, landed on the Honduran coast the following month, and led his army on a campaign that successfully reinstated Bonilla. He also supposedly served as a soldier of fortune in Nicaragua, El Salvador, and Guatemala and was a general in the armies of five Latin American republics. He offered his services to the United States when World War I began but was denied a command due to his age and instead served in military intelligence. After the war, he returned to Honduras, but ill health forced him to return to the United States, and he died in January 1924 from anemia caused by a tropical disease contracted in Central America. Barbara A. Tenenbaum, ed., *Encyclopedia of Latin American History and Culture,* 5 vols. (New York: Charles Scribner's Sons, 1996), 2:150; *New York Times,* January 22, 1924.

2. Benito Juárez served as president of Mexico from 1858 to 1872. Schrantz obviously meant to write that the Iowa couple and postcard salesman were in Juárez, not El Paso.

3. Schrantz marked out both "wordy exchange" and "brisk discussion" in the original manuscript.

4. In December 1911, Brigadier General John J. Pershing moved against hostile Moro

tribesmen on the island of Jolo in the southern Philippines. American troops surrounded several hundred Moro men, women, and children entrenched on the summit of Mount Bud Dajo. With his troops in place, Pershing used friendly Moros to convince most of the hostiles to surrender. Some holdouts clashed with Pershing's troops, but resistance quickly ended when more Moros surrendered and the Americans crushed the remaining fighters. Pershing counted only three American casualties and just twelve Moros killed. Members of the Second Cavalry were used to patrol the area and prevent the Moros from sending or receiving messages. Joseph I. Lambert, *One Hundred Years with the Second Cavalry* (Fort Riley, Kans.: Capper Printing, 1939), 181–82, 303–305; Frank E. Vandiver, *Black Jack: The Life and Times of John J. Pershing,* 2 vols. (College Station: Texas A&M University Press, 1977), 1:537–39.

Chapter 3. Joining the Regulars

1. One newspaper article states that Schrantz joined the army at the Joplin, Missouri, recruiting office on the morning of October 21, 1912. *Carthage Evening Press,* October 21, 1912. Muster roll records state that he enlisted for three years at Jefferson Barracks on October 23. Muster roll, Company F, Twenty-second U.S. Infantry, December 31, 1912–February 28, 1913, National Personnel Records Center, St. Louis, Mo.

2. The Twenty-seventh Company was a recruit training organization at Jefferson Barracks. Upon completion of their training, new soldiers were assigned to regular army units in the field.

3. Dennis P. Quinlan was born in Michigan in July 1873. He enlisted in the army in 1898 and was commissioned a second lieutenant of cavalry the following year. Quinlan was actually a captain in 1912. He retired as a brigadier general in 1934. U.S. Adjutant General's Office, *Official Army Register January 1, 1935* (Washington, D.C.: Government Printing Office, 1935), 956.

4. William H. Lang (perhaps Percy was a nickname) was a twenty-two-year-old cook from Buffalo, New York. Dave Dennis was a twenty-three-year-old farmer from Jackson County, Tennessee, and Leislly O. Apple, a twenty-year-old laborer from Sullivan's Bend, Tennessee. All three enlisted on October 23, 1912, at Jefferson Barracks, Missouri. After recruit training, Lang was assigned to Company C, Twenty-second Infantry; Dennis to Company C, Second Cavalry, and Apple to Company F, Third Cavalry. Lang and Apple were honorably discharged on October 22, 1915, and Dennis, on October 26, 1915. Registers of Enlistments in the United States Army, 1798–1914, roll 65, vol. 126–27; roll 67, vol. 131.

5. Fort Morgan, established to guard Mobile Bay, was completed in 1834.

Chapter 4. El Paso

1. Since its founding in 1848, Fort Bliss has been located at six different sites in the El Paso area. The current Fort Bliss was established in 1893 on the northeastern edge of the city.

2. The Twenty-second U.S. Infantry had already compiled an impressive record since its formation in 1866. Campaign credits included the 1873 Yellowstone expedition; Little

Big Horn (General Nelson Miles's expedition against the Sioux, 1876–1877); Pine Ridge, 1890–1891; El Caney and Santiago in 1898; the Philippine insurrection, 1899–1902; the fight in the Philippines against the Moros, 1903–1905; assistance during the San Francisco earthquake and fire, 1906; and as the Maneuver Division in 1911. A complete history of the regiment may be found in John M. Palmer and William R. Smith, *History of the Twenty-Second United States Infantry, 1866–1922* (n.p., n.d.).

3. Daniel A. Frederick was born in Georgia on June 10, 1855. He graduated from the U.S. Military Academy in 1877 and served with the Seventh U.S. Infantry from 1877 to 1899, when he became major of the Forty-fifth U.S. Infantry. He had various assignments, including service on the general staff, until he was promoted to colonel in 1911. Frederick took command of the Twenty-second Infantry in March 1912 and relinquished command on April 27, 1914. He retired from the army in June 1917 after forty years' service. U.S. Adjutant General's Office, *Official Army Register for 1913* (Washington, D.C.: Government Printing Office, 1913), 363; U.S. Adjutant General's Office, *Official Army Register January 1, 1922* (Washington, D.C.: Government Printing Office, 1922), 1245; Returns from Regular Army Infantry Regiments, Twenty-second Infantry, April 1914, Microfilm M665, roll 235, Record Group 94, National Archives, Washington, D.C. (hereafter cited as Twenty-second U.S. Infantry Returns). Edgar Zell Steever, a native of Pennsylvania, graduated from the U.S. Military Academy in 1871 as a cavalryman and was considered by the West Point authorities as "one of the finest minds that had been trained there in the last half century." In the summer of 1872, Steever and his command rounded up a band of hostile Sioux and returned them to their agency. Two years later, with another officer and twenty-two men, he succeeded in quelling an Indian outbreak at the Red Cloud agency. Steever then commanded the Palestine exploring expedition and saw action during the Spanish-American War. Steever rose steadily through the ranks and was promoted to brigadier general in August 1912. He retired the following March at the age of sixty-three, after forty-six years of continuous service, and died in January 1920 at the age of seventy. U.S. Adjutant General's Office, *Official Army Register for 1914* (Washington, D.C.: Government Printing Office, 1914), 531; *Fifty-first Annual Report of the Association of Graduates of the United States Military Academy* (Saginaw, Mich.: Seemann & Peters, 1920), 116.

4. As Schrantz implies, Steever was well aware of the volatile situation on the border. The commander of the Department of Texas did not believe that conditions would return to normal in the near future. In his June 30, 1912, report to the War Department, Steever noted "it is highly probable that a good-sized force will be needed in the district of El Paso for sometime to come," and he called for no less than three cavalry regiments to be stationed nearby for duty on the border. Ironically, portions of Steever's report were quoted in the *El Paso Herald* on the day Schrantz arrived in the city. U.S. War Department, *Annual Reports, 1912*, 4 vols. (Washington, D.C.: Government Printing Office, 1913), 3:47, 61; *El Paso Herald,* December 7, 1912.

5. The Twenty-second Infantry received orders to proceed from Fort Sam Houston to El Paso for border guard duty on February 24, 1912, nine months before Schrantz's arrival. The regiment's three battalions relieved one another and other regiments that spring, summer, and fall at various guard posts in the area. Schrantz's Company F was assigned to Washington Park on the eastern edge of El Paso on November 2, 1912, relieving troops of the Eighteenth U.S. Infantry. Palmer and Smith, *History of the Twenty-second*

United States Infantry, 133–34; *El Paso Herald,* October 31, 1912. In February 1913, the Twenty-second U.S. Infantry was dispersed as follows: Headquarters, band, and Companies A, B, C, D, and K were at Fort Bliss; Companies E and F were at Washington Park; Company G was at the Stanton Street Bridge; Company H at the El Paso Foundry; Company I at the cement works; Company L at Hart's Mill; and Company M at the Santa Fe Bridge. U.S. War Department, *Annual Reports, 1913,* 4 vols. (Washington, D.C.: Government Printing Office, 1914), 3:39.

6. Sergeant Major Henry Janz was indeed an "old soldier." A native of Strasburg, Germany, the forty-year-old entered his sixth term of enlistment on October 1, 1910. He remained with the Twenty-second Infantry until his term of service expired and he was discharged at Texas City, Texas, on September 30, 1913. Obviously enamored with the military, Janz reenlisted the following month. Twenty-second U.S. Infantry Returns, September 1913, October 1913, roll 235; Registers of Enlistments in the United States Army, 1798–1914, roll 68, vol. 129.

7. Laurence A. Curtis was born in Vermont on April 17, 1872. He served as a private in the First Wisconsin Infantry for part of the Spanish-American War and became an officer in the regular army in July 1898. He joined the Twenty-second Infantry the following year and was promoted to captain in 1904. He was detached to the Army School of the Line at Fort Leavenworth in July 1913, rejoined the company briefly in May 1914, then was appointed regimental quartermaster and ordnance and signal officer. He continued in the army through World War I and retired as a colonel in 1920. U.S. Adjutant General's Office, *Official Army Register for 1913,* 364; U.S. Adjutant General's Office, *Official Army Register, January 1, 1922,* 1258; Muster rolls, Company F, Twenty-second U.S. Infantry, August 31, 1913–October 31, 1913, and April 30, 1914–June 30, 1914.

8. The Treaty of Guadalupe Hidalgo ending the U.S.-Mexico War in 1848 named the unpredictable Rio Grande as the border between the two countries, virtually guaranteeing boundary disputes until the 1960s. The river occasionally overflowed its banks, cut new courses, and left acreage, some of it valuable, on one side or the other. The most famous boundary dispute in the area involved the Chamizal area of El Paso. There the Rio Grande changed course and added a sizable amount of land to the American side, a fact first protested by the Mexican government in the 1860s. Although the International Border Commission was created in 1889, this body did not deal with the Chamizal problem and the issue was not resolved until 1963. Oscar J. Martinez, *Troublesome Border* (Tucson: University of Arizona Press, 1988), 25–29.

9. Harry B. Elam, born in Greensboro, North Carolina, enlisted at Columbus Barracks, Columbus, Ohio, on March 30, 1911, at the age of twenty-one. A laborer in civilian life, Elam served until discharged at Texas City, Texas, on April 1, 1914. Registers of Enlistments in the United States Army, 1798–1914, roll 66, vol. 128. Elam did not serve without disciplinary trouble, however. He deserted the regiment in March 1913, surrendered a month later, and was sentenced by a summary court to six months confinement and forfeited pay. When he was absent without leave (AWOL) for a few days in June, he was sentenced again to confinement for one month and lost pay. Despite these troubles, Elam was honorably discharged and his character listed as "very good." Because of being absent without leave for three days in 1912 and three days in June 1913, he was held in service three days to make good his AWOL. He reenlisted as a private in Company L, Eleventh

U.S. Infantry, on September 13, 1914 but was transferred and rejoined Company F of the Twenty-second Infantry on December 2, 1914. Muster rolls, Company F, Twenty-second U.S. Infantry, April 30, 1913–June 30, 1913, February 28, 1914–April 30, 1914, and October 31, 1914–December 31, 1914. Charles or Charley Perry of Springville, Indiana, was also a laborer and enlisted for the first time at Columbus Barracks on March 2, 1911, at the age of nineteen. Perry deserted Company F at Washington Park on February 16, 1913, but was apprehended by civil authorities in Estancia, New Mexico, and returned to military control on August 6 at Fort Bliss, Texas. While awaiting the result of his trial by general court-martial, he escaped from Fort Bliss on September 12 and was dishonorably discharged at Fort Bliss on October 3, 1913. His character was listed as "'bad,'" his service "not honest and faithful." Registers of Enlistments in the United States Army, 1798–1914, roll 66, vol. 131; Muster rolls, Company F, Twenty-second U.S. Infantry, December 31, 1912–February 28, 1913, June 30–August 31, 1913, and August 31, 1913–October 31, 1913.

10. The name "Delbert" was written and then lined through by Schrantz in the original manuscript.

11. The exact charge against Perry is unknown, but officers could merely consult the "Articles of War" then in force to find a charge for Perry's offense against the civilian morals of the period. Possibilities include article 20, allowing for the punishment of any soldier behaving with disrespect toward his commanding officer, or article 62, calling for the punishment of all offenses prejudicial to good order and military discipline. U.S. War Department, *Regulations for the Army of the United States, 1913* (Washington, D.C.: Government Printing Office, 1913), 303, 308. If they failed to find an appropriate charge in the "Articles of War," officers could check a list of eighty-eight offenses compiled by the judge advocate general in 1912. Like Harry Elam, most men appeared before a summary court, consisting of one officer, who could sentence a soldier to be confined and forfeit pay and allowances for up to one month. Very few men escaped conviction when tried by a summary court. Edward M. Coffman, *The Regulars: The American Army, 1898–1941* (Cambridge, Mass.: Belknap Press of Harvard University Press, 2004), 119–20.

12. Schrantz is referring to Mexican bandit Pancho Villa's attack on the town of Columbus, New Mexico, on March 9, 1916. A portion of the Thirteenth U.S. Cavalry was stationed at Camp Furlong in Columbus. The Americans quickly responded and drove off the Mexican raiders. While Villa's men suffered heavily in the attack, American military and civilian casualties were relatively light. Thorough accounts of the raid may be found in a number of works, including Friedrich Katz, *The Life and Times of Pancho Villa* (Stanford, Calif.: Stanford University Press, 1998), 560–66, and Frank Tompkins, *Chasing Villa: The Story behind the Story of Pershing's Expedition into Mexico* (Harrisburg, Pa.: Military Service Publishing, 1934), 48–59.

13. Not every Mexican was reluctant to come to blows with American soldiers. Just before Schrantz's arrival, seven men were fined five dollars for attacking soldiers in Washington Park by throwing rocks and curses at them. (*El Paso Herald,* November 5, 1912)

14. Villa was definitely in El Paso in January 1913 after his escape from a Mexico City prison the month before. Villa crossed the border at Nogales, Arizona, and traveled by train to El Paso, so despite Schrantz's belief, it is unlikely he encountered the famous bandit. Villa was described as an "erstwhile refugee" in El Paso in late January, and after "sojourning" in the city, he disappeared again on February 26, 1913. Clarence C. Clen-

denen, *Blood on the Border: The United States Army and the Mexican Irregulars* (New York: Macmillan, 1969), 135; Enrique Krauze, *Mexico: A Biography of Power* (New York: HarperCollins, 1997), 309; Alan Knight, *The Mexican Revolution*, 2 vols. (New York: Cambridge University Press, 1986), 2:34–35; Katz, *Life and Times of Pancho Villa*, 185, 857; *El Paso Herald*, January 21, February 27, 1913.

15. These are references to the American assault on El Caney, outside Santiago, Cuba, on July 1, 1898, during the Spanish-American War, and to actions on March 30–31, 1899, at Malolos, in the Philippine Islands, against Filipino insurgents. The phrase "wild Moros" refers to the Muslim Filipinos who fought American occupation forces in the Philippines during various campaigns from 1902 to 1913. The Twenty-second U.S. Infantry was involved in all three actions. Palmer and Smith, *History of the Twenty-second United States Infantry*, 22–26, 40–46, 87–117.

16. The town of Alfalfa still appears on modern (1990s) U.S. Geographical Survey topographical maps. It is located about six and three-quarters miles east of downtown El Paso.

17. General José Inés Salazar operated under Pascual Orozco against President Madero's forces in the state of Chihuahua. After Orozco's army was defeated in 1912, his force divided into guerrilla bands, and one such group under Salazar continued to fight against the federals in Chihuahua. On the morning of January 23, 1913, Mexican rebels who had been raiding ranches on the American side of the border fired a volley at a three-man patrol from Troop C, Thirteenth U.S. Cavalry, near Fabens, Texas, directly across from Guadalupe, Mexico. The Americans did not return fire, and, according to the *El Paso Herald*, no American troops were wounded due to the "characteristic rebel marksmanship." The same newspaper noted that after the incident the troopers "continued to pound their beat and wiggle their fingers from their noses at the rebels." Michael C. Meyer, *Mexican Rebel: Pascual Orozco and the Mexican Revolution, 1910–1915* (Lincoln: University of Nebraska Press, 1967), 69, 77–88; Knight, *Mexican Revolution*, 1:467–68; Ralph H. Vigil, "Revolution and Confusion: The Peculiar Case of Jose Ines Salazar," *New Mexico Historical Review* 53 (April 1978): 145–70; *Carthage Evening Press*, January 24, 1913; *El Paso Herald*, January 24, 1913.

18. Horse racing was a popular pastime on both sides of the border at this time. A racetrack in Juárez's Don Alberto Terrazas Park was in operation during the Mexican Revolution, while at the turn of the century races that drew El Paso residents and area citizens were sponsored in Washington Park. C. L. Sonnichsen, *Pass of the North: Four Centuries on the Rio Grande* (El Paso: Texas Western Press, 1968), 391; Mario T. Garcia, *Desert Immigrants: The Mexicans of El Paso, 1880–1920* (New Haven: Yale University Press, 1981), 209.

19. Described as a large revolving cannon borrowed from a Mexican gunboat, "El Niño" was placed in a turret mounted on a railroad flatcar and could fire large explosive shells. The Mexican artillerymen who manned the piece gave it its unique, affectionate nickname. *El Paso Herald*, December 2, 1912. It is difficult to date the incident Schrantz describes. In late January 1913, however, General Salazar and his rebel forces, then at Guadalupe, threatened to attack Juárez. Two pieces of heavy artillery were emplaced to defend the town, and detachments of federal troops left Juárez in the direction of Guadalupe. "El Niño" eventually arrived to reinforce the garrison, and correspondents watched from

rooftops for the arrival of the rebels, but no rebel attack on the town materialized. *El Paso Herald,* January 23, 30, 1913.

20. The *El Paso Herald* issued three extra editions in one afternoon. Mexicans and Americans on both sides of the border eagerly read the news of Madero's overthrow, and the extras sold faster than any newspapers printed since the Battle of Juárez in May 1911. Army officers in the area were particularly interested in the events in Mexico City, for they "are continually watching for an increase in their business" and believed that intervention was imminent. As one officer explained, the United States had supported the established government in Mexico once Madero became its president, but now there was no longer an excuse for keeping "hands off in Mexican affairs" and "it will be up to the United States to take a hand in the game." *El Paso Herald,* February 10, 1913.

21. Nearly all American newspapers suspected that Huerta was involved in Madero's death and expressed outrage at the murder. Such widespread American indignation and calls for intervention must have been short-lived, however, for soon American businesses with significant investments in Mexico were urging President Woodrow Wilson to recognize the Huerta regime, as were Americans in Mexico, members of the U.S. Congress, and even some members of Wilson's cabinet. Michael C. Meyer, *Huerta: A Political Portrait* (Lincoln: University of Nebraska Press, 1972), 111–20; Walter V. Scholes and Marie V. Scholes, *The Foreign Policies of the Taft Administration* (Columbia: University of Missouri Press, 1970), 103–104.

22. Elbert Russell was a professional soldier. Born in Jefferson County, Tennessee, the forty-two-year-old enlisted in the army for the eighth time at Fort Sam Houston, Texas, on March 10, 1911. He was relieved as first sergeant of Company F on August 6, 1913, and made quartermaster sergeant and mess sergeant. Russell was finally discharged as a sergeant on March 9, 1914, at Texas City, Texas, but reenlisted in the company the next day and was retained as a sergeant. He left the company for duty with the disciplinary organization at Fort Leavenworth on June 14 and was not with the unit for the remainder of Schrantz's service. Registers of Enlistments in the United States Army, 1798–1914, roll 68, vol. 132; Muster rolls, Company F, Twenty-second U.S. Infantry, June 30, 1913–August 31, 1913, February 28, 1914–April 30, 1914, and October 31, 1914–December 31, 1914.

23. In September 1918, Schrantz was in command of Company A, 128th Machine Gun Battalion, Thirty-fifth Division, American Expeditionary Forces. On the night of September 28, the company came to rest in the Montrebeau Woods, near the legendary Argonne Forest, and spent a miserable evening in a cold rain similar to the one he spent at Fort Bliss. The most obvious difference between the two events is that in 1918 his command was in the midst of a bloody operation against the German army.

24. Colonel Frederick Funston (1865–1917) led the Twentieth Kansas Volunteer Infantry to the Philippines in 1898. The following year the regiment participated in the Philippine insurrection. Funston was promoted to brigadier general of volunteers and later awarded the Medal of Honor for leading the Twentieth in combat. After the regiment returned to the United States, Funston went back to the Philippines and gained even greater fame for his capture of Philippine guerrilla leader Emilio Aguinaldo.

25. The regiment received word of the move late in the evening of February 24 and was relieved the next day by the Second Cavalry. The regiment broke camp and loaded the regiment's heavy baggage in a driving rainstorm that afternoon and night. Company F

left Washington Park at 1:30 P.M. and arrived at Fort Bliss an hour later. The heavy freight and stock left El Paso at 7:00 A.M. on February 26, a second section left at 12:30 P.M., and the rest of the regiment departed about 10:20 P.M. that day. Company F also entrained about 10:20 P.M. Twenty-second U.S. Infantry Returns, February 1913, roll 235; Muster roll, Company F, Twenty-second U.S. Infantry, December 31, 1912–February 28, 1913.

26. The legendary Judge Roy Bean (c. 1825–1903) was the justice of the peace and a saloon owner in Langtry. Howard R. Lamar, ed., *The Reader's Encyclopedia of the American West* (New York: Thomas Y. Crowell, 1977), 81–82; Ron Tyler et al., eds., *The New Handbook of Texas,* 6 vols. (Austin: Texas State Historical Association, 1996), 1:437–38.

27. The regiment traveled some 870 miles by rail from El Paso to Texas City over the Galveston, Harrisburg and San Antonio Railroad. The first section of the regiment arrived in Texas City at 3:00 A.M. on February 28, the second detachment (including Company F) arrived about noon, and the heavy freight and stock at 10:00 P.M. Palmer and Smith, *History of the Twenty-second United States Infantry,* 135; Twenty-second U.S. Infantry Returns, February 1913; Muster roll, Company F, Twenty-second U.S. Infantry, December 31, 1912–February 28, 1913.

Chapter 5. Texas City

1. This "Second Division" was provisional in nature, not to be confused with the Second Division of the regular army, organized after World War I began in 1917. The "square" division consisted of two infantry brigades, each containing two regiments.

2. Hunter Liggett (1857–1935), U.S. Military Academy Class of 1879, served as an officer at various posts in the United States until he was sent to Cuba in 1899. Later that same year he went to the Philippines as major of the Thirty-first Infantry. By the time he arrived in Texas in the spring of 1914, he had served on the general staff and as president of the Army War College and been promoted to brigadier general. After commanding the Fourth Brigade in Texas, Liggett led the First Corps and First Army in France in World War I and the Army of Occupation in Germany, then retired in 1921. James T. White and Co., *The National Cyclopedia of American Biography,* 76 vols. (New York: James T. White & Co, 1893–1984), *Current Series* (1926) vol. A, 498–99. Clarence Ransom Edwards (1859–1931) graduated from West Point in 1883 and served in the Southwest. In 1899, he was named chief of staff to Major General Henry Lawton and was cited several times for gallantry during the Philippine insurrection. After serving in a number of staff positions, including chief of the Bureau of Customs and Insular Affairs and chief of the executive bureau of the Panama Canal, Edwards returned to "line" duty and was given command of the Sixth Brigade at Texas City. During World War I, he led the Twenty-sixth "Yankee" Division into combat in France. Edwards clashed with General John J. Pershing and other superiors, so he was relieved of command in October 1918 and sent home to train recruits. He continued in service after the war, was promoted to major general in the regular army in 1921, and retired the following year. Edwards was a popular commander; his men often referred to him as "Daddy." White and Co., *The National Cyclopedia of American Biography, Current Series* (1926), vol. A, 417–19; Michael E. Shay, *A Grateful Heart: The History of a World War I Field Hospital* (Westport, Conn.: Greenwood Press, 2002), 4–5, 114, 150.

3. Carter received the Medal of Honor in 1891 for his performance ten years earlier at

Cibicu, Arizona. As a first lieutenant in the Sixth U.S. Cavalry, Carter, with the assistance of two soldiers, rescued wounded men from under heavy enemy fire.

4. The Model 1903 Springfield, a bolt-action rifle, fired a .30-caliber cartridge from a five-shot internal magazine and was capable of carrying a bayonet with an impressive sixteen-inch blade. Weighing slightly less than nine pounds, the highly accurate, well made, and reliable weapon saw extensive service both in the peacetime army and in combat units during World War I. In the early 1900s the army decided to issue a new saber to replace the Model 1860. The new saber was remarkably similar to its predecessor but had a guard made of steel instead of brass. Randy Steffen, *The Horse Soldier, 1776–1943*, 4 vols. (Norman: University of Oklahoma Press, 1978), 3:184–86. The Model 1909 Benet-Mercie machine rifle was a gas-operated weapon that weighed approximately thirty pounds. Manufactured by the Colt Company and the government's Springfield Armory, the Benet-Mercie was capable of firing about four hundred rounds per minute. The gun remained in U.S. arsenals after Schrantz's service and even went to France with American troops in 1917. Because of its weight and tendency to fail under dirty field conditions, it was relegated to a training role during World War I, and U.S. troops carried more reliable machine guns in combat. Bruce N. Canfield, *U.S. Infantry Weapons of the First World War* (Lincoln, R.I.: Andrew Mowbray Publishers, 2000), 177–83. The Fourth Regiment of Field Artillery (Mountain), created in 1907, utilized the 2.95-inch howitzer. The gun, made by the Vickers-Maxim Company of England, fired 75-millimeter shrapnel or high explosive ammunition to a maximum range of forty-eight hundred yards. Thirty were obtained from Vickers-Maxim in 1900, while another ninety were built in U.S. arsenals. The small and highly mobile 2.95-inch howitzer could be disassembled into four pieces and carried by mules. Konrad F. Schreier Jr., "U.S. Army Field Artillery Weapons, 1866–1918," *Military Collector and Historian* 20 (Summer 1968): 41; Tom Jones and Fitzhugh McMaster, "1st Battalion, 4th Regiment of Field Artillery (Mountain), Mexico, 1916," *Military Collector and Historian* 36 (Winter 1984): 170–71.

5. For instance, the regiment broke camp at 5:00 A.M. on June 24, 1913, marched to Dickinson, Texas, where it arrived at 9:30 A.M., having marched fourteen miles. It pitched camp, then broke camp on June 26 at 6:00 A.M., participated in a maneuver problem on the return march, and arrived back at Texas City at 11:00 A.M. The total distance marched was about twenty-four miles. Twenty-second U.S. Infantry Returns, June 1913; Muster roll, Company F, Twenty-second U.S. Infantry, April 30, 1913–June 30, 1913. On August 11, 1913, the regiment marched to Galveston, established camp north of Fort Crockett, and engaged in annual target practice. Twenty-second U.S. Infantry Returns, August 1913. Two division maneuvers were conducted in March 1914, and there was another in August 1914. Ibid., March 1914, August 1914. Field exercises and company and battalion tests were held in September 1914. Ibid., September 1914. In addition, on August 3, the regiment marched to Galveston and participated in a street parade. Heavy rains forced the return of the regiment to Texas City on August 7. Ibid., August 1914.

6. Named for Texas City Improvement Company co-owner Augustus B. Wolvin, the Wolvin shipping line ran to Mexico and Panama.

7. Although perhaps best known as an organization committed to protecting the morality of young men in urban areas, the Young Men's Christian Association (YMCA) also helped soldiers avoid vice and moral degradation during this period. During World War

I, the organization continued to serve American troops by establishing stations in training camps where men could spend their free time enjoying wholesome activities. For a discussion of the YMCA's work with the military, see Nancy Gentile Ford, *Americans All: Foreign-born Soldiers in World War I* (College Station: Texas A&M University Press, 2001), 95.

8. John Thomas Axton, a native of Salt Lake City, was general secretary of the YMCA from 1893 to 1902, when he was appointed a chaplain in the U.S. Army with the rank of captain. Axton served two tours of duty in the Philippines and five years on the Mexican border. He was promoted to major in 1917 and was in charge of religious and philanthropic organizations at the port of Hoboken, New Jersey, during World War I, for which he received the Distinguished Service Medal. He was promoted to colonel and became chief of army chaplains in 1920 and officiated at the burial service for the Unknown Soldier at Arlington National Cemetery the following year. Axton retired from the army in 1928, then became chaplain at Rutgers University. He died in 1934 and is buried in Arlington Cemetery. *New York Times,* July 22, 1934.

9. All four transports were purchased in 1898 by the Quartermaster Department for use in the Army Transport Service. The *Sumner,* a tug formerly known as the *Major McKinley* (60 gross tons), was purchased on November 7 for $13,000 and assigned to the Atlantic fleet; the *Meade,* called the *City of Berlin* before joining the fleet, was a 5,641-ton transport purchased for $400,000 on July 13; the *McClellan,* formerly the British freighter *Port Victor* (2,792 tons), had been purchased for $175,000 on July 8 and moved to the Atlantic fleet; and the *Kilpatrick,* formerly the *Michigan,* was a 3,722-ton British ship purchased for $350,000 on July 14. Following the Spanish-American War, all underwent conversion and their tonnage changed. By 1901 the *Sumner* could carry 831 officers and men; the *Meade,* 1,264 officers and men; the *McClellan,* 255 officers and men; and the *Kilpatrick,* 1,052 officers and men. Charles Dana Gibson with E. Kay Gibson, *Over Seas: U.S. Army Maritime Operations 1898 through the Fall of the Philippines* (Camden, Me.: Ensign Press, 2002), 35–36, 128; U.S. War Department, *Annual Reports for the Fiscal Year Ended June 30, 1901* (Washington, D.C.: Government Printing Office, 1901), vol. 1, pt. 2, 287–88. The *Sumner* ran aground off the coast of New Jersey in December 1916 and was declared a total loss.

10. On the morning of July 8, 1913, Army First Lieutenant Loren H. Call was on a practice flight over Texas City when his Wright biplane suddenly tilted and he was thrown forward off the seat. Call clutched the plane and fell with it nearly a thousand feet. Finally, within a hundred feet of the ground, he fell clear and was killed instantly. More than two hundred soldiers, including Schrantz, witnessed the incident. The twenty-five-year-old aviator was originally an officer in the Coast Artillery Corps but was assigned to aviation duty at his own request. *New York Times,* July 9, 1913.

11. Charles A. Reynolds of Hocking County, Ohio, enlisted at Columbus Barracks on March 7, 1911. The twenty-one-year-old laborer was discharged from Company F as a private at Texas City on March 6, 1914. Registers of Enlistments in the United States Army, 1798–1914, roll 68, vol. 132.

12. James E. Ware, born in Mississippi on November 5, 1873, served in the Second Mississippi Infantry during the Spanish-American War and the Thirty-eighth United States Volunteer Infantry in the Philippine insurrection. He became a regular army officer in

February 1901. Promoted to first lieutenant in 1906, Ware graduated from the Infantry and Cavalry School and the Army Signal School before being assigned to the Twenty-second Infantry in April 1913 and taking command of Company F on July 20, 1913. He was transferred to Company K on January 7, 1914. Ware finally retired in November 1921 with the rank of lieutenant colonel. U.S. Adjutant General's Office, *Official Army Register for 1914*, 380; U.S. Adjutant General's Office, *Official Army Register January 1, 1923* (Washington, D.C.: Government Printing Office, 1923), 1118; Muster rolls, Company F, Twenty-second U.S. Infantry, June 30, 1913–August 31, 1913, and December 31, 1913–February 28, 1914.

13. Schrantz was appointed lance corporal on October 9, 1913, appointed company clerk on November 1, 1913, and promoted to corporal on November 26, 1913. Muster rolls, Company F, Twenty-second U.S. Infantry, August 31, 1912–October 31, 1913, and October 31–December 31, 1913.

14. Sir Lionel Carden began his thirty-eight-year diplomatic career in 1877. By the time Schrantz saw him, Carden had held a number of posts in Cuba, Mexico, and Guatemala. In 1913 he was appointed minister to Mexico. Carden ran afoul of American politicians on several occasions, most notably when he presented his credentials to the Huerta government even though President Wilson refused to recognize the regime. Carden also publicly criticized the American withdrawal from Veracruz. Forced to leave Mexico City in August 1914 after Huerta's resignation, Carden died in London in October 1915. *New York Times,* October 17, 1915.

15. Sir Christopher George Francis Maurice Craddock (1862–1914), a veteran Royal Navy officer, was promoted to rear admiral in 1910. In February 1913 he was appointed to command the North American and West Indies station, stretching from Canada to Brazil. Craddock and his flagship, HMS *Essex,* were present in Veracruz harbor during the American landings in April 1914. As Schrantz notes in the next paragraph of his memoir, Craddock engaged the German enemy on November 1, 1914, when his inferior force attacked Admiral Count Maximilian von Spee's two armored cruisers and three light cruisers off Coronel, Chile. A quick battle ensued in which two British ships were destroyed and one was able to withdraw. Craddock was killed in the action. Holger H. Herwig and Neil M. Heyman, *Biographical Dictionary of World War I* (Westport, Conn.: Greenwood Press, 1982), 122. Another profile of the admiral may be found in Jack Sweetman, *The Landing at Veracruz: 1914 — The First Complete Chronicle of a Strange Encounter in April, 1914, When the United States Navy Captured and Occupied the City of Veracruz, Mexico* (Annapolis, Md.: United States Naval Institute, 1968), 55.

16. The .303-caliber Short Magazine Lee Enfield (SMLE) was the primary bolt-action rifle used by the British army during World War I. British forces in World War II used a similar model as well, and in fact the weapon remained in service until the early 1950s. A small number of American troops were also issued the SMLE during World War I. Canfield, *U.S. Infantry Weapons of the First World War,* 98–99.

17. The regiment left Texas City and marched to Hulen (10 miles away) on April 16. The following day it marched to Webster (10 miles), and on April 18, 11 miles to south Houston. On April 19 it moved 9 miles and went into camp in Houston. As Schrantz relates, although scheduled to take part in the San Jacinto Day parade on April 21, the Twenty-second Infantry received orders at 3:25 A.M. on April 20 to return to Texas City. Starting at 8:00 A.M., the men reached Genoa at about 1:30 (distance 13.5 miles), moved

on April 21 to Shell Siding (12 miles), and returned to Texas City on April 22 (14.5 miles), a total march of 80 miles. Twenty-second U.S. Infantry Returns, April 1914.

18. *The United States Army and Navy Journal and Gazette of the Regular and Volunteer Forces* was published weekly in New York from 1863 to 1921 and was one of the most important military journals of the period. It continued to be published under a somewhat different title through the 1960s.

19. Basil D. Coleman of Edmonton, Kentucky, was a twenty-nine-year-old motorman. He ended his third enlistment with Company F in May 1912, then enlisted for the fourth time on December 12, 1912, at Fort Sam Houston, Texas. Appointed a corporal on January 14, 1913, Coleman was promoted to sergeant on September 16 and to first sergeant on September 24, 1913. He was honorably discharged on December 11, 1916. Muster rolls, Company F, Twenty-second U.S. Infantry, December 31, 1912–February 28, 1913, and August 31–October 31, 1913; Registers of Enlistments in the United States Army, 1798–1914, roll 65, vol. 127.

20. The nontransport vessels were chartered from private companies for the Veracruz campaign. The *City of Macon* (5,311 gross tons) and the *City of Memphis* (5,252 gross tons) were both chartered from the Ocean SS Company at the rate of $1,000 per day. The *Colorado* (2,764 gross tons), *San Marcos* (2,839 tons), and the *Denver* (4,549 gross tons) were chartered from the Mallory SS Company at the rate of $442, $600, and $910 per day, respectively. The *Kansan* (7,913 gross tons), *Minnesotan* (6,665 gross tons), and *Panaman* (6,649 gross tons) were chartered from the American-Hawaiian SS Company at $1,200, $900, and $900, respectively. Finally, the *Ossabow* or *Ossabaw* and the *Saltillo* or *Satilla* (both 2,667 gross tons) were chartered from the Texas City Line at the rate of $425 and $450 per day, respectively. As Schrantz reports, some ships were refitted as troop or animal transports. Gibson with Gibson, *Over Seas,* 124.

21. Discharged from government service in December 1914, the *City of Memphis* resumed service as a cargo steamer. A German U-boat sank the ship on March 17, 1917 near Fastnet, Ireland. *New York Times,* March 19, 1917.

22. James Franklin Bell (1856–1919) graduated from West Point in 1878. A career soldier, he fought in the Philippine insurrection and was awarded the Medal of Honor for heroism in Luzon. He served as army chief of staff from 1906 to 1910, then commanded the Second Division in 1914–1915. During World War I he was in charge of Camp Upton, New York, and the Seventy-seventh Division and visited the front in France. Bell was in command of the Eastern Department at the time of his death in early 1919. William Gardner Bell, *Commanding Generals and Chiefs of Staff, 1775–1995* (Washington, D.C.: Center of Military History, 1997), 98.

23. Fort Crockett was built on Galveston Island in 1897 to defend Galveston Bay.

24. Private Theodore Stelmach joined the army on April 24, 1914, and joined Company F on June 13. Twenty-second U.S. Infantry Returns, June 1914; Muster roll, Company F, Twenty-second U.S. Infantry, April 30, 1914–June 30, 1914. Private Aron Nikolonetzki enlisted on March 3, 1911, at Columbus Barracks, Ohio, for three years. Born in Russia, the twenty-four-year-old fireman was discharged from Company F on March 2, 1914, at Texas City, Texas, and reenlisted the following month. Twenty-second U.S. Infantry Returns, March 1914, April 1914; Muster rolls, Company F, Twenty-second U.S. Infantry, December

31, 1912–February 28, 1913, and February 28, 1914–April 30, 1914; Registers of Enlistments in the United States Army, 1798–1914, roll 67, vol. 131.

25. Members of the British Expeditionary Force attempting to stop the German drive on Paris established positions at Mons, Belgium. Fighting began there on August 23, 1914. Despite a stubborn defense, the outnumbered British withdrew. They continued to retreat until they reached the Marne River, then assisted French and Belgian forces in halting the German offensive.

26. The USS *New York* (BB-34) was launched in October 1912 and commissioned in April 1914. The *New York* served as Rear Admiral Frank Fletcher's flagship during the blockade of Veracruz. The ship served in European waters during World War I and was present for the surrender of the German high seas fleet in 1918. After participating in the invasion of North Africa in November 1942, *New York* served on convoy duty escorting ships to North Africa. U.S. Department of the Navy, Naval History Division, *Dictionary of American Naval Fighting Ships,* 9 vols. (Washington, 1959–1991), 5:71–72.

27. Beginning October 15, 1914, all training was suspended in the division, and passes were freely granted to enlisted men and leaves of absence to officers. Many men went hunting and fishing, and transportation was provided. Twenty-second U.S. Infantry Returns, October 1914. The regiment left for border duty in Naco, Arizona, on December 17, 1914. Palmer and Smith, *History of the Twenty-second United States Infantry,* 136.

28. Schrantz is quite correct in that few enlisted men received commissions in the pre–World War I period. The vast majority of new officers were either West Point graduates or civilian appointees. Coffman, *The Regulars,* 123–24.

29. Beginning in 1890, an enlisted man could in fact be discharged before his term of service expired by purchasing a discharge, according to rules published from time to time by the War Department. U.S. War Department, *Regulations for the Army of the United States, 1913,* 35–36.

30. Schrantz was honorably discharged as a corporal, and his service record also noted that his character was "'Excellent'" and his service "Honest and Faithful. No AWOL." Muster roll, Company F, Twenty-second U.S. Infantry, October 31, 1914–December 31, 1914.

31. Sylvester Bonnaffon III was born in Pennsylvania on October 4, 1875. Commissioned a second lieutenant in the regular army in 1899, Bonnaffon was promoted to captain in March 1911 and assigned to the Twenty-second Infantry in June 1914. He joined the regiment on July 19, 1914, and assumed command of Company F the following day. He retired from the army in October 1920 with the rank of lieutenant colonel. U.S. Adjutant General's Office, *Official Army Register for 1915* (Washington, D.C.: Government Printing Office, 1915), 394; U.S. Adjutant General's Office, *Official Army Register July 1, 1921* (Washington, D.C.: Government Printing Office, 1922), 1250; Twenty-second U.S. Infantry Returns, July 1914; Muster roll, Company F, Twenty-second U.S. Infantry, June 30, 1914–August 31, 1914.

Chapter 6. Return to Missouri

1. Schrantz's efforts must have paid off, for Company A made a fairly impressive showing during an inspection by the regular army in 1915. The company had three officers and

fifty-two enlisted men present for the inspection, with fourteen enlisted men absent. By December 31, 1915, the company had served eight consecutive days on a practice march, with an average attendance of forty-one men, and had held fifty-seven assemblies for drill and instruction with an average attendance of forty-three. Only eleven men were not present twenty-four times that year for drill and instruction, exclusive of field or camp service. The company had the largest number of assemblies and the lowest number of men not actually present twenty-four times a year of any company in the Second Missouri Infantry. U.S. War Department, *Annual Reports, 1916,* 3 vols. (Washington, D.C.: Government Printing Office, 1916), 1:1047.

2. Stray shots from the fighting between Carrancistas and the forces of Sonoran governor Jose Maria Maytorena in the Naco vicinity had killed and wounded a number of Americans, necessitating the movement of the Twenty-second Infantry. The regiment left Texas City on December 17, 1914. The Twenty-second U.S. Infantry served a few weeks in Naco, Arizona, until late January 1915, when the Mexicans withdrew from the border and the Twenty-second was ordered to Douglas, Arizona. Except for brief periods, the regiment remained at Douglas until March 1917. The Twenty-second Infantry arrived in New York City on April 1, 1917. Although the regiment as a whole did not serve overseas during World War I, three officers and four hundred enlisted men from the Twenty-second did serve in France with the First Division. Palmer and Smith, *History of the Twenty-second United States Infantry,* 136–40.

3. Schrantz was a member of the four-company "Red" contingent in this war game (July 11–19, 1915) and covered the event for a local newspaper. He is correct that the games provided some degree of realism, with skirmishing, simulated combat, prisoners, camping in adverse weather conditions, and the like. Schrantz also noted, however, that this was the first time soldiers had marched through the area since 1865, so civilian visitors thronged their camp, and he was forced to admit in one letter that the maneuvers were "a veritable picnic—'Ragtime soldierin' [sic]." At one point Company A walked into an ambush and the Carthage men were declared "out" for the day, but they redeemed themselves in the final "action" of the maneuvers. Both sides naturally claimed victory. *Springfield (Missouri) Daily Leader,* July 14, 15, 17, 20, 1915; Missouri National Guard, *History of the Missouri National Guard,* 88. Schrantz had been promoted to sergeant in the company on June 1, 1915. State of Missouri, Office of the Adjutant General, *Service of the Missouri National Guard,* 122.

4. On the night of November 1, 1915, Pancho Villa led about twelve thousand men in an attack on the Carrancista garrison of Agua Prieta. Villa expected the town to be held by a small force, but reinforcements had arrived and Carranza's soldiers had erected strong fortifications. Villa's assault failed, and he retreated to Naco. Katz, *Life and Times of Pancho Villa,* 524–27.

5. Secretary of War Lindley M. Garrison devised the Continental Plan. His plan called for an army of 121,000 regulars and 379,000 reservists with two years of regular army experience. This force would be buttressed by a volunteer reserve of 500,000 men. Garrison's plan limited the National Guard to the minor role of domestic defense. The plan faced opposition from a number of interest groups, including members of Congress who supported the National Guard, those realists who doubted the plan could be fully implemented, pacifists, and those who thought the plan did not go far enough. Presi-

dent Wilson withdrew his support and Secretary Garrison resigned. Doubler, *I Am the Guard*, 154–58.

Chapter 7. Back to the Border—As a Civilian

1. A fierce hurricane struck Texas City on August 17, 1915. The camp of the Second Division was indeed wiped out by 85- to 100-mile-per-hour winds. Ten soldiers of the Twenty-third Infantry were killed (a total of thirteen enlisted men were killed), and a number of troops were injured. Details on the losses suffered by the army may be found in *New York Times*, August 19, 1915. U.S. War Department, *Annual Reports, 1916*, 3 vols. (Washington, D.C.: Government Printing Office, 1916), 1:278.

2. Nuevo Laredo was the scene of fierce fighting beginning January 1, 1914, when Constitutionalist (Carrancista) general Pablo Gonzales launched an attack on Huerta's federal forces in the city. The citizens of Laredo watched the battle from the American side of the river, and stray shots killed or wounded several. Gonzales continued his attack the following day but withdrew after suffering heavy losses. Several hundred Mexicans were killed or wounded in the action. In late April, when the federal garrison evacuated the city, much of the business district was put to the torch. The *New York Times* reported a "sharp interchange" of shots between U.S. troops and federal soldiers and two Mexicans killed when they attempted to dynamite both the foot and wagon bridge and the railroad bridge. Jerry Thompson, *Laredo: A Pictorial History* (Norfolk, Va.: Donning, 1986), 272–79; *New York Times*, April 25, 1914.

3. Hugh Lenox Scott (1853–1934) graduated from the U.S. Military Academy in 1876. An authority on the Plains Indians, he participated in the army's last major action against them at Wounded Knee in 1890. After serving as assistant adjutant general of the First Army Corps during the Spanish-American War, Scott was superintendent of West Point from 1906 to 1910. Appointed chief of staff in November 1914, he was promoted to major general the following year and retired from active duty nearly three years later. Recalled to duty, he commanded the Seventy-eighth Division at Camp Dix, New Jersey, and retired permanently in 1919. Bell, *Commanding Generals and Chiefs of Staff*, 104.

4. The meeting with Obregón actually began in Juárez on April 30, 1916. Funston, a good soldier but no diplomat, soon bowed out of the conference. Obregón demanded the withdrawal of Pershing's Punitive Expedition from Mexico, something General Scott could not authorize, and the conference ended after two hours. Scott then met privately with Obregón. On May 3 both men worked out a tentative agreement in which Pershing would withdraw his forces to the town of Namiquipa, while Pershing himself would remain at Casas Grandes, and Wilson would set the date for the American withdrawal from Mexico. The agreement was approved in Washington, but President Carranza did not approve it, so the conference ended without success on May 11. Scott did in fact receive word that seventeen thousand Mexicans in the Pulpit Pass of Sonora were to act with another force to destroy Pershing's troops if their withdrawal was not imminent and that General Nafarete was in Tamaulipas building a bandit force for an attack on Brownsville. Scott alerted both Pershing and the U.S. commands on the border to watch for possible attacks. By early June, the Americans also had information that border raider Luis de la Rosa was recruiting in Monterrey and that recruits were being assembled near San Ygnacio,

sixty miles from Laredo, to move north and attack the Texas border towns. Clendenen, *Blood on the Border,* 275–76; Tompkins, *Chasing Villa,* 196–99; Hugh Lenox Scott, *Some Memories of a Soldier* (New York: Century, 1928), 525–28; U.S. War Department, *Annual Reports, 1916,* 1:188.

Chapter 8. Laredo

1. A total of 12 percent of the Missouri National Guard was rejected for service because of physical deficiencies. Although the data are incomplete, on a national scale at least 23,000 rejections were made from a total of 128,000 men examined, an average of 18 percent. Many of those rejections appeared to have been made because men were underweight or not the required height. U.S. Militia Bureau, *Report on Mobilization of the Organized Militia and National Guard of the United States 1916* (Washington, D.C.: Government Printing Office, 1916), 55, 132. Seven members of Company A were rejected as being physically unfit. Ultimately, more than 5,600 Missourians served on the Mexican border. State of Missouri, Office of the Adjutant General, *Service of the Missouri National Guard,* index.

2. William A. Raupp was born on November 17, 1868, in Sandusky, Ohio. A resident of Pierce City, Missouri, he first enlisted in the Missouri National Guard as a private in 1886. Discharged the following year, he entered the Second Missouri Infantry in 1890 and steadily rose through the ranks. After service in the Spanish-American War as captain of Company E and a battalion commander, he was promoted to major in 1899, lieutenant colonel in 1900, and colonel in 1906. As Schrantz indicates, after commanding the Second Missouri on the Mexican border Colonel Raupp was placed in command of two pioneer infantry regiments but did not see service overseas. He died on May 4, 1946. State of Missouri, Office of the Adjutant General, *Service of the Missouri National Guard,* 107; Missouri Secretary of State, World War I database, http://www.sos.mo.gov/archives/ww1. It may be that during maneuvers on the Mexican border in late 1916 Raupp "very deeply offended" a regular army officer who then sought revenge by having Raupp replaced as colonel of the Second Missouri and kept in the United States. On the other hand, enemies described the colonel as overbearing, arrogant, and fond of the social side of camp life. In addition, it was certainly not uncommon for National Guard officers to be examined by efficiency boards, removed from their original commands, and assigned elsewhere. Such a practice offered guardsmen like Schrantz even more evidence of a perceived anti-Guard bias on the part of regular army officers. Mahon, *History of the Militia and the National Guard,* 161–64; *Lamar (Missouri) Democrat,* October 25, 1917.

3. Clyde Alvin Narramore was born in Carthage, Missouri, on October 6, 1891. He enlisted as a private in the Second Missouri Infantry in 1908. In 1915 he was appointed battalion sergeant major and the following year he was promoted to regimental sergeant major. He served in that capacity on the Mexican border until December 1916, when he was commissioned a second lieutenant and placed in command of the supply company of the Second Missouri Infantry. During World War I he served as a first lieutenant in the 110th Trench Motor Battery and was overseas from May 1918 to April 1919. State of Missouri, Office of the Adjutant General, *Service of the Missouri National Guard,* 108; Missouri Secretary of State, World War I database, http://www.sos.mo.gov/archives/ww1.

Schrantz's fears of paperwork were borne out once the Second Missouri reached Laredo, for in one newspaper letter he wrote that Sergeant Major Narramore was "one of the busiest men in camp." *Carthage Evening Press,* August 1, 1916.

4. In his official report, Brigadier General Harvey C. Clark of the Missouri National Guard complained that only one regular army officer had been detailed to muster his men into service, and the War Department declined to authorize National Guard officers to do so. Clark also noted that the delay was due to the fact that although state officers had submitted requisitions for needed equipment, federal authorities had failed to issue the items and the guardsmen had to wait until the items were received from distant supply depots. State of Missouri, Office of the Adjutant General, *Service of the Missouri National Guard,* x.

5. According to President Wilson's call, both the Organized Militia (those units still operating under the Dick Act, who had not taken the oath required by the National Defense Act and been converted to the National Guard) and National Guard (those who had taken the new oath and been converted) were mobilized, and no man could dodge service by refusing to take the oath. Many states had not converted their units from Organized Militia to National Guard, although Missouri was arguably the first state to have proceeded with the conversion using the new oath. Under the provisions of the National Defense Act, any man who had already taken an oath to defend the Constitution and obey the president of the United States would be considered a member of the National Guard for the rest of his enlistment. Those who had signed an enlistment contract that did not contain those provisions were required to sign a new contract that included them and that made the term of enlistment six years—half in active service, half in the reserves, with credit given for time already served. Of 128,000 enlisted militia men, nearly 22,000 refused to take the new oath due to confusion about the requirements of the recently approved legislation. U.S. Militia Bureau, *Report on Mobilization,* 4, 32, 159. In a letter to the Carthage newspaper Schrantz explained that the rumor had spread that the National Guard members "were signing over into the regular army proper and would be held until the end of their enlistment, regardless of whether the Mexican quarrel developed into a war or not." The seven offenders were from Company B of the Second Missouri and included a first sergeant who had his chevrons ripped off. Dressed in overalls and jumpers and old service hats without hat cords, five of the men escaped, while members of their own company drummed the other two out of camp, as Schrantz related. Schrantz also pointed out that while none of the Carthage men refused to take the oath, two recently enlisted members of Company A deserted at Camp Clark. *Carthage Evening Press,* June 30, 1916. These men and others who refused to take the oath were not prosecuted. It could be that the men of Company B who refused were new recruits who had not yet been given the oath or perhaps experienced men who had missed their chance to take the new oath when the remainder of the company was sworn.

6. The skirmish at Carrizal took place on June 21, 1916. Two troops of the Tenth U.S. Cavalry halted outside Carrizal and met the Mexican commander, who, rather than allow the Americans to pass through, negotiated for additional time to telegraph for instructions. The outnumbered Americans deployed and advanced on the town, and the Mexicans opened fire. During the intense firefight that followed, some Americans were taken prisoner while the rest withdrew. The Americans suffered twelve killed, eleven

wounded, and twenty-three taken prisoner. Mexican losses were considerably heavier, perhaps as many as forty-five killed and fifty-three wounded. Clendenen, *Blood on the Border*, 303–10; Tompkins, *Chasing Villa*, 208–12.

7. In a letter to the *Carthage Evening Press*, Schrantz wrote that the refreshments served by the Red Cross in Enid were a welcome change from the coffee, hardtack, and "meager allowance of corned beef which monopolized the menu for the rest of the trip." The ladies of San Antonio gave the Missourians "soda pop," peaches, oranges, and watermelons "in unlimited amounts," enabling the troops to avoid visiting the local saloons. *Carthage Evening Press*, July 13, 1916.

8. A large party of Mexican raiders struck the Fourteenth U.S. Cavalry's two-company outpost at San Ygnacio about 2:00 A.M. on June 15, 1916, killing three Americans and wounding four men (one fatally), while suffering eight dead themselves. The cavalrymen pursued the bandits into Mexico but were unsuccessful in picking up their trail and so returned to the American side. U.S. War Department, *Annual Reports, 1916*, 1:188; Clendenen, *Blood on the Border*, 282.

9. As a National Guard history put it, "This being in the War Zone, war conditions prevailed in the precautions observed by those in command." Missouri National Guard, *History of the Missouri National Guard*, 90. Schrantz himself wrote that "it is common knowledge that the most dangerous man in the army is a scared recruit" with a loaded rifle. *Carthage Evening Press*, July 20, 1916.

10. Brigadier General Harvey C. Clark of Jefferson City entered the Missouri National Guard as a captain in the Second Missouri Infantry in 1888. Promoted to major in 1897, he left the regiment to serve as lieutenant colonel of the Sixth Missouri Infantry during the Spanish-American War. In 1899 he was promoted to brigadier general in the Missouri National Guard and served as commander of the First Missouri Brigade on the Mexican border in 1916. Clark commanded an infantry brigade and a depot brigade in the United States during World War I and did not go overseas. According to the Laredo newspaper, Clark was kept "quite busy" attending to "affairs" demanding his attention. State of Missouri, Office of the Adjutant General, *Service of the Missouri National Guard*, 1; Missouri Secretary of State, World War I database, www.sos.mo.gov/archives/ww1; *Laredo (Texas) Weekly Times*, July 23, 1916.

11. The Laredo newspaper noted the "hardening" process the Missourians were undergoing, including a ten-mile hike each day, followed by drill in the manual of arms or "maneuvers." *Laredo Weekly Times*, August 13, 1916. The August 18, 1916, storm saw winds in excess of 60 miles per hour and the rain fell in "veritable torrents." The men were ordered to sit in their tents in the rising water and hold guy lines and support poles, but despite their best efforts very few of the soldiers' tents were left standing. Fortunately, no men were injured or killed. *Laredo Weekly Times*, August 20, 1916. Schrantz described it as "the worst storm that most of us have ever experienced." He reported that his men were kept awake all night re-driving tent pegs and splicing ropes to keep their tents standing. Finally, at about 5:00 A.M., the wind died down, but all the tents in two companies of the Second Missouri were flattened. Rusty rifles and wet equipment were located, tents were re-erected, and by evening the camp was back to normal. *Carthage Evening Press*, August 24, 1916; Missouri National Guard, *History of the Missouri National Guard*, 90.

12. The War Department issued an order on July 18, 1916, authorizing discharges to

men with dependent relatives and another order on September 1 allowing up to fifty dollars per month per man to be paid to support the dependents of those on the border. U.S. Militia Bureau, *Report on Mobilization,* 40–41.

13. A total of eighty-six officers and men served on the border with Company A. Five were furloughed to the reserves and twelve were discharged before the company was mustered out in January 1917. State of Missouri, Office of the Adjutant General, *Service of the Missouri National Guard,* 121–28.

14. In his newspaper account of the incident, Schrantz related that three prisoners escaped. One was captured in town, another surrendered the next day, and the third, as Schrantz relates, returned secretly to confinement. "This was the most humiliating part of the whole tour of duty," Schrantz wrote, "and every one connected with the guard is standing a good deal of good natured chaffing as a result of it." Colonel Raupp, who argued that the sand storm prevented them from doing their duty, subsequently released the two negligent sentries. *Carthage Evening Press,* December 2, 1916.

15. Schrantz was not alone. According to him, there was probably not a guardsman who did not secretly resolve at some time to "buy, beg or borrow a civilian suit" to visit Nuevo Laredo so he could say he had been in Mexico, even if he could not enter the country as a soldier on duty. *Carthage Evening Press,* July 20, 1916. In August, four soldiers (three members of the Second Missouri and one from the Ninth U.S. Infantry) crossed the border in civilian clothes in order to have a "high old time" in Nuevo Laredo. They were recognized by the bridge guard on the American side as they returned across the border and then arrested and taken to the guardhouse at Fort McIntosh. *Laredo Weekly Times,* August 27, 1916. Later in the year, two members of the Carthage company were recognized and arrested by American authorities on their return from Nuevo Laredo. The men were kept under arrest in their quarters for several days. *Carthage Evening Press,* December 2, 1916. Although soldiers and customs officials guarded the bridge, civilians could cross at leisure, provided they paid the five-cent toll and left cameras behind at the customs house. Once in Nuevo Laredo a visitor found a business district mostly in ruins, but here and there a grocery store or saloon was open for business (Schrantz noted that there were about two saloons for every grocery store). Ibid., November 7, 1916.

16. Schrantz is mistaken here. There was a review held at Fort McIntosh during this period, while the Second Missouri was at the rifle range, but General Funston was not present. Funston came to Laredo in early October to review his troops, while the regiment was dispersed along the border. *Laredo Weekly Times,* September 3, October 8, 1916.

17. According to Schrantz, Zapata had a population of about 250 and was the county seat of twelve-hundred-square-mile Zapata County, said to have only 7 white civilian inhabitants. The First Battalion established its headquarters at Zapata, along with Companies B and D, with Company A at Ramireño and Company C at Urabeño. *Carthage Evening Press,* September 7, 15, 1916; Missouri National Guard, *History of the Missouri National Guard,* 91.

Chapter 9. Ramireño

1. In a letter home, Schrantz gave details about the skirmish on June 14–15. According to locals, the twenty-four members of the Fourteenth U.S. Cavalry had their camp on

the river bend at the southern edge of town. After a week of careful planning, a band of about seventy Mexican raiders, supposedly reinforced by men on the Texas side of the river, crossed the river on the night of June 14 and moved to attack the town. Much to the surprise of the bandits, a troop of the Fourteenth Cavalry had arrived in town at nine o'clock that evening, bringing the total in the American garrison to more than a hundred. Although the Americans suffered three killed in the initial stages of the attack, they soon organized and drove the bandits away, killing twelve or thirteen and capturing five. The remainder crossed back into Mexico. *Carthage Evening Press,* September 15, 1916.

2. Ramireño had a population of about seventy. With no Americans in the town, and no Mexicans able to speak English, Schrantz and several of the other members of Company A who could speak some Spanish served as interpreters. The other Missourians used sign language with the locals but also began studying Spanish. Although impressed by the friendly nature of the locals, the men of Company A were instructed to "be friendly to everyone and trust no one." *Carthage Evening Press,* September 15, 1916. Despite these instructions, both the civilians and the National Guard troops were on their best behavior while Company A was there, with no incidents on either side. Ibid., October 16, 1916.

3. Even Schrantz admitted that the meager stock of groceries in the village and the ranch's horses and cattle were not much incentive for bandits to attack the garrison, but he also wrote that it would be foolhardy to neglect the town's defenses. *Carthage Evening Press,* September 23, 1916.

4. Other false alarms occurred. One night, two Missourians saw five horsemen riding toward the camp, only to discover they were in fact long-horned cattle. On another occasion, about twenty cowboys driving thirty cattle arrived in town, but upon investigation the suspicious looking cowboys proved to be just what they claimed. *Carthage Evening Press,* September 23, 1916.

5. Schrantz is quite correct about Roos being "a chronic citizen soldier." The Carthage native was born on December 9, 1890. He first enlisted in Company A in 1907 and was promoted to sergeant before being discharged in 1910. He reenlisted, was commissioned a second lieutenant in 1912, and resigned the following year. He reenlisted again and was promoted to first sergeant of the company in 1915. While serving on the Mexican border he was furloughed to the reserves. He entered the army again late in World War I (September 1918) and served with the Medical Department, and although promoted to sergeant, he spent the war stateside at Camp Greenleaf, Georgia, and Camp Eustis, Virginia. State of Missouri, Office of the Adjutant General, *Service of the Missouri National Guard,* 121; Missouri Secretary of State, World War I database, http://www.sos.mo.gov/archives/ww1.

6. John M. Curlee joined Company A in 1910. He rose to the rank of mess sergeant in June 1916, then to sergeant two months later. He was furloughed to the reserves in November 1916. State of Missouri, Office of the Adjutant General, *Service of the Missouri National Guard,* 121.

7. San Ygnacio Viejo was established by Spanish settlers perhaps one hundred years before Schrantz's time in the area. It was situated about two or three miles north of Company A's camp. *Carthage Evening Press,* September 23, 1916.

8. The *Laredo Weekly Times* reported that the "the camplife and incidental drilling and

marching" had hardened the guardsmen into "virile men" and "better specimens of real men," with the weaklings in the ranks converted into specimens of "physical manliness capable of doing any hard drilling or manual work." *Laredo Weekly Times,* October 1, 1916. The deployment of the Second Missouri from Laredo along the border taught the Missourians "much of what would be expected of them if they had to do this kind of work in the event of hostilities" and familiarized them with "what they had never before come in contact and preparing themselves for efficient service in the event trouble should break and become of a serious nature wherein their services as border patrolmen would become necessary." *Laredo Weekly Times,* November 26, 1916.

9. Marcus Bell was born in Fredonia, Kansas, in 1893. He came to Carthage in 1896 and graduated from Carthage High School in 1912. Bell earned a BS degree in agriculture from the University of Missouri in 1916. His military career began in March 1916 when he became a private in Company A, Fourth Missouri Infantry. Although promoted to corporal the same month, Bell transferred to Company F that July. He served with that company on the Mexican border, was promoted to sergeant in August 1916, and was mustered out in February 1917. When World War I began, Bell was given a commission, and in September 1917 he was promoted to command of Company H, Fiftieth U.S. Infantry. He went overseas with that unit in September 1918. In the interwar years he had a variety of assignments and graduated from the Command and General Staff College in 1934 and the Army War College in 1942. At the beginning of World War II, he was chief of staff of the Eightieth Division. He then became assistant division commander of the Eighty-first Division and saw action in the Pacific theater. Promoted to brigadier general in 1943, Bell was also awarded the Silver Star and Legion of Merit for his service. He served in Korea after World War II, was assigned to Fort Riley in 1950, and retired as a brigadier general in 1951. He died in 1981. *Carthage Evening Press,* June 28, 1961; State of Missouri, Office of the Adjutant General, *Service of the Missouri National Guard,* 352.

Chapter 10. The End of Border Service

1. Such alerts must have been relatively common. In early November, for instance, a midnight haystack fire in the camp of the Fourth Missouri Infantry caused the fire alarm to be sounded, and many soldiers rushed to the scene, "thrown completely out of equilibrium and off their guard." *Laredo Weekly Times,* November 5, 1916.

2. In addition to guard duty, the Missourians engaged in various maneuvers between different battalions of the Second Missouri, with other Missouri regiments, and with the Second Florida Infantry and the Third U.S. Artillery in December 1916. The men of the Second Missouri also formed their own regimental football team and enjoyed games in Laredo, along with musical programs at the YMCA building. *Carthage Evening Press,* November 16, 1916, December 7, 15, 19, 1916; *Laredo Weekly Times,* December 17, 1916.

Chapter 11. Editor's Postscript

1. Missouri National Guard, *History of the Missouri National Guard,* 92–93; State of Missouri, Office of the Adjutant General, *Report of the Adjutant General of Missouri,*

January 1, 1917–December 31, 1920 ([Jefferson City, Mo.?], 1921), 89, 108. The Missourians bitterly resented the dissolution of the old Second Missouri, and even the Carthage city council sent letters of protest to Washington, to no avail.

Appendix A. The U.S. Army, the National Guard, and Mexico

1. U.S. War Department, *Regulations for the Army of the United States, 1913,* 161–68.

2. U.S. War Department, *Annual Reports, 1913,* 1:252–53.

3. Ibid., 1:246–54. Annual rejections from 1900 to 1916 ranged from 70 to 81 percent. About 12 percent of recruits were foreign born. Most were laborers or farmers. Coffman, *The Regulars,* 97–98, 102.

4. *Laredo Weekly Times,* October 22, 1916.

5. Two of the finest studies of army life during the Indian Wars period are Don Rickey Jr.'s *Forty Miles a Day on Beans and Hay: The Enlisted Soldier Fighting the Indian Wars* (Norman: University of Oklahoma Press, 1963), and Edward M. Coffman's *The Old Army: A Portrait of the American Army in Peacetime, 1784–1898* (New York: Oxford University Press, 1986). Dr. Coffman continues his earlier study through this period in *The Regulars: The American Army, 1898–1941.*

6. Edward Coffman examines the gulf between the regular army soldier and society in the pre-1898 period in his book *The Old Army* and in the 1898–1941 period in *The Regulars,* 96, 139–40, 192–93, 416.

7. Tompkins, *Chasing Villa,* dedication.

8. Clendenen, *Blood on the Border,* 139.

9. For instance, an officers' school for elementary instruction was established at each post, in addition to special service schools at Fort Monroe, Virginia (artillery), Washington, D.C. (engineers and medical), Fort Totten, New York (submarine defense), Fort Riley (cavalry), and the general service and staff school at Fort Leavenworth, Kansas. Marvin A. Kreidberg and Merton G. Henry, *History of Military Mobilization in the United States Army, 1775–1945* (Westport, Conn.: Greenwood Press, 1975), 203–204.

10. William Harding Carter, *The American Army* (Indianapolis: Bobbs-Merrill, 1915), 78–79.

11. War Department expenditures in 1912 went to support not only a regular army but also a National Guard force of nearly 122,000 men. Allan R. Millett and Peter Maslowski, *For the Common Defense: A Military History of the United States of America* (New York: The Free Press, 1984), 302.

12. Carter, *The American Army,* 66. A concise summary of the army's attempts to "modernize" during this period may be found in Timothy K. Nenninger's essay, "The Army Enters the Twentieth Century, 1904–1917," in *Against All Enemies: Interpretations of American Military History from Colonial Times to the Present,* ed. Kenneth J. Hagan and William R. Roberts (New York: Greenwood Press, 1986), chap. 11. Also see Peter Karsten, "Armed Progressives: The Military Reorganizes for the American Century," in his book *The Military in America: From the Colonial Era to the Present* (New York: The Free Press, 1986), chap. 24; Edward M. Coffman, *The War to End All Wars: The American Military Experience in World War I* (Madison: University of Wisconsin Press, 1986), 11–19; Coff-

man, *The Regulars,* chap. 5; Weigley, *History of the United States Army,* chaps. 14 and 15; and Millett and Maslowski, *For the Common Defense,* chap. 10.

13. Brian Linn, *Guardians of Empire: The U.S. Army and the Pacific, 1902–1940* (Chapel Hill: University of North Carolina Press, 1997), 59. Linn's excellent study examines the army's many difficulties in maintaining a large force in overseas possessions.

14. William Harding Carter (1851–1925), a native of Tennessee, served as a twelve-year-old dispatch bearer with Federal forces during the Civil War. After his graduation from West Point in 1873, Carter served first as an infantry officer, then with the cavalry in the West during the Indian Wars. He was awarded the Medal of Honor for bravery against the Apaches in 1881. After the turn of the century, Carter saw service in England, France, and the Philippines. He rose steadily through the ranks and was commissioned a major general in 1909. He commanded the Maneuver Division in Texas in 1911 and mobilized the Second Division for service in Texas in 1913. Carter was retired from the army because of his age in 1915, but when the United States entered World War I he returned to command the army's Central Department in Chicago. Carter retired again on the fiftieth anniversary of his entry into the army and was awarded the Distinguished Service Medal for his World War I service. In addition to his distinguished military career, Carter authored a number of books and articles. White and Co., *The National Cyclopedia of American Biography* (1931), 21:37.

15. Frederic Louis Huidekoper, *The Military Unpreparedness of the United States* (New York: Macmillan, 1915), 392–93.

16. John M. Palmer, *America in Arms* (New Haven: Yale University Press, 1941), 152–54.

17. John Dickinson, *The Building of an Army* (New York: Century, 1922), 5.

18. U.S. War Department, *Annual Reports, 1913,* 1:9, 3:64.

19. Ibid., 3:65. American presidents used the application and lifting of the arms ban to favor factions they supported during the Mexican Revolution. Woodrow Wilson, Taft's successor, continued the arms embargo, although his dislike of the Huerta regime led to more lax enforcement of the measure, and Wilson finally repealed the ban in February 1914. Wilson reimposed the ban later in 1914. Knight, *Mexican Revolution,* 2:30–32; Katz, *Life and Times of Pancho Villa,* 175–76, 210–12, 354–56; Henry F. Pringle, *The Life and Times of William Howard Taft,* 2 vols. (New York: Farrar & Rinehart, 1939), 2:706; Scholes and Scholes, *Foreign Policies of the Taft Administration,* 92; U.S. War Department, *Annual Reports, 1913,* 3:58–65. In addition, according to historian Robert E. Quirk, "smuggling was carried on by respectable American firms . . . and winked at by the American customs officials." Quirk, *The Mexican Revolution, 1914–1915: The Convention of Aguascalientes* (New York: Norton, 1970), 11.

20. U.S. War Department, *Annual Reports, 1913,* 3:60.

21. Excellent accounts of this part of the revolution may be found in Knight, *Mexican Revolution;* Krauze, *Mexico;* Meyer, *Huerta;* and Katz, *Life and Times of Pancho Villa.* A popular history of American military involvement in Mexican affairs during this period is John S. D. Eisenhower's *Intervention: The United States and the Mexican Revolution, 1913–1917* (New York: Norton, 1993).

22. U.S. War Department, *Annual Reports, 1913,* 3:113.

23. Ibid., 3:40, 113–20.

24. *Infantry Journal* quoted in Huidekoper, *Military Unpreparedness,* 420.

25. The initial landing party on the morning of April 21 consisted of 787 Americans. The Mexicans were able to assemble about one thousand regular troops and three hundred volunteers to oppose them. As Mexican resistance increased, U.S. reinforcements were landed, so that ultimately more than thirty-seven hundred American sailors and marines were involved in the two-day action. Historian Robert E. Quirk believes Mexican casualties were much higher (at least two hundred killed and three hundred wounded). Quirk, *An Affair of Honor: Woodrow Wilson and the Occupation of Vera Cruz* (New York: McGraw-Hill, 1964), 103.

26. U.S. War Department, *Annual Reports, 1914,* 3 vols. (Washington, D.C.: Government Printing Office, 1914), 1:179. A detailed account of the Veracruz incident may be found in Jack Sweetman's *The Landing at Veracruz.*

27. Sweetman, *The Landing at Veracruz,* 158.

28. U.S. War Department, *Annual Reports, 1915,* 3 vols. (Washington, D.C.: Government Printing Office, 1915), 1:211–12; U.S. War Department, *Annual Reports, 1916,* 1:278.

29. U.S. War Department, *Annual Reports, 1915,* 1:7, 151–52; Kreidberg and Henry, *History of Military Mobilization,* 198.

30. An excellent, concise account of these events is Quirk's *The Mexican Revolution, 1914–1915,* first published in 1960.

31. To further confuse the issue, according to the Volunteer Act of 1914, *individual* guardsmen could volunteer for service outside the continental United States. If three-fourths of any National Guard unit volunteered for overseas service, that unit would be accepted before any other volunteers were raised and the unit would be kept intact. Weigley, *History of the United States Army,* 340.

32. Schrantz hints at this acrimony in his memoirs. After his enlistment in the regular army, for example, he disguised the fact that he had formerly been a member of the Missouri National Guard.

33. Missouri was fortunate in that both state and federal funding to the National Guard increased during the early years of the twentieth century. In 1903, the state's National Guard received nearly $36,000 in federal and $23,500 in state funds, while by 1913 that funding had increased to $113,000 in federal money and $66,000 in state funds. Cooper, *The Rise of the National Guard,* 181, 183.

34. The largest number of National Guard members on duty occurred on July 31, 1916, when more than 110,000 were on the border and more than 40,000 were in state mobilization camps. The largest number actually to be on the border (112,000) was during the following month. U.S. Militia Bureau, *Report on Mobilization,* 10, 156.

35. The editor of one Texas newspaper proved to be remarkably perceptive in an editorial of October 1916 in which he analyzed the National Guard troops on the border. He wrote that the spirit of the guardsmen in answering President Wilson's call was "all that could be expected" and they were "good material" but were unfortunately "not all that could be desired, or needed." Their morale was lacking, the newspaper editor explained, because they had not been sent into Mexico and "the only powder they have burned so far has been in target practice." The guardsmen failed to realize, according to this Texan, that they did far more efficient service in merely being prepared than many an army had

done in actual fighting. Compared to the regular, who realized he must "buckle down and soldier" until his discharge, the guardsman was always thinking of the family or business he left behind and wondering if there was a way to secure a discharge to get back where he was needed. *Laredo Weekly Times,* October 22, 1916.

36. U.S. Militia Bureau, *Report on Mobilization,* 6, 150–51. This analogy is not entirely accurate, for the regular army discovered their own deficiencies and shortcomings during this period as well. Supply transportation problems were serious during the initial stages of the pursuit of Villa, for example, until sufficient motor vehicles were secured. As historian Clarence Clendenen explained, Pershing's men were adequately supplied, but "soldiers and officers never received the comforts and amenities of the American Expeditionary Forces in either World War." Clendenen, *Blood on the Border,* 227.

37. Major Westley Halliburton of the Second Missouri offered a defense of the National Guard's border service after his return home in 1917. He argued that the regulars had thought the Missourians "sufficiently efficient" to patrol a lengthy stretch of the border, that even the regulars had been surprised in a bandit raid on their unfortified camp at San Ygnacio, Texas (while the guardsmen had fortified their camp to prevent such an attack), and that the Missourians had put a battery of regular artillery out of action during field maneuvers on the border in December 1916. *Carthage Evening Press,* January 16, 1917.

38. Quoted in Tompkins, *Chasing Villa,* 229.

39. U.S. Militia Bureau, *Report on Mobilization,* 5.

40. U.S. War Department, *Annual Reports, 1917,* 3 vols. (Washington, D.C.: Government Printing Office, 1918), 1:854.

41. Clendenen, *Blood on the Border,* 297–98. Excellent accounts of the National Guard's experience on the Mexican border may be found in chapter 15 of Clendenen's *Blood on the Border;* U.S. Militia Bureau, *Report on Mobilization;* John K. Mahon, *History of the Militia and the National Guard,* 151–52; and Doubler, *I Am the Guard,* 159–62.

42. Cooper, *The Rise of the National Guard,* 108–72; Doubler, *I Am the Guard,* 136–63; Mahon, *History of the Militia and the National Guard,* 138–53. For a well-written summary of an Ohio National Guard regiment during this period, see John Kennedy Ohl's *Minuteman: The Military Career of General Robert S. Beightler* (Boulder, Colo.: Lynne Rienner Publishers, 2001), 5–21.

Appendix B. Schrantz's Letters to the Carthage Evening Press

1. Captain William M. Fassett was born in New Hampshire on January 28, 1876. He graduated from West Point in 1897 and was promoted to captain in 1902. After graduation from the Army School of the Line and Army Staff College, Fassett joined the Twenty-second Infantry at Fort Bliss on December 19, 1912. He assumed command of Company E and the Second Battalion of the regiment the same day. In March 1913, he transferred to the signal corps. He returned to the infantry in 1915 and was temporarily promoted to brigadier general during World War I and awarded the Distinguished Service Medal. He retired in January 1924 with the permanent rank of colonel after thirty years' service. Twenty-second U.S. Infantry Returns, December 1912; U.S. Adjutant General's Office, *Official Army Register for 1914,* 104; U.S. Adjutant General's Office, *Official Army Register January 1, 1925* (Washington, D.C.: Government Printing Office, 1925), 712.

2. Schrantz was quite correct when he predicted that a peaceful solution would not be found. On April 25, 1914, ambassadors from Argentina, Brazil, and Chile offered to mediate peace between the United States and Mexico. The mediators and U.S. representatives met at Niagara Falls, Canada, on May 20, but by late June they had made little progress and had failed to resolve the Veracruz incident. Eisenhower, *Intervention*, 130–34.

Bibliography

Unpublished Materials

Missouri Secretary of State. World War I Military Service Record Database. http://www.sos.mo.gov/archives/ww1.

Muster rolls, Company F, Twenty-second U.S. Infantry. December 31, 1912–December 31, 1914. National Personnel Records Center, St. Louis, Mo.

Registers of Enlistments in the United States Army, 1798–1914. Microfilm M233, Record Group 94. National Archives, Washington, D.C.

Returns from Regular Army Infantry Regiments, Twenty-second Infantry. Microfilm M665, Record Group 94. National Archives, Washington, D.C.

Thirteenth Census of the United States. 1910. Population Schedule for Carthage, Marion Township, Jasper County, Missouri. Microfilm T624, roll 791.

Twelfth Census of the United States. 1900. Population Schedule for Carthage, Marion Township, Jasper County, Missouri. Microfilm T623, roll 866.

Published Works

Bell, William Gardner. *Commanding Generals and Chiefs of Staff, 1775–1995.* Washington, D.C.: Center of Military History, 1997.

Canfield, Bruce N. *U.S. Infantry Weapons of the First World War.* Lincoln, R.I.: Andrew Mowbray Publishers, 2000.

Carter, William Harding. *The American Army.* Indianapolis: Bobbs-Merrill, 1915.

Clendenen, Clarence C. *Blood on the Border: The United States Army and the Mexican Irregulars.* New York: Macmillan, 1969.

Coffman, Edward M. *The Old Army: A Portrait of the American Army in Peacetime, 1784–1898.* New York: Oxford University Press, 1986.

———. *The Regulars: The American Army, 1898–1941.* Cambridge, Mass.: Belknap Press of Harvard University Press, 2004.

———. *The War to End All Wars: The American Military Experience in World War I.* Madison: University of Wisconsin Press, 1986.

Conard, Howard L., ed. *Encyclopedia of the History of Missouri.* 6 vols. New York: Southern History Company, 1901.

Congressional Quarterly, Inc. *Guide to U.S. Elections.* Washington, D.C.: Congressional Quarterly, 1975.

Cooper, Jerry. *The Rise of the National Guard: The Evolution of the American Militia, 1865–1920.* Lincoln: University of Nebraska Press, 1997.

Dickinson, John. *The Building of an Army.* New York: Century, 1922.

Doubler, Michael D. *I Am the Guard: A History of the Army National Guard, 1636–2000.* Washington, D.C.: Government Printing Office, 2001.

Eisenhower, John S. D. *Intervention: The United States and the Mexican Revolution, 1913–1917.* New York: Norton, 1993.

Fellman, Michael. *Inside War: The Guerrilla Conflict in Missouri during the American Civil War.* New York: Oxford University Press, 1989.

Fifty-first Annual Report of the Association of Graduates of the United States Military Academy. Saginaw, Mich.: Seemann & Peters, 1920.

Ford, Nancy Gentile. *Americans All: Foreign-born Soldiers in World War I.* College Station: Texas A&M University Press, 2001.

Garcia, Mario T. *Desert Immigrants: The Mexicans of El Paso, 1880–1920.* New Haven: Yale University Press, 1981.

Gibson, Charles Dana, with E. Kay Gibson. *Over Seas: U.S. Army Maritime Operations 1898 through the Fall of the Philippines.* Camden, Me.: Ensign Press, 2002.

Herwig, Holger H., and Neil M. Heyman. *Biographical Dictionary of World War I*. Westport, Conn.: Greenwood Press, 1982.

Huidekoper, Frederic Louis. *The Military Unpreparedness of the United States*. New York: Macmillan, 1915.

Jones, Tom, and Fitzhugh McMaster. "1st Battalion, 4th Regiment of Field Artillery (Mountain), Mexico, 1916." *Military Collector and Historian* 36 (Winter 1984): 170–71.

Karsten, Peter. *The Military in America: From the Colonial Era to the Present*. New York: The Free Press, 1986.

Katz, Friedrich. *The Life and Times of Pancho Villa*. Stanford, Calif.: Stanford University Press, 1998.

Kennedy, David M. *Over Here: The First World War and American Society*. New York: Oxford University Press, 1980.

Knight, Alan. *The Mexican Revolution*. 2 vols. New York: Cambridge University Press, 1986.

Krauze, Enrique. *Mexico: A Biography of Power*. New York: Harper-Collins, 1997.

Kreidberg, Marvin A., and Merton G. Henry. *History of Military Mobilization in the United States Army, 1775–1945*. Westport, Conn.: Greenwood Press, 1975.

Lamar, Howard R., ed. *The Reader's Encyclopedia of the American West*. New York: Thomas Y. Crowell, 1977.

Lambert, Joseph I. *One Hundred Years with the Second Cavalry*. Fort Riley, Kans.: Capper Printing, 1939.

Linn, Brian. *Guardians of Empire: The U.S. Army and the Pacific, 1902–1940*. Chapel Hill: University of North Carolina Press, 1997.

Mahon, John K. *History of the Militia and the National Guard*. New York: Macmillan, 1983.

Martinez, Oscar J. *Troublesome Border*. Tucson: University of Arizona Press, 1988.

Meyer, Michael C. *Huerta: A Political Portrait*. Lincoln: University of Nebraska Press, 1972.

———. *Mexican Rebel: Pascual Orozco and the Mexican Revolution, 1910–1915*. Lincoln: University of Nebraska Press, 1967.

Millett, Allan R., and Peter Maslowski. *For the Common Defense: A*

Military History of the United States of America. New York: The Free Press, 1984.

Missouri National Guard. *History of the Missouri National Guard.* N.p.: November 1934.

Nenninger, Timothy K. "The Army Enters the Twentieth Century, 1904–1917." In *Against All Enemies: Interpretations of American Military History from Colonial Times to the Present,* edited by Kenneth J. Hagan and William R. Roberts. New York: Greenwood Press, 1986.

Ohl, John Kennedy. *Minuteman: The Military Career of General Robert S. Beightler.* Boulder, Colo.: Lynne Rienner Publishers, 2001.

Palmer, John M. *America in Arms.* New Haven: Yale University Press, 1941.

Palmer, John M., and William R. Smith. *History of the Twenty-second United States Infantry, 1866–1922.* N.p., n.d.

Payne, James E. *History of the Fifth Missouri Volunteer Infantry.* Privately printed, 1899.

Pringle, Henry F. *The Life and Times of William Howard Taft.* 2 vols. New York: Farrar & Rinehart, 1939.

Quirk, Robert E. *An Affair of Honor: Woodrow Wilson and the Occupation of Vera Cruz.* New York: McGraw-Hill, 1964.

———. *The Mexican Revolution, 1914–1915: The Convention of Aguascalientes.* New York: Norton, 1970.

Rickey, Don, Jr. *Forty Miles a Day on Beans and Hay: The Enlisted Soldier Fighting the Indian Wars.* Norman: University of Oklahoma Press, 1963.

Scholes, Walter V., and Marie V. Scholes. *The Foreign Policies of the Taft Administration.* Columbia: University of Missouri Press, 1970.

Schrantz, Ward L. "The Battle of Carthage." *Missouri Historical Review* 31, no. 2 (January 1937): 140–49.

———. *Jasper County, Missouri, in the Civil War.* Carthage, Mo.: Carthage Press, 1923.

Schreier, Konrad F., Jr. "U.S. Army Field Artillery Weapons, 1866–1918." *Military Collector and Historian* 20 (Summer 1968): 40–45.

Scott, Hugh Lenox. *Some Memories of a Soldier.* New York: Century, 1928.

Shay, Michael E. *A Grateful Heart: The History of a World War I Field Hospital.* Westport, Conn.: Greenwood Press, 2002.

Sonnichsen, C. L. *Pass of the North: Four Centuries on the Rio Grande.* El Paso: Texas Western Press, 1968.

State of Missouri. Office of the Adjutant General. *Report of the Adjutant General of Missouri, January 1, 1917–December 31, 1920.* [Jefferson City, Mo.?], 1921.

———. *Report of the Adjutant General of the State of Missouri for the Years 1907–8.* Jefferson City, Mo.: Hugh Stephens Printing, 1908.

———. *The Service of the Missouri National Guard on the Mexican Border.* Jefferson City, Mo.: Hugh Stephens Printing, 1919.

Steffen, Randy. *The Horse Soldier, 1776–1943.* 4 vols. Norman: University of Oklahoma Press, 1978.

Sweetman, Jack. *The Landing at Veracruz: 1914—The First Complete Chronicle of a Strange Encounter in April, 1914, When the United States Navy Captured and Occupied the City of Veracruz, Mexico.* Annapolis, Md.: United States Naval Institute, 1968.

Tenenbaum, Barbara A., ed. *Encyclopedia of Latin American History and Culture.* 5 vols. New York: Charles Scribner's Sons, 1996.

Thompson, Jerry. *Laredo: A Pictorial History.* Norfolk, Va.: Donning, 1986.

Tompkins, Frank. *Chasing Villa: The Story behind the Story of Pershing's Expedition into Mexico.* Harrisburg, Pa.: Military Service Publishing, 1934.

Tyler, Ron, et al., eds. *The New Handbook of Texas.* 6 vols. Austin: Texas State Historical Association, 1996.

U.S. Adjutant General's Office. *Official Army Register for 1911.* Washington, D.C.: Government Printing Office, 1910.

———. *Official Army Register for 1913.* Washington, D.C.: Government Printing Office, 1913.

———. *Official Army Register for 1914.* Washington, D.C.: Government Printing Office, 1914.

———. *Official Army Register for 1915.* Washington, D.C.: Government Printing Office, 1915.

———. *Official Army Register for 1916.* Washington, D.C.: Government Printing Office, 1916.

———. *Official Army Register July 1, 1921.* Washington, D.C.: Government Printing Office, 1922.

———. *Official Army Register January 1, 1922.* Washington, D.C.: Government Printing Office, 1922.

———. *Official Army Register January 1, 1923.* Washington, D.C.: Government Printing Office, 1923.

———. *Official Army Register January 1, 1925.* Washington, D.C.: Government Printing Office, 1925.

———. *Official Army Register January 1, 1935.* Washington, D.C.: Government Printing Office, 1935.

U.S. Department of the Navy. Naval History Division. *Dictionary of American Naval Fighting Ships.* 9 vols. Washington, 1959–1991.

U.S. Militia Bureau. *Report on Mobilization of the Organized Militia and National Guard of the United States 1916.* Washington, D.C.: Government Printing Office, 1916.

U.S. War Department. *Annual Reports for the Fiscal Year Ended June 30, 1901.* Washington, D.C.: Government Printing Office, 1901.

———. *Annual Reports, 1912.* 4 vols. Washington, D.C.: Government Printing Office, 1913.

———. *Annual Reports, 1913.* 4 vols. Washington, D.C.: Government Printing Office, 1914.

———. *Annual Reports, 1914.* 3 vols. Washington, D.C.: Government Printing Office, 1914.

———. *Annual Reports, 1915.* 3 vols. Washington, D.C.: Government Printing Office, 1915.

———. *Annual Reports, 1916.* 3 vols. Washington, D.C.: Government Printing Office, 1916.

———. *Annual Reports, 1917.* 3 vols. Washington, D.C.: Government Printing Office, 1918.

———. *Regulations for the Army of the United States, 1913.* Washington, D.C.: Government Printing Office, 1913.

Vandiver, Frank E. *Black Jack: The Life and Times of John J. Pershing.* 2 vols. College Station: Texas A&M University Press, 1977.

Vigil, Ralph H. "Revolution and Confusion: The Peculiar Case of Jose Ines Salazar." *New Mexico Historical Review* 53 (April 1978): 145–70.

Weigley, Russell F. *History of the United States Army.* New York: Macmillan, 1967.

Weinstein, James. *The Decline of Socialism in America, 1912–1925.* New Brunswick, N.J.: Rutgers University Press, 1984.

White, James T., and Co. *The National Cyclopedia of American Biography.* 76 vols. New York: James T. White & Co., 1892–1984.

Williams, Walter. *The State of Missouri: An Autobiography.* Columbia, Mo.: E. W. Stephens, 1904.

Witwer, Reverend George, and Ananias Clime Witwer. *Witwer Genealogy of America.* South Bend, Ind.: L. P. Hardy, 1909.

Index

Cornman, Col. Daniel, 18, 60, 162–63*n* 15
cowboys, 58, 80
Craddock, Sir Christopher George Francis Maurice, 71, 173*n* 15
Curlee, John M., 112–13, 182*n* 6
Curtis, Capt. Laurence A., 33, 68–69, 166*n* 7
customs border patrol, 44–45

daily life of soldiers: accidental shooting at Texas City, 67–68; busyness of Texas City training, 64–65; and European war buzz, 78–79; fear and trigger-happiness, 15; marching songs, 14, 77, 149; in regular army, 125; training vs. operational standards, 34; women bathing episode, 101. *See also* border guarding; field conditions; off-duty activities
demographics of pre-WWI enlistees, 124
desertion problem, 125
Díaz, Felix, 52
Díaz, Porfirio, 20, 129
Dick, Charles W. F., 137
Dick Act (1903), 137–38, 162*n* 10
Dickinson, Texas, Sixth Brigade camp at, 74
discharges, 7, 25, 82, 175*n* 29
discipline of soldiers: drunkenness issue, 37, 57, 145; Garrison's report on border guards, 135; and gay Lothario characters, 38–39, 166–67*n* 9, 11; inconsistencies in National Guard, 94; laxness on border guard duty, 42–43; and problem of rushing to enlist, 144–45; at Texas City, 66
Dolores Creek, 106, 114
dress and appearance, 13, 16, 68
drill: at Carthage, 14; corporal's leadership in, 69; reviews before commanding officers, 62, 71; Schrantz's familiarity with regulations of, 17–18, 69; at Texas City, 63

drunkenness, 37, 57, 145
dust storms at Laredo, 101

E Company, 22nd Infantry Regiment. *See* Company E, 22nd Infantry Regiment
Edwards, Brig. Gen. Clarence R., 60, 62–63
18th Infantry Regiment, 2nd Division (provisional), 31, 52
Elam, Harry B. "Silkhat Harry," 38, 166–67*n* 9
"El Niño" cannon, 52, 168–69*n* 19
El Paso, Texas: army organization in, 36–40; cannon at, 36, 52, 168–69*n* 19; Fort Bliss, 30–31, 54, 56–57; guard duty, 2, 6–7, 34–36, 38, 40–48; Huerta's takeover of Mexico, 52–54; 22nd Infantry's deployment to, 31, 33–35, 165–66*n* 5; Red Flagger activity, 40, 48–52; Rio Grande, 35–36; Schrantz's description, 36, 146; Villa's arrival in, 167–68*n* 14
enlistment duration, 25–26, 124
entertainment, camp, 64–65, 171–72*n* 7
Essex, HMS, 71
ethnicity of pre-WWI enlistees, 124

Fassett [Kassett], Capt. William M., 145, 187*n* 1
F Company, 22nd Infantry Regiment. *See* Company F, 22nd Infantry
federal army vs. Maderista volunteers in Mexico, 22–24, 40, 48, 51–52, 53
federal government, U.S., and control over National Guard, 91–92, 95, 137–41, 162*n* 10, 179*n* 4–5, 186–87*n* 31–35
field conditions: billets/lodging, 30–31, 33–34, 35, 56; Dolores Creek flood, 114; at Fort Bliss, 30–31, 56–57; at Laredo, 101, 180*n* 11; near El Paso, 56–57; at Ramireño, 108; at Texas City, 60, 61–63, 148–49, 153–54; at Washington Park, 33–34, 35. *See also* food/rations
field firing problem/exercise at Texas City, 69–70, 151–53, 176*n* 3

Tampico incident, 71

Texas City: aircraft at, 66–67, 150–51; characters and incidents, 67–68; divisional unit organization, 60–61, 72, 75, 170n 1; field conditions, 60, 61–63, 148–49, 153–54; Gen. Carter, 65–66; longshoremen's strike, 79–80; marches to and from, 71–72, 77, 156–57, 171n 5, 173–74n 17; Mexican events building up to Veracruz, 70–71; off-duty environs, 64–65; overview, 2, 7, 132–33, 135; San Jacinto Day parade, 71–72; Schrantz's civilian trip back to, 89–90; Schrantz's disenchantment with lack of action, 81–82; Schrantz's journalistic letters on, 146–58; training at, 63–64, 63–65, 69–70, 149–50, 151–53, 176n 3; train trip to, 57–59; and Veracruz mission preparation, 72–74; weather, 60, 61–63, 149–50

Texas-Mexico border, 2, 8. *See also* border guarding; Punitive Expedition

3rd Field Artillery Regiment, 97

13th Cavalry Regiment (U.S. Army), 86

35th Infantry Division in WWI, 119–20

Tompkins, Frank, 127

training: for border guard duty, 35, 98; Mexican border deployment as, 141–43; National Guard unit, 14–16, 17–18, 83, 84–85, 93–94, 95; vs. operational standards, 34; at Texas City, 63–65, 69–70, 133, 151–53, 176n 3. *See also* maneuvers

transport craft, 66, 75, 120, 122, 172n 9

22nd Infantry Regiment, 2nd Division (provisional): in Arizona, 84, 85, 135, 176n 2; Company E, 34, 36, 52, 67–68; El Paso deployment, 31, 33–35, 165–66n 5; historical sketch, 164–65n 2; and Huerta's counterrevolution, 53; waiting for Veracruz duty, 75–79. *See also* Company F, 22nd Infantry Regiment

uniforms, 13, 16

The United States Army and Navy Journal, 17, 174n 18

Veracruz, Mexico, battle of: American strength at, 186n 25; build-up to, 70–71, 72–74; events of, 74, 134–35; 7th Infantry's participation, 28

veterans, regular army, in National Guard, 126–27

Vicksburg, Mississippi, 87–89

Villa, Francisco "Pancho": Agua Prieta attack, 85–86, 136, 176n 4; Columbus, NM attack, 8, 86, 136–37; in El Paso, 167–68n 14; vs. Huerta, 46, 130, 133; Naco, Sonora attack, 84; Schrantz's fantasy encounter with, 46–47

war: anticipation among soldiers, 148, 151, 154–56, 157; as dangerous but romantic, 5, 57, 74, 146–47

Ware, 1st. Lt. James E., 69, 70, 172–73n 12

war stories from old soldiers, 37–38

Washington Park area, El Paso, 33–38, 50–51

weaponry: antiaircraft artillery, 66; Benet Mercier machine guns, 61; blank cartridge ammunition for training, 18; cannon at El Paso, 36, 52, 168–69n 19; Mexican army, 22; regular army issue, 34; SMLE rifle, 71, 173n 16; Springfield rifles, 13, 61, 160n 3, 171n 4; summary of 2nd Div, 61

weather: and camping out at Fort Bliss, 56–57; hurricanes, 89–90, 101, 177n 1; in Laredo, 101, 180n 11; in Texas City, 60, 61–63, 149–50

Whitsett, Capt. George Pentzer, 11–12, 161n 6

Wilson, Woodrow: vs. Huerta, 133–34; initial avoidance of military action against Mexico, 54, 61; National Guard call-up, 8, 91–92, 186–87n 35; recognition of Carranza government, 136; and Veracruz battle, 72, 75–76

Wood, Charles P., 5

Wood, Maj. Gen. Leonard, 130

World War I: and Craddock, 71; German submarine warfare, 75, 84; Mexican border action as preparation for, 9, 141–43; news and speculation on beginning, 76–79; Schrantz's service in, 1, 95, 119–20, 169n 23; and Stemmons, 112; Whitsett and Schrantz in, 12

World War II, 1, 120, 122

YMCA, 65, 171–72n 7

Zapata (town), Texas, 113, 181n 17

Zapata, Emiliano, 136

Zapata County, Texas, 105–15, 181n 17

ISBN-13: 978-1-60344-096-7
ISBN-10: 1-60344-096-8